PHANTOM
REFLECTIONS

The Stackpole Military History Series

THE AMERICAN CIVIL WAR

Cavalry Raids of the Civil War
Ghost, Thunderbolt, and Wizard
Pickett's Charge
Witness to Gettysburg

WORLD WAR I

Doughboy War

WORLD WAR II

Armor Battles of the Waffen-SS, 1943–45
Armoured Guardsmen
Army of the West
Australian Commandos
The B-24 in China
Backwater War
The Battle of Sicily
Beyond the Beachhead
The Brandenburger Commandos
The Brigade
Bringing the Thunder
Coast Watching in World War II
Colossal Cracks
A Dangerous Assignment
D-Day Deception
D-Day to Berlin
Destination Normandy
Dive Bomber!
A Drop Too Many
Eagles of the Third Reich
Eastern Front Combat
Exit Rommel
Fist from the Sky
Flying American Combat Aircraft of World War II
Forging the Thunderbolt
Fortress France
The German Defeat in the East, 1944–45
German Order of Battle, Vol. 1
German Order of Battle, Vol. 2
German Order of Battle, Vol. 3
The Germans in Normandy

Germany's Panzer Arm in World War II
GI Ingenuity
Goodwood
The Great Ships
Grenadiers
Hitler's Nemesis
Infantry Aces
Iron Arm
Iron Knights
Kampfgruppe Peiper at the Battle of the Bulge
Kursk
Luftwaffe Aces
Massacre at Tobruk
Mechanized Juggernaut or Military Anachronism?
Messerschmitts over Sicily
Michael Wittmann, Vol. 1
Michael Wittmann, Vol. 2
Mountain Warriors
The Nazi Rocketeers
On the Canal
Operation Mercury
Packs On!
Panzer Aces
Panzer Aces II
Panzer Commanders of the Western Front
The Panzer Legions
Panzers in Normandy
Panzers in Winter
The Path to Blitzkrieg
Penalty Strike
Red Star under the Baltic
Retreat to the Reich
Rommel's Desert Commanders
Rommel's Desert War
Rommel's Lieutenants
The Savage Sky
A Soldier in the Cockpit
Soviet Blitzkrieg
Stalin's Keys to Victory
Surviving Bataan and Beyond
T-34 in Action
Tank Tactics

Tigers in the Mud
Triumphant Fox
The 12th SS, Vol. 1
The 12th SS, Vol. 2
The War against Rommel's Supply Lines
War in the Aegean
Wolfpack Warriors

THE COLD WAR / VIETNAM

Cyclops in the Jungle
Expendable Warriors
Flying American Combat Aircraft: The Cold War
Here There Are Tigers
Land with No Sun
Phantom Reflections
Street without Joy
Through the Valley

WARS OF THE MIDDLE EAST

Never-Ending Conflict

GENERAL MILITARY HISTORY

Carriers in Combat
Desert Battles
Guerrilla Warfare

PHANTOM REFLECTIONS

AN AMERICAN FIGHTER PILOT IN VIETNAM

Mike McCarthy

STACKPOLE
BOOKS

Published in paperback in 2009 by
STACKPOLE BOOKS
5067 Ritter Road
Mechanicsburg, PA 17055
www.stackpolebooks.com

Cover design by Tracy Patterson

Printed in the United States of America

10 9 8 7 6 5 4 3 2 1

ISBN 0-8117-3554-0 (Stackpole paperback)
ISBN 978-0-8117-3554-4 (Stackpole paperback)

The Library of Congress has cataloged the hardcover edition as follows:

McCarthy, Mike, 1941–
    Phantom reflections : the education of an American fighter pilot in Vietnam / Mike McCarthy.
        p. cm.
Includes bibliographical references and index.
ISBN 0-275-99327-2 (alk. paper)
1. Vietnam War, 1961–1975—Aerial operations, American. 2. Vietnam War, 1961–1975—Personal narratives, American. 3. Fighter pilots—United States. 4. McCarthy, Mike, 1941– I. Title.
DS558.8.M33 2007
959.704'348092—dc22
[B]   2006028550

To all those I flew with who were not as fortunate as I
and did not have the opportunity to reflect on these events with
the perspective that the passage of time provides.

Contents

Acknowledgments

First, to my mother, Henrietta, who first instilled in me the love of reading and the pleasure of writing. God rest her soul. R.L. Penn, aviator superior, reviewed one of the very first drafts and made numerous comments that were right on target. He'd been to Ubon about a year and a half before me. Many thanks to Lee Brazell, who was also at Ubon with Penn. The three of us had numerous e-mail discussions over a period of a year and a half, about the efficacy of the war and how we now felt about it. Lee had several insightful comments and encouraged me to put my thoughts down in a book, as did Penn. Greta Bishop (Bishop Literary Services) read the first draft of the manuscript and gave me a professional editor's view on the work. She made numerous comments, which I later incorporated in this book. B/G Pete Hayes also read an early version of the draft and even called me up one weekend to pass on his comments. Pete and I went through pilot training together and he also went to Ubon and Korat, Thailand, a few months after I had left the base. The last sentence in the book is Pete's idea and it accurately expresses my view.

The Southwest Valley Writers Group in Phoenix proved to be incredibly helpful and actually reviewed about a third of the chapters in this book. Each month we would meet to review each other's work, and I learned many valuable writing tips from this friendly group of writers. Chuck Cook, a neighbor, Army aviator and veteran of Korea and Vietnam, read the first draft and gave many useful comments. The Mayborn Non Fiction Writers Conference selected Phantom Reflections as one of the top twenty submittals and gave it a very useful review. The Arizona Statewide Writing Contest also selected the manuscript as one of the top twenty submittals and provided several encouraging comments that gave me the impetus to continue.

John Wagner, a fellow fighter pilot, who is also a writer, swapped manuscripts with me and we each reviewed the other's work. John had several cogent comments. Our stalwart friends, Jim and Marie Wells, read one of the first drafts and encouraged me to continue. My sister Pat Voss was prescient enough to keep some of my letters from Ubon that allowed me to go back and see how I was feeling at that time. She was also an excellent research assistant in finding the actual newspaper accounts of the Gulf of Tonkin Incident that I had read about in Big Spring, Texas, when it happened. George Marrett was a major factor. I've detailed how I came across him in the book, but he was also kind enough to read the chapter summary and recommend me to Elizabeth Demers, the senior acquisition editor for Praeger Security International. I can't thank you both enough. Lastly, to my good wife, the Fair Linda, who kept urging me on despite my doubts and misgivings to "get the show on the road" and finish this work.

Introduction

April 30, 2003
A Hotel Room in California

I wasn't sure what to expect as I clicked "Play" on my laptop screen. Radio conversations that took place over 30 years ago filled my small hotel room.

"Chuck, this is Lead, do you read? I've got your smoke. Where are you in relation to the smoke?"

A garbled response follows this radio transmission.

"Are you okay?"

A burst of static on a radio is the only answer to the question.

"Are you in high karst?"

More static in the reply.

"Waterboy, this is Roman Lead, I haven't got much fuel left. Do you have my position marked?"

"Everybody stay off Guard, I'm having trouble reading them. This is Roman Lead."

"Roman Lead, this is Misty 51. Can you direct me to your position? We've just refueled and can take over."

Several more minutes of fragmented, confused, and overlapping radio transmissions follow.

At this point my wife Linda called. In 2003, I commuted between Phoenix, where we live, and the FAA Regional Office in Lawndale California, where I worked during the week as a Lockheed Martin contractor.

"You absolutely won't believe what I'm doing," I said. I then placed the phone next to the laptop computer so she could hear my voice on a tape that recorded a rather remarkable rescue mission in North Vietnam — 35 years earlier. The incident was indelibly etched in my memory, even after all these years. She'd heard me talk about the rescue numerous times, and was somewhat familiar with the story. The reflections, which had always hovered in the background of my mind, flowed back in vivid detail.

The experience began in April of 2003, when we went to San Jose, California, to visit our daughter, Erin, and her husband, Scott, at Easter. During a trip to a nearby mall, I stopped at the Barnes & Noble bookstore and had to pass down a narrow aisle to get to the main part of the store. A book display, strategically placed, caught my eye. I noticed a book in the center with an illustration of an A-1 Skyraider airplane and a rescue helicopter on the cover. The title was *Cheating Death* by George Marrett, which was about the rescue of downed aircrews in both North Vietnam and Laos during the Vietnam War. Of course, I picked the book up. As I thumbed through the pages, I recognized some of the people and places. I came across a map of North Vietnam and Laos that depicted the location of the rescues that the author had been involved in. As I scanned this, my gaze settled on the name of one site—Roman 2 A&B. My jaw dropped. Roman 2 was my wingman that had been shot down on July 8, 1968, in the lower part of North Vietnam.

I had seen the airplane crash. We were in the process of bombing some trucks on a road, and at the time I didn't think that either the front- or back-seater had ejected. I made a low pass over the area, but saw only the burning wreckage of the F-4D from Ubon Royal Thai Air Base. I climbed, orbited the area, and then radioed a radar site in South Vietnam to mark the location, so we could have an accurate position of the crash site. Incredibly, after a few moments, the voices of the two pilots filled my headset! Miraculously, they had ejected and were both on the ground. I made the necessary radio calls to launch the vast rescue effort, but it soon became apparent that it would be dark in less than an hour, and a helicopter pickup would not be possible until first light the next morning.

It was a particularly poignant moment for me. I was low on fuel and had to depart after they had been told they would have to spend the night in a very bad part of North Vietnam. Enemy soldiers were all around their positions. The only saving grace was that their locations in the rocky terrain were difficult to reach from the ground. In all honesty, I thought I'd never see either of them again. But I was wrong. They were rescued early the next morning. The author of the book I held in my hands at Barnes & Noble was one of the A-1 Skyraider pilots who provided cover for the helicopters in the successful rescue.

As I continued to read the book, I discovered there was an entire chapter on their rescue. I was absolutely fascinated. I never knew all the details of what happened on the second day of the recovery, only that they returned to our base at Ubon, alive and well. The author, George Marrett, had also never met the two rescued pilots, since they landed at different bases after the mission. In his book he comments that if they ever do meet, they owe him a few drinks. I was astonished to discover that George was very concerned that he wouldn't make it back from this rescue mission. He had been on a similar harrowing operation near the same place a month before with major losses of the rescue aircraft. George had even written a letter to his wife in case he did not return. Thus, it was a major event in his life, as well as mine.

Intrigued by this revitalized major memory of my Vietnam combat tour, I began to search the Internet for more articles by George. In the course of my search I came across a Web site that dealt with rescues during the war. As I browsed, I was again stunned to see a hyperlink to "The Roman 2 SAR (Search and Rescue) Day 1, and Day 2." I clicked on the link, and had a surreal experience. Suddenly, I was listening to an audiotape of the actual rescue. It had been recorded in the cockpit of a two-seat F-100F "Misty" Forward Air Controller jet that had arrived at the site a few minutes after the crash and had pinpointed the exact location of the two pilots. They had the fuel to initially direct the rescue effort and were also on the scene the next day. As I listened to the first part of the recording, I heard myself several decades ago. I was awestruck. I had no idea the tape existed. My vivid recollection had been frozen in time.

In the spring of 2003, my wife Linda and I were preparing for an Alaskan cruise, which would also be a reunion of all the Canadian pilots who had flown the CF-104 Starfighter, the Canadian version of our F-104 fighter. I had the good fortune to be a USAF exchange pilot with the Canadian Forces during the early seventies. In the process of e-mailing back and forth about the arrangements, one of my Canadian friends, Bill Ross, wrote and asked my opinion about the Iraq War, which had just started. We had been friends for a long time and he was my daughter's godfather. Bill's a bit of a curmudgeon, and since I hadn't replied immediately, he was afraid he'd offended me. As I answered his e-mail, I tried to explain how I felt about the Vietnam War when he first met me in 1972. I was pretty conservative in those days. I also discussed how my attitude evolved to what it is now. I thought that was significant, because for many people my age, the Vietnam experience has a great deal to do with how we look at things today, such as Iraq. It's a lens that colors how we view events.

The words just tumbled out. I was amazed at how much I wrote in that reply. I was also surprised at how much emotion I felt as I was writing. The idea of a book began to take hold. I have tried to take that very significant period; explain how I came to be in that place, at that time, and describe my feelings and thoughts during the events. The stories in the chapters ahead are the most significant events that I recall. Some still seem like they happened a few minutes ago, although it's been many years since they took place. As I've related them, I've tried to describe what it was like to be there. My intent was not to write a book about the glorification of war, or showcase what fearless heroes we were, but to show what it felt like. As time marched on, my views underwent a gradual metamorphosis and are different today than they were in 1968. As I'll explain, this viewpoint evolved after considerable reflection.

It was a difficult period. There were many proud moments, yet other memories brought back great feelings of sadness. The war had a significant impact, not only on me but also on the entire country. Some of the effects still linger today. As I think back, one of the amazing things about my combat tour was that we never talked about many things—such as how we truly felt. It wasn't macho, or maybe we just didn't want to open Pandora's Box. After a while, the abnormal became the normal, and that's how we coped with the situation. But after several decades, one has the luxury of reflection, and that's what I've written about in this memoir.

CHAPTER 1

A Very Restless Night

I was more worried about this mission than any of the others I had flown. At the ripe old age of 27, I had a total of sixty-six combat missions, 1,936 flying hours in the USAF, of which 121 were in combat. I'd never had an accident, and had never been involved in a crash, or been hit on a combat mission. I had been at Ubon Royal Thai Air Base in Thailand since mid-December 1967, assigned to the 433rd Tactical Fighter Squadron, known as "Satan's Angels." With a name like Mike McCarthy, I felt that I was the veritable personification of the "Luck of the Irish." Nonetheless, on April 1, 1968, as I was about to brief for my target that day in the Hanoi area, I was apprehensive. After a restless night, I was not at all sure my age, number of missions, or flying hours would continue to increase.

The cause of my apprehension had begun the day before. Around 3:00 PM, I looked at the schedule board to see what I would be doing the next day. It wasn't particularly good news. The mission directive message had come in early from 7th Air Force Headquarters in Saigon. A big strike was scheduled to hit Phuc Yen Airfield, north of Hanoi, in the morning. This was one of their main MiG fighter bases and was heavily defended. The MiGs had been more aggressive of late, and attacks on our aircraft had increased significantly. Although the airfield had been struck before, the attacks had been sporadic. Now, approval had been received from Washington to strike the target in force. This was great news for a strategic military thinker, because it meant we would finally deliver a strong blow directly to the enemy's ability to hinder U.S. air strikes in the Hanoi and Haiphong areas. The attack would be a major step in that direction. I imagined that the leaders who had planned the mission had high expectations. Finally, the gloves were off.

However, strategic policy looks different when you are the one who must implement the plan. I was not overjoyed, especially when I discovered that I was to be the number four or trailing member in the flak suppression flight that would

1

precede the actual strike flights by a few seconds. This position usually received more flak, although there was certainly enough to go around at this target.

Our task would be to roll in slightly ahead of the main formation of fighters that would dive-bomb the target. The bomb load for our flight would be either 1,000-pound bombs, or cluster bombs, which would split open and dispense little baseball-size fragmentation bombs that would explode upon contact with the ground. The 1,000-pound bombs were fused to explode in the air, since this would cause even more shrapnel. The net effect would be a huge amount of shrapnel near the antiaircraft guns and SAMs or surface-to-air missiles. We would find out which weapons we would carry at the morning brief.

Pilots had learned early in the war that a duel with antiaircraft guns was not conducive to longevity. The guns had a major advantage since we had little angular change once we were stabilized in a dive aimed directly at them. This made it easier for the gunners to track us. We had to get almost a direct hit on the guns to knock them out, which was very difficult to do even under the best of circumstances. But—all this shrapnel flying around would cause them a bit of distraction, and might even take out the crews and destroy some of the equipment as well. The strike flights would roll in about 30 seconds behind us. Hopefully, our efforts would suppress the guns and SAMs enough to allow the bombers to hit their targets without all that nasty, distracting flak.

In practice, this tactic was fairly effective. However, there was no one to perform this suppression for us. The gunners on the ground would be able to shoot at the flak suppression flight unimpeded as we dove down to deliver our bombs. Since a huge number of guns and SAMs were clustered around the airfield, we could expect a ferocious response as we rolled in on the flak sites at the airfield. In my position as "Blue Four," the last to attack the target, I could expect to receive much flak. There would be no element of surprise, since the North Vietnamese would have picked the strike force up on radar several miles from the target and be primed for our attack.

To paraphrase Caesar's comment about Gaul, "All North Vietnam is divided into six parts." These partitions were called Route Packages, and Package VI, the area around Hanoi, was the worst. I had been to Package VI before, but this was different—very different. The other times had been either as MiG Combat Air Patrol (CAP), or as part of a strike flight using radar-bombing tactics above the overcast. These were not uneventful aeronautical feats by any stretch of the imagination, but we didn't have to roll in on a huge number of guns clustered around a primary target.

For the past several weeks, the weather had been awful in the Hanoi area because of the monsoons. There had been no opportunity to conduct this type of attack on the airfield for several weeks. The monsoons had ended, and the forecast for the next several days was for clear skies in our target area. I was certain

I would go on the mission. It was difficult for me to think of anything but the impending strike tomorrow, and my thoughts were not those of an eager, optimistic fighter pilot. The Hanoi area was a place to be feared.

The fighter wings developed effective tactics to cope with the heavy defenses around targets such as major airfields. By late 1967, Electronic Counter Measure (ECM) pods were available, which helped greatly. These little beauties replaced a weapon on the bomb rack and looked like a small bomb with antennas hanging down. There were two kinds: a barrage noise jammer that made it difficult for the North Vietnamese radar to pick us out individually from the 2-degree jamming strobe that each airplane emitted. Should that technique fail, and the enemy radar lock on to us, we also carried a beacon downlink jammer that would cause the SA-2 SAM's guidance signal to fail, and prevent an intercept. On the strikes into Hanoi, each airplane carried both.

In order for these pods to be effective, we had to fly an ungainly formation that was difficult to maintain, but gave us the best benefit from the ECM jamming pods. Each flight member in a flight of four had to fly much further apart, 1,500 feet laterally, and 500 feet vertically, than they were used to. Normally, in close-formation flying, small changes are easy to detect and can be corrected instantly. When you are quite far apart, it is very difficult to maintain a precise position because small changes are not detected as quickly. To judge what 1,500 feet looked like was no simple task, yet it was crucially important. Each pod emitted a jamming strobe of 2 degrees that looked like a wide band of "snow" or interference on the enemy radarscope. The flight of four created an eight-degree swath of interference across the radarscope with four of these strobes together. The radar controller knows there is a target in there somewhere, but he can't tell exactly where, and doesn't have enough data to lock on and launch a missile. The jamming coverage is what dictated the 1,500-feet distance that we had to maintain. If I exceed that 1,500-feet distance, then I'd be separated from my fellow flight members' strobes and become exposed. A lone strobe made the task of the SAM radar operator easier, since he might be able to single the target out from the jamming noise and launch a missile. If I moved in too close, then the flight was not emitting an 8-degree strobe. So, 1,500 feet is what we strived for.

The other limitation with pods was the bank angle. We could only bank 15 degrees. Any more than that and our pods would not radiate properly—we showed up as a regular target that the SAM operator could easily lock on to. Not good. This lack of maneuverability made "pod formation" hard to fly. If we wanted to make a large turn, the entire flight made a max performance turn all at once to the desired heading. This minimized the time the pods weren't giving us protection. These tactics would get us to the target area, but then what?

At the target, we'd have to roll in for a dive-bomb pass. That's when the mission got interesting. The pods would not protect us during the attack because of the extreme maneuvers. It was the flight leader's job to get us in position for the attack, and then we all rolled in all at once. The old World War II movies of all the fighters peeling off one by one look good on the screen, but it was a good way to get killed, since they were attacking in trail, sequentially.

The objective was to attack simultaneously so the gunners would have to pick which one to shoot at. In essence, we diluted their fire and tried to overwhelm the defenses. The number two wingman closed up on the leader to about 500-feet separation a few miles from the target. Numbers three and four moved slightly ahead of the leader and closed in with 500-feet separation. At the roll-in point, the leader would abruptly roll into a 60-degree dive, steeper than normal. When he did this, he rolled directly into his wingman number two, who would do a barrel roll into and slightly over the leader to join him inside the turn. The other two wingmen, numbers three and four would roll in simultaneously with the leader, and since they were ahead of him at that point, the net result was that the entire flight of four would end up in a steep dive (45 to 60 degrees) in about the same positions they had been in before the roll-in, essentially still in pod formation, but going downhill rapidly. It was a violent maneuver, and you had to see it to believe it. A real toe curler! While it may be difficult to visualize, the entire maneuver was precisely choreographed.

This method of attack gave us a few seconds to find our target, put the gun-sight pipper on it, drop our bombs, and start the pullout. Lead would try to turn hard into the number two wingman to give him a chance to catch up, and then turn into numbers three and four for the same reason. As a matter of survival, we wanted to get back into pod formation as quickly as possible, get some altitude, and get the hell out of there as fast as we could.

If the gunners used barrage fire and merely shot up over the target, we gritted our teeth and went through it. A high bomb release altitude minimized the time we were in the effective range of the flak concentrations, but it also decreased accuracy. These complex tactics were only used to attack targets in the heavily defended areas around Hanoi. On less dangerous targets, we each rolled in singly, albeit from different directions, and joined up afterward. However, for targets in the Hanoi area, the "pod roll in" as we called it, seemed to work best. I'd seen it, I'd practiced it in training, and I thought I knew how to do it, but I'd never actually done it over a Package VI target in the Hanoi area. Tomorrow would be the first time. We would get the final details tomorrow at the briefing, which would start at 3:00 AM, but I'd already learned enough to know that I would have a very restless night.

By now, it was about 5:00 in the afternoon of March 31 and I had to get something to eat and try to get some sleep before the early morning briefing. I walked along the dusty road to my hootch, dropped a few things off in my room, and then went to the Officer's Club.

My thoughts were consumed with the mission tomorrow, and they weren't optimistic musings. This would be a tough one. I stopped at the bar first for a couple of scotches to see whether that would brighten my dour disposition. It didn't. In retrospect, this was one of the strangest aspects of my combat tour. You could walk into the Officer's Club, and it didn't look any different from any other bar where guys would get together after work for a few drinks. There was a jukebox in the bar, and the songs I remember most were "Downtown," to which we had our own lyrics, and "You've Lost That Loving Feeling." If someone listened to the conversations that swirled around, it would generally be about some rather inane topic, seldom anything controversial. Crews seldom talked about what was really on their minds! For at least a third of us in the bar that evening, there were real concerns about even being alive at this time tomorrow—but nobody mentioned anything close to that thought. Yes, I know, fighter pilots are supposed to have aggressive personalities and relish the chance for combat, all the while immersed in very positive thoughts about how they will emerge triumphant in the battle to come. Perhaps others did, but I can only report with certainty how I felt, and it certainly wasn't very positive that night. Conversations over the years, however, lead me to believe that perhaps I wasn't the only one who had these feelings. At any rate, we didn't talk about these things . . . too unmanly. You just pretended everything was fine, and tried to act as if you didn't have a care in the world.

Eventually, I went to the dining room to get something to eat. I generally didn't drink too much, since I needed to be sharp for the next day, and besides, the drinks didn't seem to have much effect anyway.

I don't remember what I had for dinner that night, or even who was at the table. Obviously, I was preoccupied. I went back to my room early, around 8:30 PM. My roommate, Major Tony Doran, wasn't there; perhaps he was flying a night mission. I tried to read a bit, but couldn't concentrate. Finally, I set the alarm for 2:00 AM, turned out the light, and tried to get some sleep.

Sleep simply wouldn't come. I considered myself a reasonably confident person, but most of my thoughts were negative. At this point, I was a relatively experienced pilot. But I wasn't naive. I knew what I was up against. I'd seen people get shot down. I'd heard their plaintive Emergency Locator beeper signals on the emergency frequency as they frantically hoped they'd be found and rescued. I'd even heard some of the radio conversations of the survivors on the ground. Some were picked up; others weren't.

On my previous trips to Hanoi, the weather had been overcast, so the threat from visually aimed antiaircraft guns was less, although SAMs were always a major concern. The last time I had been there was the previous week on a MiG CAP mission, and the North Vietnamese fired 37 SAMs at the strike force. The weather had been extremely hazy, which made it difficult to see the SAMs in time to avoid them. Now the weather was excellent. Did this mean more SAMs would be launched? I still can't explain the negative feelings I had, even today, but it was an overwhelming sense of doom. I couldn't imagine myself coming back unscathed from this mission. Never before or since have I felt this bad about a mission. I was convinced that, at the very minimum, I would get hit, and hopefully could make it to a safe area, most likely in northern Laos or the Gulf of Tonkin. At the worst, we would be shot down, captured, and end up as POWs, which terrified me even more than the thought of being killed.

At this point in the war, we had enough intelligence to know that POWs were being horribly treated. I didn't know whether I could stand up under that kind of torture. I wasn't sure if I would behave with honor in that situation. I prayed. I made what Catholics call an Act of Perfect Contrition, where we ask forgiveness for our sins and vow to receive normal confession with a priest as soon as possible. I prayed that I would be up to the task ahead of me, and that if bad things happened, I would conduct myself in a proper way. I prayed that I would not let my fellow aviators down and jeopardize them or the mission.

As all these thoughts were churning through my mind, I pondered the series of events and actions that caused me to be in this situation. How did I come to be at this place, at this time? This moment was a long way from the University of Miami and the AFROTC commissioning ceremony almost 6 years earlier, where I raised my right hand and promised to defend America against all enemies, foreign and domestic. This was real, and the simple fact was that I had gone to great lengths to make sure I would be a "player" in this drama that was about to unfold. I hadn't arrived here by accident. It had been quite an effort to get to this point. Had I made the right decisions? I mentally reviewed the last few years as I eventually drifted off to sleep.

CHAPTER 2

Clouds Gather

Williams AFB, November 1963

Like many significant events in your life, you don't always realize the true impact until many years later. In retrospect, several dates about the Vietnam War stand out in my memory. One of the first took place on November 2, 1963, at Williams AFB, just outside Phoenix, Arizona.

I had just graduated from USAF Pilot Training at Laredo AFB in Texas a few months prior to this. It was the fulfillment of a dream as I grew up in Upstate New York. At around age 10, I decided I should be a pilot instead of a train engineer. And not just any pilot, but a fighter pilot. To me, they represented the epitome of the profession. Some of my first heroes were the fighter pilots of the Battle of Britain—the legendary "Few." I was born in February 1941, just a bit after the famous conflict in the skies had taken place. As a boy, it was still recent history. Airplanes fascinated me but I had never been in an airplane.

When I was 12, my father's boyhood friend, Pat Murphy, a fine Irishman, took both my father and me up for a ride in his Cessna 180, a tail dragger. My suspicions were confirmed! It was everything I had hoped it would be, and more. Whatever doubts I may have had faded away, and I knew what I wanted to be when I grew up. I confess to having had a somewhat one-track mind, something my mother tried to cure me of, but with only partial success. My father was a doctor, who had been a flight surgeon in World War II at an Army Air Corps Pilot Training Base at Lemoore, California. He did not want me to be a pilot! He had seen too many crashes of young men, just like me, and while he sympathized with my desires, he didn't think that was the path I should take. He hoped I'd be a doctor like himself, and to motivate me he often took me on house calls and to see operations when he did the surgery. I had a slight problem in that I got sick at the sight of all that gore. Who wanted to be a doctor if you puked all the time? Not me! Nope. I wanted to fly.

As soon as I graduated from high school, my family moved to Sarasota, Florida, and I started college at the University of Miami in the fall. At that point, AFROTC entered my life and provided the focus I needed. A month after graduation, with a degree in business, I went for pilot training at Laredo AFB in Texas and completed the difficult course a little over 1 year later. To have those silver wings pinned on my uniform was, and still is, one of the high points of my life.

But there was a downside. The assignment we received out of pilot training was based on class standing. Those at the top of the list had the first pick of assignments. Fighters usually went first. There were only eleven F-102 fighter assignments split among six bases like ours that flew the T-33 during our training. I was peeved at this, but an F-102 was OK, even though it was really an inter-ceptor. I would have preferred the F-100. They got to dogfight, bomb, and strafe, which seemed to me to be the role of real fighter pilots. I wasn't too worried though, since I had graduated fourth in my class of twenty-six. The number one guy in our class selected a "Deuce," as the F-102 was known, and the numbers two and three wanted to come back to Air Training Command as instructors. Surely I'd get the one of the other "Deuces" . . . right?

The answer turned out to be "no." I was crushed. I received an assignment as a T-37 Instructor Pilot at Webb Air Force Base, along with Dave Kurshan (the number two guy), who would be my roommate for the 4 years that I was there. The struggle in Southeast Asia had begun to pick up, and the need to produce more pilots was apparent. Since you had to be in the top quarter of your class to be an instructor pilot, the volunteers and a few others were selected, including yours truly. To say that I had a chip on my shoulder about the assignment would be an understatement. With this huge chunk of timber on my shoulder, I proceeded to Williams AFB, near Phoenix, Arizona, to attend Pilot Instructor Training. By November 2, 1963, we had almost completed the course.

I finished flying that afternoon and had dinner, by myself, in the Officer's Club around 6:00 or 7:00 PM. I don't know why, but even today I can still remember what I ate as I watched the NBC Evening News on TV: a hamburger with "HP Steak Sauce" and a "Budweiser" beer. Maybe it's because I usually use "A-1 Sauce." There was a bit of excitement. It turned out that President Diem of South Vietnam had been assassinated the day before, during a coup in Saigon. I remember the pictures of his shot-up body in the trunk of the vehicle. Pretty ugly. I should mention that Vietnam was not an entirely unknown place. I even knew of a few pilots who had been sent over there as "advisors" to the South Vietnamese Air Force. There was considerable commentary on TV that night as all the newscasters speculated what the assassination might portend. While I remember the incident, I had no idea at the time about how much of an impact it would later have on my life. I finished my beer and went back to my room in the Bachelor Officer's Quarters.

At that point, the thought of flying in combat was somewhat of an abstraction. Sure, we new 2nd Lieutenants were aware of what we had signed up for when we joined the Air Force, and we knew that it might someday involve combat, but at that particular moment, it didn't seem like a reality. Not yet.

Big Spring, Texas, August 2, 1964

And so, it came to pass that I arrived in Big Spring, Texas, in the late fall of 1963. Big Spring was where Webb AFB was located, and it had been a major pilot training base for the USAF for some time. I had heard about the place while I was still at Laredo. The base was located in dry, flat, West Texas, not too far from Midland. Some classmates in pilot training, who had lived in the area, were quite happy to regale me with stories of incredible cold fronts that would sweep through the area during the wintertime and caused dark brown dust clouds up to God knows how high. I'd never seen anything like that in Upstate New York, or Florida, so I assumed they exaggerated for my benefit. They had not. When the first major storm arrived, visibility and winds were soon out of limits. Sure enough, below 14,000 feet, visibility was terrible. However, it wasn't clouds I saw, but dust that had been kicked up to that altitude. I became a believer, and repented for my lack of faith.

Despite the massive chip on my shoulder because I was not a fighter pilot, I had become accustomed to my new instructor pilot duties, and, if I were honest with myself, even liked it. At least I was the boss, to some extent. Years later, I would look back at this period and realize how much I had learned and matured. I became more aware of human nature, and why people react the way they do, because I watched students make mistakes repeatedly until the light dawned. Perhaps that's rationalization, but I don't think so. I also built up quite a bit of flying time in a short period, which would serve me well in the years to come. As the old adage goes, "It takes about 2,000 hours to gain 2,000 hours of experience." There's not a lot of ways to shorten the process. In addition to flying, I also taught navigation and instrument procedures in the ground school portion of the program. Any Irishman likes a captive audience that has to listen to his great thoughts, or they won't pass. Life wasn't too bad. I still longed to get into fighters, but I flew a lot, the people were friendly, and I had all the lack of concern of a 24-year-old bachelor.

My roommate was Dave Kurshan, whom I had gone with for pilot training at Laredo and the instructor course at Williams AFB. Dave was a little unusual in that he had gone to the Naval Academy at Annapolis, but upon graduation, decided to take his commission in the Air Force. We arrived together at Webb and soon found a duplex. Later, we moved to a slick apartment called the Ponderosa, which was considered pretty upscale in 1964 for Big Spring, Texas.

And that's where I was on Sunday, August 2, 1964, when the Gulf of Tonkin incident began to unfold. Dave and I were glued to my brand-new color TV— one of the few in Big Spring at the time. The incident had our undivided attention. Events in Southeast Asia had been picking up steam, and it had become a pretty well-known area. But now, something major was in progress. The papers in the morning had not hinted at anything momentous. Due to the time zone differences, many events had already transpired. It was too late for the morning papers, but the attack on the U.S. destroyer *Maddox* had extensive TV coverage. Most of the major events in the crisis would play out over the remainder of the week. A major attack on U.S. Navy warships didn't happen every day. I was excited! Maybe this would somehow change my situation and get me into fighters and even into the action, where I thought I belonged.

I confess to Churchillian thoughts of great glory at that moment.

The following days brought more excitement. By Monday morning, the papers were quite full of events in the Tonkin Gulf. A second nighttime attack by North Vietnamese boats was reputed to have taken place, although events were confused. Small wonder, even today, there is no proof that this second raid ever took place. What it did set in motion, however, was a decision by President Johnson to launch a retaliatory strike against North Vietnam. When asked what U.S. policy was, Dean Rusk, the secretary of state, said, "The U.S. Policy on Vietnam is victory without a great war or military orgy in winning it."

By Wednesday, our time, the papers and TV had details of the raid on North Vietnam, which turned out to be rather contentious because the president announced it on TV before the aircraft hit the target. During the attack, two navy planes, an A-4 Skyhawk and an A-1 Skyraider, were shot down, with one pilot killed and the other captured. The captured A-4 pilot was Everett Alvarez, who thus became the first POW of America's longest war. Little did I know that 9 years later, I would sit near him at the Red River Valley Fighter Pilots Association's First Real Reunion in Las Vegas as the "River Rats" celebrated the return of the POWs after the U.S. role in the war came to an end.

The last time I had seen a similar amount of war-related activity was during the Cuban Missile Crisis. President Johnson was on TV, and it sounded as if we were about to go to war. I watched all these events with intense interest, and deep down in my pancreas, I knew I wanted to be a player.

Why? What were my thoughts? Excitement? Adventure? A chance for glory, perhaps to live out my fantasy to be a fighter pilot? I was also somewhat of an idealist, and to some extent, still am.

It's of interest to note the mood of the country at the time. As I researched this book, I went back and read the newspapers of that critical time period. The *Arizona Republic* had a quote in an editorial on August 6, 1964, the day after the air strikes: "The U.S. has nothing to fear if it remains united, determined, and strong." The overwhelming opinion was that the country should stand up to the Communists and show resolve. The decision to broaden the war was not looked upon with disfavor—quite the contrary.

As the events of that early week in August escalated, the mood at Webb AFB was one of excitement. This sort of thing is, after all, what a pilot trains for in the military, the result of a very expensive process. This was what military power was used for, and I think all of us thought we were on the side of the angels and that we were the "good guys."

To understand the mood, I think you have to view events from the perspective of the times. World War II, the most massive conflagration in history, had ended just 19 years earlier, and if ever there was a "good war," I think most Americans felt that was the one. The war had ended with "Unconditional Surrender" from both Germany and Japan. The United States emerged as a superpower, even though it was between Romania and Portugal in terms of military strength when Hitler invaded Poland. The industrial strength of the United States had prevailed. Despite differences, America was the most united that it has ever been when faced with a common threat. Korea, 5 years later, was not so conclusive.

Since most of the pilots at Webb were in their twenties and thirties at the time, this was pretty much our frame of reference: we were the good guys; Communism was bad, Democracy was good, and, therefore, we would prevail. We had proved what American power could do, and some of us, yours truly included, couldn't wait to get in on the action. Many of the excited, young instructor pilots and students would soon be players in the war, although they didn't realize it at the time. It was a moment of high excitement.

On Friday, August 7, 1964, Congress passed the Gulf of Tonkin Resolution, as requested by President Johnson. In essence, it was a blank check to proceed with a greatly widened war. As Caesar said when he crossed the Rubicon, "Jacta alea est." We had crossed our Rubicon, and, as with Caesar, it would not be possible for us to go back. The die was indeed cast. Our lives would forever change in the months and years to come.

CHAPTER 3

The Long Wait

W hile the United States may have crossed the Rubicon that week in August 1964, it would be many long months, 31 to be exact, before I was a direct player in the drama that had erupted in Southeast Asia. I was convinced that the war would be over before I was assigned to fighters and had a chance to participate. I tried to hurry things along.

I sent for information on Air America, a clandestine airline run by the CIA in Laos and Vietnam. It had an aura of mystery and swashbuckling excitement to it, but the "Company" flew mainly transports and had a few clauses about dropping you immediately if you didn't fly certain "special missions," which paid far more than normal flights. I was adventurous, but not that adventurous so I didn't pursue that option any further.

My next attempt at self-insertion into the war effort took place when I was on a cross-country flight to McConnell AFB, in Wichita, Kansas, which trained F-105 Thunderchief pilots for the war. We had landed there for fuel, and I ran into another pilot I knew from another base. As I vented my frustrations, he told me about a new program the Air Force had started, and said that they needed F-105 pilots. He didn't have many details, but said the training was being conducted at Nellis AFB in Nevada. Why didn't I give them a call? He mentioned that it was called the "Wild Weasel" program, which meant nothing to me at the time.

As soon as I got back to Webb, I called Nellis, and asked to speak with someone about the Wild Weasel program. In what seemed like 13 picoseconds, I was on the phone with some full Colonel! He wanted to know how I learned of the program, why I had called, and so on. He wasn't too friendly. I explained how I wanted to get into fighters, make the world safe for democracy, and free the beleaguered South Vietnamese from oppression. He thought those were all noble goals, but then he wanted to know how much "Thud," or F-105 flying time I had. When I told him zero, he was less than impressed. Later, I learned all about "Weasels." They had one of the most dangerous missions of the air war, since they would fly ahead of the strike force and attempt to get the North Vietnamese to launch surface-to-air missiles at themselves. As soon as the "Weasel" picked up the SAM radar signals, the F-105 would launch a missile that would home in on the North Vietnamese site. What the good Colonel needed was high-time pilots who knew the airplane like the back of their hand. Alas, I couldn't fill that square. The program was still pretty classified at the time, which was the cause of his angst toward me. He wished me well, and that was the end of that. Would my time ever come? Would I ever get a chance to prove myself?

Inexorably, the war began to make its presence felt on our little base and community. More and more student pilots began to get assignments that would lead to the war as soon as they graduated. As they finished their training tours, several of the instructor pilots also began to get Vietnam assignments. Word had come back of pilots we knew who had been shot down. Some were missing, and we hoped they had survived and become POWs. The romantic image of war had become a little more realistic.

Soon, my good friend, Joe Burley, got his assignment: an F-4 to George AFB. We had both arrived at Webb about the same time and flew together quite often. Next, his roommate, Scott Stovin, also received orders to go to F-4s. How long would it be before I got an assignment like that? The F-4 Phantom II was the absolute latest and greatest fighter around in the early sixties. Capable of speeds of Mach 2, or twice the speed of sound, it was an awesome machine and was involved in more and more of the strikes against the heavily defended areas of North Vietnam. The venerable "Thud," or F-105 Thunderchief as it was for- mally known, had taken heavy losses over the North. In fact, by the time I ar- rived in Thailand, our sick joke was, "What's the definition of a supreme optimist?" Answer: "A Thud driver that gave up cigarettes so he wouldn't die of lung cancer!" We thought it was very funny at the time. Still, I wanted to fly fighters.

What was I like at the time? What was I thinking? As I look back, I suspect I was insufferable in many respects. I had the arrogance of someone who was convinced that our involvement in the war was totally correct and was not tolerant of those who didn't share that view. I had a vague, if not shallow, understanding of what Saint Augustine's "Just War Criteria" was all about. In reality, I didn't think too much about the morality of the war. I was just convinced that the United States was right; therefore, it had to be just. I was more concerned about the excitement, the glory, and the adventure of it all. I was also not married. I had been engaged, but there were a few problems, and I think I knew deep down in my pancreas that it was a marriage that would never be. I had broken off the engagement twice because of my misgivings. I think, in many respects, this made me all the more eager to go off to the great adventure.

And then, one day in late spring 1967, my yearning was answered. The squadron commander called me to announce that I had just been promoted to Captain and that I had an assignment to go to F-4s at George AFB in a few months. I was ecstatic! It was everything I had hoped for all wrapped up in one package. I was to fly one of the best airplanes that we had, in a war I thought was for a most noble cause, and I'd get to prove that I had the "right stuff." If there were ever a day when I could have leapt over tall buildings in a single bound, that would be one.

A few changes took place along the way to my rendezvous with destiny. My assignment was changed from George AFB in California to Homestead AFB, just south of Miami, Florida. This was good news. I had gone to college at the University of Miami, not very far away, in Coral Gables, so this would be familiar ground.

The reality of the war became a little more apparent when my friend George McKenna and I went to survival school at Fairchild AFB in Spokane, Washington. George was also an instructor at Webb and would train with me at Homestead, as soon as we finished the survival course. We had been in the same instructor pilot course at Williams, and he shared my desire to get into the war. It would be good to have his smiling, Irish face and sense of humor available in the months ahead. Neither of us relished the idea of survival training. It was like having a root canal. You knew it was necessary, but that didn't make it enjoyable. At least it was a step toward flying fighters.

If the survival instructors had just told me I'd have an intense hunger if I didn't eat for a week, or that I'd be exhausted if I didn't sleep for 3 or 4 days, I'd have believed them. The course was designed to test your mental and physical limits, and it accomplished that without a doubt. Under pretty realistic conditions, we learned what it was like to evade capture, and lived off the land. We also experienced what it was like to undergo capture and interrogation. It definitely was not pleasant. Not to worry. I was 26 years old, God's gift to aviation, and, besides, I was Irish. What harm could come to me? At last, the survival course ended and George and I headed back to Webb AFB glad to have the experience behind us.

The long-awaited day arrived. I packed my bags and got ready to go off on the great adventure. My roommate, Dave Kurshan, received an offer from Pan American Airlines, which he accepted, and in a few months would be based in San Francisco. I said goodbye to all my friends, put some of my bulkier items in storage, and packed most of my things in my Pontiac LeMans. I took a last look in the rearview mirror as I left Big Spring, Texas, and headed east to Florida. Things had worked out the way I hoped, and I was eager to participate. While I had some apprehensions about what was in store, I was pretty sure I was bullet proof. Ah, the arrogance of youth!

Homestead and "Double Ugly"

As I chugged off to my new life that fine day in May of 1967 and drove through the rolling hills of East Texas, Arkansas, Louisiana, Mississippi, Alabama, and finally into Florida, it got greener every mile of the trip. This was all right; and a welcome change from the dry, brown West Texas desert. I had plenty of time for reflection, and, as I recall, they were pleasant thoughts. I would soon check out in a new, impressive airplane, and revisit scenes I was familiar with in Miami. As I drove along, the thought of checking out in the F-4D dominated my thoughts. The war was far away, and how I would react in combat was still unknown. I would deal with that "monster" later.

I drove on the base and checked into the Bachelor Officer's Quarters, a rather nondescript, two-story concrete building where transient and bachelor officers stayed. It was right next to the Officer's Club, so that was convenient. The rooms were rather Spartan: a bed, a dresser, some chairs, and a small bathroom. Later, I would look for an apartment off base. But there was much to do of a more immediate nature, as I checked into the 306th Tactical Fighter Squadron. Oh, how I loved to be able to say that I was now part of a tactical fighter squadron!

There was a lot to do. It was somewhat complicated by the fact that we were the first class of F-4 students to go through this program at Homestead. The original fighter wing, the 31st Tactical Fighter Wing (TFW), had already deployed to South Vietnam with their F-100s. Our F-4s were brand-new and had just arrived at the base. We took over the old fighter wing's buildings and became known as the 4531st TFW. The first two digits meant we were a Provisional Wing and would function as a Replacement Training Unit (RTU) that checked pilots out in the airplane before they went to Southeast Asia. All the instructor pilots were veterans of the war, and would pass on their experiences as we progressed through the program. I distinctly remember one of the welcome briefings that the Wing gave to our new class. It was presented in a briefing room not far from the flight line. I later learned it was where President Kennedy was briefed on prospective operations during the Cuban Missile Crisis. Homestead would have been one of the major launch bases if the situation had come to that. I was suitably impressed.

Homestead AFB was named after the nearby town, a few miles away. As is typical in South Florida, the terrain was very flat, but the base was located right on the edge of Biscayne Bay. As soon as we took off, we were flying over beautiful beaches and the Florida Keys. Quite a change from flying over the parched, arid soil of West Texas. I had learned to fly light airplanes in this same area while a student at the University of Miami and it felt good to be back.

When I arrived, the base was actually a Strategic Air Command base, full of B-52 bombers. Tactical Air Command, which I belonged to, was what is known as a tenant on the base. Later all that changed, and the base became a Tactical Air Command fighter base. A good thing too, since each group had different personalities and viewpoints. Besides, those big bombers screwed up the traffic pattern as they lumbered along.

We had a lot to learn in a short time. Although I had eagerly looked forward to this day for many years, the program was often daunting. A good half of the class, like myself, had only flown Air Training Command airplanes for the last 4 years. While we had a lot of flying time, we knew nothing of dive-bombing, dog-fighting, intercepts, or aerial refueling. It was exciting, but a lot to master.

I can't say the airplane was good-looking, like a P-51 Mustang, or an F-104 Starfighter, which are things of elegant beauty, at least to pilots. Those aircraft were a perfect form optimized for a specific task. But the F-4 made its own statement! It was big—58,000 pounds of big, when it was fully loaded. The wings tilted up at the end, and the tail drooped down, unlike most airplanes. It had two huge air intakes on the sides of the two-man cockpit. It looked mean. Its official name was Phantom II, which was appropriate, since McDonnell Aircraft, the manufacturer of the first Phantom at the dawn of the jet age, had built it. Like its predecessor, it was first designed as a Navy carrier airplane. The Air Force bought it also, in an attempt to buy a common fighter for the military services. While we called it "Double Ugly" because of its massive, unusual shape and size, it was said with pride. While it's true that for most fighter pilots—the best fighter is the one they're flying now—it was a fine airplane. Faults yes, but none that were critical once they were understood.

The first ride was a never to be forgotten experience. I had not flown an airplane with an afterburner before, and it was quite a thrill. An afterburner adds additional thrust when raw fuel is injected behind the turbine section of the engine and then ignited. This causes a huge increase in power, almost double what the basic engine produces without an afterburner, but it comes at a price. The fuel consumption at low altitudes increases almost four times. At higher altitudes, fuel consumption decreases, but the bottom line is that you use it when you need a lot of extra thrust, or "smash" as we call it, for a short time. As the next months would show, it would prove its value many times.

Since the F-4 was originally a Navy airplane, it was a little different from most Air Force fighters. One of the most obvious features was the tail hook, a massive hunk of iron that hung below the aft fuselage, just below the drooped-down tail. This was designed for carrier landings, but a lot of air force fighters of that time began to sport these devices, in case they had to abort a takeoff at high speed. The F-4 hook was a massive affair. Without question this would stop the big fighter if it snagged the wire that was strung across the ends of most runways. The airplane also had an angle-of-attack indicator system that was quite different from anything I had experienced. Air Force pilots learned to fly a precise airspeed on final approach, and controlled this with power, and used the stick (pitch) to change the rate of descent. On the other hand, the Navy trained pilots to fly a consistent angle of attack, which they controlled with pitch and manipulated descent rate with power. Airspeed is an indirect indicator of angle of attack, so it's a kind of a chicken-or-egg type argument, since whatever you do with one parameter will change the other, but it represented a new way of thinking, at least for me, and it took a while to get used to this system.

The first few rides got us accustomed to the airplane. We learned how to land in different configurations and how to fly the fighter under maximum performance conditions. This, in itself, was a major change. In Air Training Command, with new students who had little experience, safety was a major concern. All that changed in the Tactical Air Command. Safety was still a concern, but overriding that, was the fact that we would soon find ourselves in combat where our very survival might depend on our ability to fly the airplane to the maximum of its capabilities against a foe who was determined to kill us. The world looked different from that vantage point.

So the days progressed, and what had seemed unfathomable a few months earlier became second nature. A flight to Mach 2, twice the speed of sound, was a major milestone. In the sixties, very few people had ever traveled that fast. We felt pretty special to have joined that exclusive club. The F-4, for its day, had a sophisticated airborne radar system, which is one of the reasons it was so big. We had air-to-air missiles that could be fired at an enemy without the necessity to see his airplane visually. Before we finished the course, we all had an opportunity to fire a Sparrow missile over the Gulf of Mexico at a towed target. We mastered the art of intercepting another aircraft using our own radar. This was a new experience for most of us, and was also quite exciting. We soon discovered that everything in the tactical fighter world was done in formation, and virtually every flight, after the initial aircraft checkout, was flown with at least one other fighter, and often a flight of four. Again, this became old hat after a while.

On my first dive-bombing mission at Avon Park Gunnery Range in central Florida, I thought I would pack it in right there! We rolled into a 45-degree dive-bomb pass from 10,000 feet, with a planned bomb release altitude of 4,000 feet, which would allow us to pull out at a reasonable height above the ground, around 1,500 feet. Now, 45 degrees may not sound like it's steep, but the first time I d: ' I felt I was headed straight down. I was comfortable with the vertical i~ ' other aerobatic maneuvers, but they were always at much higher .

this. And things happen fast! There are just a few seconds to make some quick corrections before it's time to pickle the bomb and pull out. It takes a lot of rapid mental computations to compensate for all the errors and changes. We learned all the standard tactics and techniques that fighter pilots have used for generations: high- and low-angle dive-bombing, rocket attacks, low-altitude skip bombing and strafing, with the huge 20-mm cannon that was hung under the belly of "Double Ugly." Strafing was a kick, and is what most people associate with fighter pilots attacking targets on the ground, because of all the World War II gunnery films. As we were later to learn, while it may be fun to practice it, low-altitude ground attack can be a very dangerous pastime when other people shoot back. Nonetheless, it was a great exhilaration.

When most people think of fighter pilots, I suspect the main thought that comes to mind is two aircraft flying against each other in a dogfight. That was certainly my concept, and I eagerly looked forward to this phase of training. I soon learned that it's much harder than it looks. For one thing, it's a violent affair, since the essence is to fly the airplane aggressively, which translates into very high "G forces." To prevent the other airplane from getting into a position to shoot me down meant I had to turn hard enough to prevent him from bringing his guns or missiles to bear on my aircraft. So I could be in a sustained turn of six to seven "G's," or more, for a long time. And 30 seconds at seven G's is tough! Conversely, to shoot someone down, the attacker must turn even tighter than the target to achieve a tracking solution. Again, this means a lot of G's for an extended period. It is hard to breathe, and to even turn your head is difficult because a force that's six to seven times the force of gravity weighs it down. A major problem is to not black out, since the blood in your head will drain to your lower body. To overcome this, fighter pilots wear "G suits," which consist of inflatable bladders worn around the lower abdomen, thighs, and lower legs. When we pulled G's, the pants inflated, and helped keep the blood in the upper parts of the body. After a while, we learned to tense our neck, stomach, and leg muscles to fight the effect of high G's. Naturally, after an intense dogfighting training mission, I was quite tired. The entire mission might last for just 45 minutes from takeoff to landing, but a good portion of it would be flown at maximum performance.

It's difficult to describe just how intense an air-air engagement really is. Moving any part of your body is hard. You're probably sweating profusely. The helmet and oxygen mask have a tendency to slip down, which makes it hard to breathe and see. There is a tremendous amount of conversation between airplanes, which you have to assimilate and act upon, and your mind has to operate at a feverous pitch to keep track of everything that's taking place. And that's just in training. In combat, the other airplane is trying to kill you. An engagement might last 3 to 5 minutes, but you are using an afterburner most of the time. Fuel and stamina diminish quickly.

One of the most difficult things to master in Aerial Combat Maneuvers, the official name for a dogfight, was to learn to think and visualize the battle in three dimensions. To imagine a modern jet dogfight, think of an egg-shaped piece of sky that's about 5 miles wide, narrower at the top of the egg than at the bottom because of the effect of G's on the turn radius of the airplane. This imaginary egg will go from the ground to 40,000 feet and during the course of a battle, we might go between those extremes several times. The other difficult aspect is to keep everyone in sight during the fight. This may sound simple, but it's incredibly hard. If you are looking at an airplane against a clear, blue sky, and take your eyes off it for just a moment to check something in the cockpit, when you look back out, you may well have lost the target. This is because after the eyes have focused in the cockpit, and then the gaze returns to the outside world, the eyes will automatically tend to focus a little bit in front of the nose of the airplane, a phenomenon known as "empty field myopia." If there are clouds near the target, then the eye will tend to focus on the clouds, and you might pick up the target pretty easily. To lose sight of your opponent at a critical moment will most likely mean you'll lose the fight, hence the age-old dictum of fighter pilots, which states, "lose sight, lose fight." We quickly learned *never* to take our eyes off our opponent, but like the admonition to keep your eye on the ball in golf, it's more easily said than done, and takes a lot of practice. The other problem is that there are several aircraft involved: often four in our flight and at least two of the enemy, sometimes more. Both attacker and defender are usually supersonic when the battle starts, so it is not like the movie *Top Gun*, where the good guys and the bad guys are always in plain sight.

But it felt good when I mastered the concepts. In retrospect, we didn't get enough Air Combat Tactics training, but it was one of the major highlights of the F-4 checkout program. We all imagined ourselves as the next aces once we got into combat.

Most of us had never refueled in the air. Jet aircraft burn fuel at a prodigious rate, and aerial refueling was a way around this limitation. Again, it's harder than it looks, but once mastered, it became routine. The F-4 was easier than some fighters since it used a refueling receptacle on top of the fuselage. We rendezvoused with the KC-135 aerial tanker, dropped below and behind, and opened the refueling door. Then we closed to a predetermined position in relation to the tanker, and stabilized there while the boom operator in the back of the tanker flew the refueling boom into the receptacle. Once he connected, we had to hold that position until we had all our fuel. When connected, we had a limited range of motion sideways, fore, and aft, as well as up and down. Refueling took several minutes, and required that we fly a very stable formation position, which is what sometimes made it difficult. It was hard to learn to relax enough to avoid porpoising, but with practice, we got the hang of it.

To find and join up with the tanker was often the other difficult part. It wasn't too bad in the clear skies over Florida, but later, during the war, we would have to do it at night, in thunderstorms, and often "on fumes," as the lads used to say. This rejoin would require that we do an airborne intercept with the tanker so that we would end up slightly in trail and 1,000 feet lower than the tanker. Throw in turbulence and lightning, and it made for a quite exciting experience. Most of the missions over the more northern parts of North Vietnam and Laos required refueling en route to the target, and sometimes on the way back.

We had one more skill to master before we would be unleashed on the enemy, and that was the gentle art of attacking a target at night. Most pilots don't like night ground attacks. The mission was quite dangerous, and I quickly learned this wasn't something that I felt a burning desire to do a lot either. So why do it? In Vietnam, most of the enemy supplies were being moved at night down the Ho Chi Minh Trail in Laos and North Vietnam. Night ground attack tactics were developed to counter the flow of supplies to the south. One aircraft would carry flares, which could be dropped over the target area and provide illumination for several minutes. While the target was illuminated, the wingman would roll in and try to hit the target before the flares went out.

This probably sounds pretty simple, but from the time pilots learn to fly on instruments in pilot training, they are taught to avoid abrupt movements so as not to induce spatial disorientation, a phenomenon where you feel, sometimes very strongly, that the airplane is doing something different from what the flight instruments indicate. At times, it can be an almost overpowering sensation, and many an aircraft has been lost because the pilot became so disoriented that he lost control of the airplane. So now, having had it drilled into our heads *not to ever* use more than 30 degrees of bank, or 10 degrees of pitch, *when flying at night, or in weather*, we were doing everything we were trained not to do; and with a vengeance! We would roll almost inverted, and then pull down into a 30- to 45-degree dive just as in day dive-bombing. Once we dropped the bomb, or fired the rockets, we pulled off with four G's in 2 seconds, and went back and did it again. The cockpit lights were dimmed in the front cockpit so we could see outside better, which made it difficult to read the flight instruments. The danger of spatial disorientation was always present. No wonder our masters saved this part of training for the end of the course! Be that as it may, we mastered that final phase and soon our time at Homestead drew to a close.

October 1967. Now what? We'd finished the RTU Training Program, and it was time for assignments. The war had raged on in Southeast Asia while we checked out in the Phantom. Strikes into North Vietnam had escalated, and the aircraft losses had increased. That got my attention. Would I soon be one of the statistics? My initial thoughts during the Gulf of Tonkin Incident, that the war would be over before I could participate in it, were obviously ill founded. In 1967, there were a total of ninety-seven F-4s lost in the war. This did not add to one's sense of immortality. We had some choice in our fate. I chose Ubon Royal Thai Air Base in Thailand as my first choice. That was where the action was, and I wanted to be part of it.

It wasn't a flippant decision. I was unmarried, so I didn't have a family to worry about, but still, I tended to be rather conservative in the way I made decisions. I wasn't reckless, but felt the war was a noble cause and that I could play a major part in coming events, perhaps even make the "world safe for democracy." It sounds like a trite phrase today, but I actually felt that way at the time. Like a lot of people, I felt that our government was on the side of the angels, and I had no reason to distrust the stated goals of our endeavor.

While I was concerned about my future, I was also confident. Perhaps I wasn't the most experienced pilot in the world, but I felt I was good. I was aware of my limitations and knew what I could do and what might be overreaching. As the maxim goes in aviation circles, "There are Old Pilots, and There are Bold Pilots, but There are No, Old, Bold Pilots." I knew what I was about to do was risky, but I felt that I would survive it. I looked for all the things that young men seek in war: glory, excitement, a chance to prove my mettle, adventure, an enhanced career opportunity, and, ultimately, an opportunity to see how I would react when I met "The Monster," that is, how would I behave when I was in combat for the first time?

The flesh peddlers in fighter assignments rolled their dice, and I got what I had requested, Ubon Royal Thai Air Base in Thailand. The base had shot down the most enemy MiG aircraft of the war but also had high losses. Not as bad as the F-105 Thud bases, but bad enough. If I wanted to be in the thick of things, then that was the place to be. The point here is that I was in the Vietnam War of my own volition. I wasn't drafted. I didn't get sent there against my wishes. Quite the contrary. Further, I wasn't uneducated about the conflict and felt I had as reasonable a grasp of the situation as most Americans did at the time. Bottom line: I wanted to go. Nobody forced me into the Vietnam War. I was a True Believer, anxious to right the wrongs of the world. Stand by for adventure!

CHAPTER 4

The Die Is Cast

So, this was it. The event I had dreamed about, wished for, and anticipated with all my might had come to pass. I was an official fighter pilot. I even had an AFSC (Air Force Specialty Code) that proclaimed it so—1115F—Pilot, Tactical Fighter, F-4.

So what did I feel when I finished my F-4 checkout at Homestead? To a certain extent I dreaded it, but also looked forward to it, if that makes any sense, which I suspect it doesn't. The thought that I might be a POW was my biggest dread. I wasn't sure I could withstand the torture and degradation. Some pilots I had known had been shot down and were prisoners. I imagined what they were going through, and it filled me with trepidation. Still, I felt a sense that I was bulletproof. Surely a fate such as that would not happen to a nice guy like me? It was the same feeling I had when a sudden, major emergency presented itself while I was flying. My first reaction was one of stunned disbelief. This can't happen to me! Then, after reality set in, I would deal with the problem. I remember I could not go for very long without thinking about what the next year had in store for me. It was a constant thought that never quite went away.

So, as these often-contradictory thoughts ran through my anxious brain, I cleared out of my apartment, put most of my belongings in storage once more, said goodbye to my friends, and sallied forth to meet my fate. By now, it was mid-November, and I packed the few items I would take with me in my 1964 Pontiac Lemans and drove up to Syracuse, New York. My mother had moved there a few years after my father died, my first year in college. I would spend Thanksgiving there with my family, and then head west to Travis AFB, just outside San Francisco, and catch the plane that would take me to Clark AFB in the Philippines for the Jungle Survival Course. Once that was completed, it would be on to Ubon Royal Thai Air Base in Thailand, where I was scheduled to report in the second week of December 1967. As on the drive to Homestead 6 months ago, there was plenty of time to think. The war was imminent. I was anxious to see my family, but also eager to get on with things.

The time in Syracuse was awkward. My mother had since remarried and had moved into a house across the street from my grandmother. I had two sisters — one, Nancy, who still lived at home in Syracuse, and Pat, a stewardess with American Airlines, based in Dallas. I also had two stepbrothers and a stepsister, who I didn't know very well at all. Most of the relatives on my mother's side were in the Syracuse area, and it was good to see them all again, but there was still that sense of lost family unity. I took care of a few items of business that remained and sold my car to some dealer downtown. The sale of the car brought the finality of my assignment home to me, and to top it off, I didn't get very much for it either. Events had gone too far to turn back; I was headed for the war.

Most of all, I remember that I was restless. I just couldn't relax. We had Thanksgiving dinner, and I recall it as a rather somber event. Everyone tried to make it a dinner-as-usual affair, but I, for one, had a difficult time with that. As I look back, I think about my mother quite a bit. Here I was, her only son, about to go off to war in a few weeks. While I was anxious, it was still a big adventure, and one where I had gone to great lengths to insure that I would be a player. The headlines could not have been a comfort to her. They often reported that several F-4s had been shot down on raids over North Vietnam. Not the sort of thing that would put a mother's mind to rest. Now, as I look back, I try to imagine what she went through while I was gone. I also shudder at how insensitive I was to her situation. It wasn't until many years later, when I became a parent myself, that I began to realize what she must have endured and how little I did to ease her plight.

Ultimately, I could stand the restiveness no more and decided to go to Travis AFB by way of Big Spring, my previous base before I checked out in the F-4. Even though I had been very anxious to leave the place, I yearned for something comfortable and familiar before I embarked on the great adventure, and it would also allow me to see my sister Pat in Dallas before I went on to San Francisco.

So I said goodbye to my mother, sister, stepfather, and relatives and started on my way. From the vantage point of the present, it bothers me now that I did that. It must have hurt my mother a great deal to have me choose not to spend my few remaining days in the United States with her, but instead go back to visit friends in Big Spring. But that was her way. She never interfered in my decisions and always supported me in whichever direction I chose to go. She was not particularly thrilled that I wanted to be a pilot, but never tried to talk me out of it. This situation was no different. She was far more stoic than I would have been had the situation been reversed.

I arrived at Big Spring a few days after Thanksgiving, quite full of myself, but also a bit perplexed. Here I was, a certified fighter pilot, quite a change from when I left the same place about 6 months earlier. But I hadn't tasted combat yet, so I was somewhat between phases. Still, it felt comfortable. I had already detected a sentiment that would grow more pronounced in future months. The war didn't seem to have much meaning unless you were directly involved. It had been hard to carry on conversations about Vietnam with people in Upstate New York. If a relative was drawn into the spreading conflict, then the war seemed to affect them. If not, then life went on as usual.

One memory stands out in my mind after all these years and, in fact, is the main reason I wrote this chapter. Jack Magee and his wife Carrie were very good friends while I was stationed at Big Spring. They were an older couple (older in this case meaning Jack had been in World War II), which meant he was around 45 or so in 1967. But Jack was a bit different. He had been a B-17 pilot during World War II, and if memory serves, was wounded before he finished twenty-five missions, a normal tour at the time. After the war, he returned to college, became a pharmacist, and practiced in Big Spring. For reasons that seem strange to me now, I never thought of him as a pilot. He never talked about his war experiences, except in very general terms which was typical of "The Greatest Generation." He and Carrie were very involved in life at the base, but always as interested bystanders. I just didn't think of them as players in one of the most cataclysmic events of the twentieth century, although I'm amazed now that I didn't. We, the young pilots at the base, thought the world revolved around us, and never gave much thought to what some of these people might have gone through.

Jack had recently become a part owner of a Cessna 172 light airplane and asked if I wanted to go flying with him while I was there. Of course, I said yes. I must admit I was a bit obtuse. As I look back upon it, Jack knew far better than most of my peers what I was about to go through as I experienced combat for the first time. The flight was enjoyable, and uneventful, but I'm amazed, as I think back now, that I still didn't think of Jack as a pilot. He was the sympathetic pharmacist who was always ready to listen to us. In fact, my roommate, Dave Kurshan, went out with his daughter Susan for a while. Jack phoned me several times at Homestead, while I checked out in the F-4. I always considered it a pleasant call, but now, I think it was more than that. Jack didn't have a son, and in some respects, I might have represented the son he never had. As I mentioned earlier, my father died while I was still a teenager, so in the same respect, Jack was the "father" I wanted to talk to in difficult times. But I remember the flight because we never talked about the most obvious thing: what would I experience in the next few months? I wanted someone to reassure me that this adventure would end well. Although today, I can't imagine what I could say to some young pilot to ease his mind as he is about to go off to combat. I never saw Jack and Carrie again after this trip, which I regret. Wisdom often comes late.

The days passed. It was time to leave Big Spring and start the trek to Travis, and then to the war. I caught an early morning Trans Texas Airlines DC-3 flight (yes, they still flew them!) to Dallas, where I would transfer to an American Airlines 707 to San Francisco. My sister Pat was a stewardess for American Airlines, and although she had to fly that day, we were able to meet for a few moments to say goodbye. I still think about that moment. An old acquaintance from Webb came up to us just as I was about to board the flight to San Francisco. Frank had left the Air Force about a year earlier and was now a copilot for American Airlines. I was in uniform, so Frank asked me where I was now assigned. I told him I was headed for Ubon Air Base in Thailand to fly F-4s. Frank was not the subtle type. He commented, "Wow! They're really getting their ass shot off over there!" My sister Pat had done pretty well up to that point, but the remark brought reality home to us. Frank wished me well and left for his flight. Pat and I said our goodbyes, and I boarded the 707 to San Francisco. My sister, fine lass that she is, had arranged with Bobbie Fowler, a stewardesses on my flight, to keep me in drinks for the entire trip! When I went to pay for a drink, I was informed that Pat had arranged for everything to be taken care of. It was a nice gesture that I always appreciated and helped take the sting of departure away.

I spent the last few days in San Francisco with Dave Kurshan, who had gone with Pan American Airlines. We reminisced about the times we'd had at Webb as he showed me the local sites. Finally, it was time to go. Four members of my F-4 class from Homestead were scheduled to head off for the war on the same flight. We had agreed to meet at the "Top of the Mark," a cocktail lounge at the Mark Hopkins Hotel in San Francisco, for one last drink in the States, and then go together to Travis AFB for the flight to Clark Air Base in the Philippines. We were all scheduled to attend the Jungle Survival Course, the final step before we went into combat. We all met as planned, had more than a few drinks as I recall, and took a cab to Travis. We checked in for our flight, a World Airways DC-8 that was under contract to the Air Force. It was very much like a departure on any other flight except; in this case, we were all very well aware that we might not come back. It was a weighty moment that the earlier drinks did not ameliorate. We each seemed locked in our own private thoughts, and I don't recall a lot of discussion. It was late when we departed for an intermediate fuel stop in Hawaii, then onto the Philippines.

Late in the afternoon, we arrived at Clark AB, tired but eager to get on with the next phase, which was Jungle Survival Training. This was the last step, and the instructors did not find it difficult to keep our attention, since we might well need this knowledge soon. After a few brief classes on the base, we were all taken into the jungle where we would spend the next few nights. If we were shot down over Vietnam or Laos, the only way out was to avoid capture until a helicopter could pick us up. There was no way to walk back to friendly lines and not be captured. If we could not evade and were captured, we faced a very uncertain future indeed. The situation in Laos was quite grim, since they were a guerilla force.

A prisoner was a liability that had to be fed and taken care of. More than likely, we would be killed soon after capture. If we were not rescued in Laos, there was little hope. For all these reasons, the instructors did not have to force us to pay attention. I must say it was a most useful and well-conducted course.

At last, the course was over. We were trucked back to Clark, cleaned up, and the next day I said goodbye to my good friend George McKenna, who would head to DaNang Air Base in South Vietnam, while I boarded my own flight to Bangkok. I never forgot that moment. George and I first met at Williams AFB for the Instructor Pilot Course in 1963 and had been together since then. The great adventure was about to begin, and neither of us was sure how it would turn out.

The long-anticipated flight to Bangkok's Don Muong Airport was uneventful. Located on the outskirts of the city it was a dual-use airfield. The main portion was a regular civilian terminal, but across the field was Don Muong Royal Thai Air Base, a military facility that shared the runways with the civilian air terminal. We landed at the terminal, and immediately became aware of the huge military presence in Thailand. There were all sorts of signs and notices that told arriving military personnel where to go and how to contact their organizations. We soon retrieved our bags, which for me included one entire year's worth of clothing and flying gear packed in a green, canvas B4 bag. I've never been able to pack in such an efficient manner since then. Sure enough there was transportation already arranged, and we headed for the Chao Phaya Hotel in downtown Bangkok. There were three of us headed to Ubon. None of us had been to Asia before, so this was all very new to us.

The drive into the city took about 30 minutes and included many sights that we had never seen before: canals alongside the road; water buffalo everywhere; an exotic language that was meaningless to us; and a very ripe, pungent smell, reminiscent of a farm, and caused by open sewage. After much horn honking by our driver, we arrived at the Chao Phaya Hotel in downtown Bangkok. This was a pleasant surprise. The hotel had pretty much been taken over by the U.S. military, and might as well have been a Bachelor Officer's Quarters. It was very nice indeed, with rich mahogany wood everywhere (which was quite common in Thailand) and very well-appointed facilities. It had a nice restaurant, several bars, and a quite pleasant staff; what more could one want? The Air Force dominated the place, and there were pilots in flying suits everywhere. This was not your average hotel, by any stretch of the imagination.

We had a little bit of time for some sightseeing, then had a quick dinner, and got ready for an early morning ride back to the military side of Don Muong Air Base, where we were scheduled to catch an Air Force C-130 transport that made rounds of the different air bases in Thailand every day to drop off supplies and personnel. Ubon was about 150 miles northeast of Bangkok, and we were scheduled for the midmorning flight.

We arrived around 8:00 AM, got a quick breakfast, and went to the terminal to await our flight. Our introduction to combat was about to happen! Regardless of what had brought each of us to this war, we would soon be actual participants, not mere observers. We were eager but also apprehensive. We had a vague idea of what the future held in store for us, but there were a lot of unanswered questions.

And so it was that I came to meet the first two people from Ubon: Chuck Mosley and Gary Magnusson. They were both back-seaters who had been down to Bangkok for a few days' respite and were headed back. They were both very outgoing and were more than eager to share their experiences with us. Chuck had a patch on the shoulder of his flying suit that read, "SA-2 Flight Examiner," and showed a picture of "Snoopy" from the "Peanuts" comic strip, sitting on top of his doghouse with a look of fright on his face as a Soviet SA-2 surface-to-air missile was going past. The meaning was obvious. Chuck had seen one of these missiles up close and personal. He'd been in combat and was still standing. I was impressed. Maybe this wouldn't be so bad after all.

Soon, the C-130 arrived and we took off. We made one intermediate stop at Korat Royal Thai Air Base to drop off some other passengers and cargo. Korat at that time was pretty well known for its role as one of the two F-105 "Thud" bases that had conducted the majority of the deep interdiction strikes against the very high threat targets in North Vietnam. Consequently, they had high losses. The F-4s had begun to pick up a lot of those missions, and, of course, we wondered if we would have to contend with the same sort of loss rate. It was my one and only visit to the base, whose inhabitants claimed to be "Shit Hot from Korat." I have no idea how the phrase came about, but in the Vietnam War, everything that was good was known as "Shit Hot." Exceptional things were touted as "Super Shit Hot." Everyone knew what you meant, and the phrase didn't require any explanation. But on this particular day, there was very little activity during our brief stop. The morning strike force was most likely in the target area at the time we were there, and the flight line was very quiet. We discharged our cargo and were soon on our way to Ubon Ratchathani, about 180 miles northeast of Korat. My first visit to an actual combat base was decidedly anticlimactic.

Around 2:00 in the afternoon on December 13, 1967, we touched down on Runway 25/07, the single runway that served Ubon Royal Thai Air Base. My combat tour was about to begin. As I researched this book, I dug through several files. I found my travel voucher when I checked into Ubon. I left Homestead on November 5, 1967, took some leave in Syracuse, New York, Big Spring, Texas, and then went to Clark for the Jungle Survival Course before I arrived at Ubon, Thailand. For all of that travel, I received a grand total of $237.78. Don't go to war to get rich. If that's your goal, there are better ways.

Ubon had been around for quite some time. During World War II, the Japanese had used it. In the 1960s it was a base of the Royal Thai Air Force, and their armed T-28 aircraft used it to fight any border incursions from Laos, which was about 60 miles to the east. When the USAF fighter wings first deployed to Ubon in 1966, there was very little in the way of infrastructure. By the time I arrived, it was a substantial facility and resembled a Stateside Air Force Base, with all the amenities such as movie theatre, base exchange, Officer's Club, post office, and so on. In fact, as I reflected later, that was one of the great ironies: I found it difficult to make the transition every day from a relatively normal existence on the base to taking off for a combat mission that, for several minutes at least, might be a pulse-pounding, tension-filled, abnormal situation. But all that lay ahead. For the moment, we had to check in and become part of our new world.

Members of the squadrons we had been assigned to met us at the C-130 when we arrived. Our orders just said that we were assigned to the 8th Tactical Fighter Wing, which consisted of four squadrons. The Wing parceled us out to the various squadrons based on their manning strength at the time. While this may seem like a simple human resources type of personnel function, one of the major drivers of this process was how many pilots had been shot down or completed their tours when we arrived. That's what determined who went where.

In short order, we were all taken to our individual squadrons and introduced around. We "new guys" were assigned to separate squadrons, so to make new friends was the order of the day. It felt good to be in a squadron again, and since everyone had been in the same situation just a few months earlier, they went out of their way to make a "new guy" feel at home. Two squadrons were located on either side of the Wing Headquarters in a low-slung, mahogany building. The other two squadrons were just across the street to the north, and everyone was right on the flight line. The noise and activity were intense, as strikes departed or returned. As I was to learn soon, the big strikes into the Hanoi area involved a large number of aircraft, and they all took off or landed at the same time. Quite a feat on a single runway, since some aircraft might have suffered battle damage and almost everyone was short of fuel. Now I felt that I was in a combat zone! There was no doubt that things were different here.

After a quick tour of the squadron, I was assigned a room in a "hootch," our name for the low, mahogany rooms we lived in. I was given Maj. Tom Kirk's bed, which I took as a good sign, since he'd shot down a MiG and had just finished his tour. These were pretty nice quarters. The rooms were air-conditioned, with two officers to a room that included a refrigerator, a sink, beds, and upright lockers. I had no trouble finding a place to store all of my one bag's worth of worldly possessions. It was a week or two before my roommate, Maj. Tony Doran, arrived, so I had the whole place to myself. I had a few drinks at the Officer's Club that night as I tried to assimilate all that was happening to me. The fighter-pilot world is a pretty small fraternity, so if you don't know someone, you make friends quickly and often find that your new acquaintances know somebody that you know. Of course we "new guys" wanted to know what it was all about. How was the war going, and what could we expect when we started flying in a few days? In a sense, I was encouraged because here, right in front of me, were pilots who had been in my situation just a few weeks ago. If they could survive all the threats, then I could too. At least, that's what I tried to tell myself. I would find out soon enough. A few more drinks and I went to bed at the end of my first day in a combat zone.

The next day orientation got underway in earnest. I had to get a mug shot, or, as we called them, our "Shoot Down Photos." There was a grim reason for this. If you were unfortunate enough to get shot down and captured, your best chance to come out at the other end was to make sure that it was known you were a prisoner. So, if possible, any opportunity to be photographed in captivity was a good thing, and therefore, a recent photo was required. We also had to develop three authentication questions that the rescue crews would ask us before they would attempt a pickup in enemy territory. These questions were to verify that you were the person you said you were. The North Vietnamese and Pathet Lao had been known to use captured survival radios to sucker the rescue forces into a flak trap. The seriousness of what I had gotten myself into began to dawn on me.

Next stop was my new squadron, the world-famous, highly respected 433rd Tactical Fighter Squadron, to be fitted with all my personal equipment. My white helmet that I brought with me was repainted with camouflage colors. I was issued two survival radios; a survival vest with extra batteries and survival equipment; a .38-caliber Smith & Wesson pistol along with a holster and a gun belt; a tree letdown device in case you got hung up in the triple jungle canopy, and couldn't reach the ground; and, to top it all off, a couple gruesome-looking knives, one sewed to the back of my G suit, the other on a belt with my new .38-caliber cannon. By the time I got all this stuff strapped on, I looked like Matt Dillon, about to have a shootout on the main street of Dodge City. It also weighed about 60 pounds, which soon became apparent when I walked around in the hot, humid climate. This was getting more serious by the minute.

Then it got even more serious. You couldn't fly combat in the Great Patriotic War (my term . . . apologies to real historians) until you passed a test on the Rules of Engagement. At first, I thought it was a bit of a joke. Some of it made sense, but some didn't. You couldn't shoot down an enemy airplane unless you had positive visual contact and had identified it as such. Later, we had special aircraft that could verify that the target was indeed an enemy. In that case, it was OK to launch a missile without ever having sighted the target. I could see the logic in that because an air battle can be very confusing. Others didn't. Laos was quite puzzling. It was often a very dangerous place, but you couldn't drop bombs on a flak site unless it was within a certain distance from the highway, in which case it was OK to blow it to bits. Much, much later, when I was at the Pentagon and had to help formulate such rules, I developed a bit more empathy, but at the time, it was very perplexing and seemed inane. We had several briefings by the intelligence folks and then had to take a test that signified we understood all the rules; then we were good to go. I had one more hurdle to overcome. I hadn't flown in over a month and needed a recurrency and orientation check flight.

I'll never forget that flight. Major Hank Zimke, a senior pilot within the squadron, gave me my check ride. This is a pretty normal event. Flying, in essence, is a series of very elaborate habitual responses that are constantly reinforced. You can lose proficiency in a short time if you don't fly often. Air Force policy was that after 30 days you had to fly with an instructor pilot if you hadn't flown during that period. It was also an orientation ride so I could become familiar with the local area and learn the landmarks and procedures. An added feature was to introduce me to what "real combat flying" was all about. We took off, did a tour of the immediate local area, then climbed to altitude. Then we got serious. Hank showed me what a SAM break was like. A bit of explanation: The SA-2 was the Soviet surface-to-air missile that the North Vietnamese would fire at us to try to shoot us down. It was very fast, but you could outmaneuver it if you saw it in time. The SAM was a very fast rocket, but at any given airspeed it could only pull so many G's. If you could pull more G's than it could, the missile couldn't match the change and would miss you. Believe me, it's easier to write about this than to do it!

Hank proceeded to demonstrate what it was like. In a very loud, terror-filled voice, he shouted, "SAM . . . take it down!" With that, he shoved the stick full forward, which resulted in about two to three negative G's. Here's what it feels like: 1 G is the normal force of gravity, what you feel every day. Zero G is weightlessness. When you see the astronauts floating in space, that's 0 G. Negative G is much more unpleasant. Blood rushes to your head. You are jammed up against the canopy and your shoulder straps. It's hard to move. It's disorienting. It's uncomfortable, to put it mildly. It was also something I was familiar with. As an instructor in T-37s, I had to practice inverted spins often, in case a student inadvertently got me into one. Still, this was more violent than anything I had ever experienced. The idea was to make it so violent and sudden that the missile couldn't follow you through the maneuver. If you did it prematurely, or not aggressively enough, then the missile might arc above you, and then come down on you. In that case, there was only one recourse: pull up aggressively into the missile, just as you would if it were an enemy aircraft trying to get a tracking solution on you. Hank described the imaginary SAM attack as if he were a back-seater, watching the whole thing. I paraphrase, but it sounded like this, "It's coming down; still tracking us! TAKE IT UP!!!" With that, he slapped on about six to seven G's in a violent pull-up. This was all very exciting, except for one thing. My anti-G suit hose had pulled out during the aggressive negative G pushover, and wasn't connected. Several things happen when you pull high G's. The blood in your head is pulled down to the lower extremities. One of the first senses to go is vision. Your field of view starts to narrow and gets much smaller. Color disappears, and things become gray. Eventually, you can't see anything, but you are still conscious. If you keep it up, you eventually lose consciousness, or black out. It takes about 10 to 20 seconds to regain consciousness, and you may or may not realize that you have been unconscious. I went out like a light. Without the G-suit, and not expecting anything as violent as this, I was totally caught by surprise. I soon came to my senses, but I had learned a valuable lesson indeed. Suitably humbled, we completed the check ride and I was pronounced good to go for my first combat mission. I wasn't totally sure I was ready, but a few days later, I was scheduled to fly my first mission.

CHAPTER 5

First Mission

Friday, December 22, 1967. The culmination of several years of preparation was about to take place. I had completed all the hurdles and prerequisites and was scheduled to fly my first combat mission. I had been paired with Lt. Dave Carter as my back-seater (or GIB—Guy In Back as they were known in the F-4 business). The 8th Tactical Fighter Wing had a pretty sensible policy to check a new guy out in combat. They paired the neophyte with a back-seater who was pretty experienced, and had, on average, sixty to eighty missions under his belt. They had seen enough combat to know what to look for, and they were quite familiar with the procedures that would insure survival. As I was about to find out, there were many things that I was not aware of, and for which my training had not prepared me.

When I first arrived at Ubon, most of the GIBs were pilots, and this was their first assignment out of pilot training. The front-seaters, or aircraft commanders, were a bit older, and had more flying experience. Pilots who read this will understand that the GIBs weren't pleased with their situation. They wanted to be up in the front seat, where they could run the show. In most cases, they had graduated high in their pilot training class and hoped that they would get a fighter assignment. So, it was a bit of a letdown when they found themselves in the backseat. We had a few pilots who had been GIBs on their first combat tour, and volunteered for a second tour just to become front-seaters. That's how big an issue it was with them.

A few words about how things worked in the F-4 might clarify the situation. Although it was a two-seat aircraft, it was not like most multiengine transport or bomber aircraft where the pilot and copilot sit side by side and have a similar instrument panel in front of them. The two F-4 cockpits were as different as night and day. True, it had flight controls in the back, and you could fly it from there, but the controls were very rudimentary. The Navy version of the F-4 didn't even have flight controls in the backseat, since it was occupied by a Radar Intercept Officer (RIO) who wasn't a pilot. You couldn't put the throttles into afterburner; the front-seater had to do that for you. Same with the landing gear, flaps, and tail hook. You could blow the gear and flaps down with compressed air in an emergency, but that caused another set of problems, since it would often rupture the hydraulic system. Worst of all was the visibility from the back. It was quite difficult to see forward, since the front-seater and his ejection seat were in the way. To land the Phantom from the back was always a bit of a thrill. When you couldn't see the runway from either side, you assumed you were lined up on the runway. Later, I became an instructor pilot in the F-4 at Homestead and became intimately familiar with what a monster it was to land from the backseat, especially at night. Formation flying from the back was not much different from the front, and refueling was also not too difficult.

The GIBs did have a bit of an empire in that they had sole control of the radar system, as well as the inertial navigation and some weapon delivery functions, including the nuclear radar delivery settings. The front-seater also had a radarscope, just below the gun sight. So he could see what the back-seater was doing, but he couldn't determine what to scan and could not lock on to a target unless it was directly in front of the aircraft and in the gun sight. The same was true for the inertial navigation system. The front-seater could read the output, but the GIB controlled the system. This piece of equipment relied on accelerometers to determine where you had gone in relation to where you had started. It was pretty sophisticated at the time, and gave us roughly the same capabilities that Global Positioning Satellite systems do today, although by no means as accurate. There were numerous interceptor aircraft with cockpit layouts similar to the Phantom, but this was the first time a tactical fighter had been built that way.

Prior to the Phantom, most tactical fighters were single seaters, and the fighter pilot did everything. So it represented quite a change when they put pilots in the backseat. They didn't like it, and they resented the fact that they were assigned navigator duties rather than pilot duties. They did not want to be known as the best radar operator, they wanted to have the reputation as the "best stick," and be recognized for their flying skills, not their weapon-system expertise. Most front-seaters let their pilot GIBs fly the airplane as much as they could, but in combat, each crew member had distinct duties to perform. Midway through my tour, the Air Force changed its policy and assigned navigators to the F-4 backseat, and changed the name to WSO (Weapon Systems Operator), similar to what the Navy had done. The pilot GIBs didn't complain a bit.

In spite of these problems, it made good sense to team new pilots up with an experienced back-seater, and Dave Carter was no exception. He was a pilot and had several missions under his belt, and I was glad for that. We'd learned that we were to fly together that morning, and I was both excited and nervous. It was hard to believe that I was about to go on a real combat mission. How would I do? Would I handle myself well, or make a complete mess of things? After all, as a fighter pilot, this is what I had been trained for. Would I be a coward? Worse yet, if I were, would I put my flight members in jeopardy as well? As I look back, I think I was more concerned about that than anything else. When I became a pilot, I accepted that it was a more hazardous profession than the others. But a large part of the self-image of fighter pilots is tied up in how they perform under stress, and combat was one of the ultimate stresses. Would I be up to the task? I would soon find out.

We started to brief for the mission shortly after noon. The mission planning rooms were located in the middle of the brown mahogany Wing Headquarters building just off the flight line, and this is where we obtained all the maps and target intelligence data. We were to be part of a four-ship flight led by Capt. Willy Flood, an Air Force Academy graduate who was one of those back-seaters who'd volunteered for another tour to get in the front seat. This was old hat to him, but all new to me. The target was a suspected truck park on the now famous Ho Chi Minh Trail in the southern part of Laos, not too far from Mu Gia Pass in North Vietnam. The North Vietnamese would run their supplies at night down this trail to resupply their forces in South Vietnam. During the daylight hours, they stayed hidden in camouflaged truck parks on the sides of the trail in Laos. We would rendezvous with a Forward Air Controller (FAC) who was in an O-2 aircraft and was familiar with the target area. Strikes in Laos required a FAC because of the Rules of Engagement. A bizarre set of directives if there ever was one. We gathered up all our data, plotted our routes, and received an intelligence briefing about the area and any other developments that we needed to be aware of. Once that was completed, we went to our squadron briefing area, which was next door, and went over what our flight was to do in great detail. Every Air Force flight goes through this process, even on peacetime training missions. No detail is left to chance, and you go over everything: what frequencies to check in on, taxi, take off, join up, en route, target tactics and procedures, what to do if emergencies arise, and so on. My mind raced to assimilate all this information. The whole event had an air of unreality. I heard the words and understood what they meant, but it was hard to believe I was about to go do this. Prior to this point, I had never dropped a real, live bomb. All my training had been with either inert or practice bombs that would simulate the ballistics of a real weapon. The thought that I might kill someone, or, conversely, that they might try to kill me, was sort of an abstract concept at this point. I knew what I was supposed to do and hoped to be able to complete my mission and not make too many mistakes. It was exciting, yet strange, all at the same time. This whole process took about 2 hours, and soon it was time to get our personal equipment on and go to the airplanes. I felt awkward as I put on my new survival equipment and strapped on my pistol and knife belt, since I had never worn anything like this before. I was well aware of the reason to wear all this gear. Should I be shot down, I'd need it to survive. The tension ratcheted up a notch!

The squadron used a van to drive the crews out to the planes, and soon, Dave and I arrived at the revetment where our airplane was parked. It was a crystal clear day and rather cool, which was not what I had expected. I had imagined Southeast Asia as hot. I wasn't entirely wrong. The cool temperatures on this day were just a brief change from the normal hot and humid climate. "Double Ugly" looked every bit like its nickname. There were two 370-gallon drop tanks, three 500-pound bombs under each inboard pylon station, and six more 500-pound bombs hung on the centerline multiple ejector rack, for a total of twelve. That was more than a B-17 bomber carried in World War II. And that was just my airplane. The other three airplanes had the same bomb load. I began to preflight the airplane and the weapons. This part was pretty familiar except for the check of the bombs, which the Wing weapons officer had taught me how to do a few days earlier during my orientation training.

I started to settle down and relax a bit at this point. As I was to learn later, the worst part of every mission was the briefing and preparation that led up to it. One could imagine all sorts of dire possibilities. When I got to the airplane, that was normal. I had some control over the machine, and it was also a well-ordered, predictable routine. It kept my mind occupied with tangible steps that had to be accomplished, and there was less time to dwell on the negative aspects of flying combat. After the preflight, we strapped in, started the engines, and finished our system checks in the cockpit. That portion of the mission was accomplished in about 30 minutes, and soon the flight leader called for us to check in on the radio, "Honda Flight, check in." That was followed by a crisp "Two," "Three," "Four" from each flight member. As the newest of the new, I was number four, or tail-end Charlie. Lead got our taxi instructions from the tower and we started to taxi out to the arming area near the runway. Since we were all in separate re-vetments, or shelters, this was my first opportunity to see all the flight members at once. I verified that I had the correct tail numbers and then got into the proper sequence (no small problem when thirty-six airplanes might all be taxiing at once!).

The last step before takeoff was to have the airplane inspected by maintenance personnel for any problems such as cut tires or hydraulic or fuel leaks, and to pull the safety pins on the tanks and pylons so that you could jettison them if you had to. Any problem that couldn't be fixed right away would be cause for that airplane to abort the flight. This was a common practice, even in peacetime. In combat, however, they also had to arm all the weapons, which carried a higher risk. The entire flight would taxi into a line-abreast position, just short of the runway. Each crew member would then put his hands up on the canopy rail and keep them there while his airplane was checked. This was to show the ground crewman that we weren't touching anything, since many of the ground checks required a check for stray voltage. If you turned on switches and there was a short circuit, or bad ground connection, you might cause something to activate that shouldn't. I used to think this was somewhat overcautious until one day the F-4 next to me had a pylon with six 500-pound bombs drop off the wing and fall to the ramp. Since the bombs don't arm until you drop them from the pylon, nothing blew up, but it made a believer out of me. Since I was number four, I was the last one to get checked. I had a few more moments to contemplate what we were about to do. As I recall, my emotion was one of anticipation more than fear. It's hard to be afraid of what you don't know. Besides, wasn't this what I had always wanted to do, and taken great pains to accomplish?

Then I was armed, and it was time to go. Lead called for takeoff clearance, and we were cleared on the runway. We lined up on the runway in normal Finger Four formation: Lead first, number two to his left, number three to Lead's right, and me as four to the right of number three. At many bases, Lead and two would take off in formation, followed in 30 seconds by three and four. Unfortunately, the single runway at Ubon was rather narrow (125 feet wide instead of the normal 150 feet), so we took off one at a time, with 30-second spacing. This allowed enough time for the plane ahead to abort and not have to worry about being hit from behind by the wingman. It also lengthened the time required for all four to rejoin, but not by much. We ran the engines up, did our checks, and when we were all ready we signaled with a nod of our heads. Finally, it was my turn. I lit the afterburners, felt the surge of acceleration, and we rolled.

The F-4 didn't take off like a lot of airplanes. In most planes, as you get near takeoff speed, you can feel the airplane through the stick. It just feels as if it wants to take off, as the controls stiffen and gradually become more effective. In the F-4, we started the roll with the stick all the way back, as far as it would go. This gave us the most effective angle of attack and resulted in the shortest takeoff distance. At light loads, you could feel when the airplane was about to fly. Heavy loads were another matter. You computed takeoff speed carefully, and as you approached it, the airplane just sort of left the ground, in pretty much the same attitude you'd been in. There wasn't the normal rotation and liftoff like a lot of airplanes. Once airborne, it felt like I'd popped the speed brakes when I came out of the afterburner, since we were much heavier than normal, and the drag with all the bombs and tanks was much higher. I joined on number three and we proceeded on our way to the target area, in Laos, about 120 miles away. Since the target was close, there was no need to refuel in the air. If all went well, the mission would take about an hour and a half.

The flight to the target area was uneventful, not much different from a training mission back in the States. The weather was perfect, very clear, and there was not a cloud in the sky. I reviewed everything I had to do: what switches to set up, what gun-sight settings to dial in, what dive angle and release altitude to achieve for our particular load, and so on. At 8 miles per minute, it didn't take too long to reach the rendezvous point, and soon the flight lead called us all over to that frequency, and he made a radio call to the FAC. Lo and behold, a voice came up on the radio as if he'd been waiting all day for us to show up! The FACs flew light, propeller aircraft such as the O-2, a converted civilian airplane that had been modified for this unique role. They had a lot of loiter time in the area and numerous radios to contact all the control agencies and fighters. They also flew at much lower altitudes than we did, around 5,000 or 6,000 feet, sometimes lower. This gave them a better view of the ground, but it was also more dangerous. This danger was somewhat offset by the fact that the enemy often would not fire at them because they knew that to do so would soon result in an air strike as the FAC directed any orbiting fighters to strike the guns. These controllers knew the area they were assigned to in great detail, and would often immediately pick up any changes from earlier flights over the area. Once they thought they had found a target, they would describe it to the flight of fighters assigned to them. This is often a lot more difficult than it sounds. The FAC is much lower, and it's difficult to describe a target that may be camouflaged. Once the target was described, he'd insure that everyone had him in sight and then he would roll in and fire a white phosphorous rocket to mark the target. The FAC then got out of the way and directed each flight member to drop their bombs at a certain distance and direction from either his marking rocket or where the bombs hit. It's sort of like trying to direct a blind person through a door, but if he had a target and gave an accurate description, it usually worked. On occasion, there may be friendly forces or civilians nearby, so no fighter could drop a bomb unless cleared to do so by the FAC.

This last part was giving me fits! As our flight spread out and flew in a circle at 18,000 feet, the FAC wanted to know whether everyone had him in sight. Try as I might, I couldn't find him. I began to get quite concerned. Would I mess up this entire mission because I couldn't acquire a visual on the FAC? Fortunately, Dave Carter was used to this, and he politely mentioned that the FAC was at ten o'clock low near a feature on the ground. Whew! Saved from total embarrassment and humiliation. Now I saw why they paired an old head GIB with a newbie front-seater. I armed up my bombs and dialed in the mil settings on the gun sight. This was stimulating. I was about to drop a live bomb on a real target. We had briefed to make about three or four passes on the target. Lead was cleared in and soon dropped some bombs. The FAC called out corrections for two and three in relation to the leader's bombs. Now it was my turn. I could see where three's bombs had hit and thought I knew where the FAC wanted me to drop. I rolled into a 45-degree dive angle and prepared to pickle my bombs at 7,500 feet, which would allow me to bottom out at 4,500 feet, above the effective range of the lighter antiaircraft guns. You don't have a lot of time to make corrections on a high-angle dive-bomb pass. I never did see an actual target, just an estimation of the point on the ground where the FAC had told me to bomb.

Down we went! Airspeed 450 knots, dive angle OK, pipper about where I thought it should be, and release altitude coming up...rapidly! I pickled (pressed the release button on the control stick) and started a four to five G pull-up as I felt the bombs leave the airplane with a big thump. As I pulled up and looked for the rest of the flight, I distinctly remember thinking, "I don't remember all those small cumulus clouds being there when I rolled in. Maybe I was concentrating too much on finding the target." About a second after that thought formed in my head, Dave Carter, in a rather excited voice, said, "Jink! Jink! They're shooting at us!" What I had perceived to be clouds were numerous bursts of antiaircraft fire. My innocence shattered, I immediately started to jink— random changes in all three dimensions so you are not where the gunners had predicted you would be when they fired at you. Often, these storage areas were very well defended, and we had obviously stumbled across one of those. I wasn't as afraid as I thought I would be, because I didn't know what I didn't know. I did look back in time to see my bombs explode, but they appeared to have blown holes in the jungle, and there were no secondary explosions, which would have meant we had hit something lucrative. Somewhat more aware of my surroundings, we all made another pass and dropped the remainder of our bombs. The FAC flew over and took a look at what our handiwork had accomplished. As I recall, he gave us credit for some "possible storage areas" destroyed for our BDA (bomb damage assessment). Such was the frustrating nature of this war. We would often bomb targets that weren't readily visible, and often with inconclusive results. But no one had been hit, and I was now a combat veteran! In a way, it was like a John Wayne movie except that I had a major role in it. While I had seen some flak, there was still an aura of unreality about it. I hadn't seen enough yet to realize that this whole process could get very ugly, and that there were people on the ground who very much wanted to blow me out of the sky.

As we rejoined, one of the airborne command posts asked our flight to fly into Package I, the lower part of North Vietnam, to see whether we could get a radio fix on a crew that had been shot down in that area a few days earlier. There had been some sporadic contact, and if a survivor could hear us fly overhead and come up on his survival radio, we could take a fix on the transmission, which could locate his position. The area was only about 50 miles from our target, so we headed over there and circled for about 10 minutes. We broadcast on the Guard Emergency frequency several times, but never received a response. It had been too long; the crew was probably either dead or captured. This war had become a little more real to me with each passing moment. Although we were unable to find any trace of the crew, it did give me confidence that everything possible would be done if there were any hope at all that someone could be rescued.

Rather short of fuel by now, we headed back to Ubon. I was still in one piece, and nobody in the flight had been hit. Maybe this wouldn't be so bad after all. It still felt somewhat strange, but at least I had completed my first combat mission. Shortly before I wrote this piece, I read "Flyboys" by James Bradley. This is a rather well-known book about nine crewmembers who were shot down in World War II near the island of Ichi Jima, just north of Iwo Jima. Eight of the nine were captured and eventually executed on the island. The ninth, who survived after a harrowing rescue, was President George H. W. Bush, then a very young Navy TBF Avenger pilot. Several of the eight men who did not survive that mission were on their first mission as well. "There but for the grace of God, go I."

CHAPTER 6

Christmas and New Year's 1967

Now that I'd survived my first combat mission, there was another major event to look forward to. The Bob Hope Show was coming to Ubon! I had seen these shows before on television back in the States, but now the actual show was scheduled to be at our base a few days before Christmas, on the 23rd. It's amazing, now that I look back upon it, but even then, Bob Hope had entertained military troops away from home ever since World War II. The recent shows were broadcast on TV, and families Stateside eagerly looked forward to the show since it made them feel a little closer to their loved ones in far-off locations. Although I had only been on the base a short time, it was pretty obvious that everyone was quite excited. This show may have looked pretty spectacular when seen on TV for an hour or so, but when you saw the entire production in person, it was unforgettable.

For one thing, it was a remarkable logistical operation in itself. The military was more than happy to provide transportation for the entertainers, and I was astounded at how much they could accomplish in a short time. A few advance people would arrive a few hours before the scheduled showtime and gather enough data about some of the local events and personalities so that they could write some gags and jokes that had a local flavor. In essence, the show was personalized for each location. This may sound like a trivial matter, but it was tremendously effective and very much appreciated by all of us. A few hours later, the main contingent would arrive, by C-130 or C-141 cargo planes and start the main preparations. The show was scheduled to start at around 1:00 in the afternoon and last for about 2 hours. There was time for a few pictures and autographs after the show, while all the equipment was packed up and reloaded, and then the cast and crew moved to the next location. You couldn't help but admire their stamina. Did I mention that they had some pretty slick females with them? In the show that I saw, Raquel Welch and Joey Heatherton looked pretty foxy. A lot better than seeing a bunch of guys in flying suits every day, but I digress.

I had flown a night mission to Laos the evening before. We landed rather late, and by the time I woke up the next morning, the excitement about the show was quite evident. At any rate, I was hungry around noontime and went to the O Club to get something to eat. We knew the Bob Hope Show was scheduled at 1:00 PM, and we sure as hell didn't want to miss that! We'd already seen them start to set up the stage right in front of the control tower, which was at the midpoint of the airfield. I remember we had plenty of time for a leisurely lunch, and we all talked about how great the show would be. Maybe this war would not be so bad after all? About a half hour before the scheduled showtime, we headed down toward the flight line so we could get good seats.

We arrived about 20 minutes before the show started, and had decent seats, not too far from the stage, on the right-hand side. Gradually, the rest of the squadron congealed around the people they knew. The show started, and for the next 2 hours, it was one of the most wonderful entertainment experiences I've ever witnessed. The show was fabulous, and the fact that a lot of the jokes and references were specific to our base at Ubon really made it special. The timing was perfect, and the entire show just flowed from one segment to the next. The jokes were great, the girls were tremendous, and the entire event took your mind off the war. As the show was about to finish, Bob Hope summoned the entire cast on stage, and the mood suddenly became a bit somber and serious. We'd had our fun. Now Bob reminded everyone of why the show had come at this particular time. He motioned to the orchestra to play "Silent Night." The entire cast started to sing, and, spontaneously, the entire audience joined in. Thirty-six years later, I still get a bit misty-eyed when I think about it. In fact, whenever I hear the familiar refrain, that particular moment at Ubon, Christmas 1967 is the image that pops into my mind with razor-sharp clarity. I usually have to turn my head to avoid the embarrassment.

All of a sudden, you realized just how lonely and far away from home you were. No matter how good a face we tried to put on, we all knew how we felt. We were grateful that Bob Hope and his entertainers had given up their Christmas holiday to entertain us, but it was still a very poignant moment that lingers with me even today. I don't think there was a dry eye in the entire crowd, including the entertainers; I felt tears run down my cheeks and I didn't care. Whatever individual religious beliefs people may have held, the moment had a profound impact on all who were there.

On that note, the show drew to a close. Just as it was ending, several flights of F-4s took off, right in front of the stage. I think Bob thought that this was part of our contribution to the show. In reality, the guys had taken off for a combat mission. Since some of this was filmed for TV back in the States, it must have provided a fitting end to the show. There was time for a few autographs and photo shots with the stars, and I was able to get a few shots of Raquel Welch, all dressed up in an orange Australian flying suit and bush hat in the Base Operations building. It was the end of a spectacular show, and one I'll never forget, for a couple of reasons.

Unbeknownst to me, while I was having lunch in the O Club, the show had been looking for me! Since I was the newest guy in the Wing, and had just flown my first combat mission, they wanted to have me on stage with someone who had completed their 100th mission, and were now about to go home. I guess that would have provided contrast: the oldest and the newest. Alas, they didn't find me in time. As Marlon Brando would say, "I coulda been a contender!" But it was not to be. Instead of being launched on a show-business career, I was relegated to finish my tour, unknown to the public. Such was the lot of the fighter pilot ... so near and yet so far. My lack of stardom notwithstanding, it was a wonderful show that I have not forgotten over many decades. I still value the effort that all those entertainers made on our behalf during those difficult years. Believe me, it was well appreciated.

The pleasant interlude over, the war continued unabated. President Johnson had declared a bombing moratorium for North Vietnam in the vain hope that they might reciprocate in some way. Like my 15 minutes of potential fame with the Bob Hope Show, it was not to be. We still flew missions over the Ho Chi Minh Trail though, since that was definitely not off-limits. If anything, the North Vietnamese took advantage of our benevolent gesture to increase the flow of supplies down the "Trail." I have a vivid memory of my mission on Christmas Eve. Major Tony Doran, my roommate, was the flight leader, and we took off around 9:00 in the evening for a night mission over Laos. I couldn't get over the incongruity of flying a combat mission on the night that's celebrated worldwide to commemorate the birth of Christ, with the message of peace on earth to men of goodwill. And here we were, in the middle of the night, about to bomb folks and war supplies to smithereens. Tony switched our flight over to the frequency to check in with the FAC, call sign Blindbat, a C-130 that had special night-vision equipment, to get our target data. Tony called the FAC, "Blindbat, Honda. Flight of two F-4s." Right on cue, the FAC answered, "Honda, this is Blindbat. Merry Fucking Christmas." That summed up my attitude at least, and I think he spoke for all of us that night. It was dark, it was lonely, and we all wondered what the hell we were doing there on this particular night, of all nights. We bombed where he directed, with no visible results. We flew back to

Ubon, landed, and then went to the Club for a few drinks. I can't remember a more bizarre Christmas Eve.

The next day, Christmas, was about the same except that it was daylight, which made it a little bit more tolerable. I went to Christmas Mass in the chapel, which was said by Father Rydel, the Catholic chaplain. It was hard to reconcile the message I heard at mass with the role I was playing. Later, Tony Doran again led our two-ship strike into Laos. Again we dropped the bombs where directed with no visible results. There was very little flak, or at least I didn't see much. Again, I experienced the same bizarre sentiment I'd had the night before. We landed back at Ubon, and downed a few more drinks to wash away what was left of the rather morose day. I was starting to get the impression that maybe things didn't change much in this war. Did I mention that it was only my fourth combat mission?

The week between Christmas and New Year's flew by (no pun intended). New Year's Eve was a replay of Christmas, but not quite so morose. We had a night mission in southern Laos and landed around 10:00 PM. There was still time to go to the club and have a couple belts to celebrate the New Year. The Wing Commander at the time was not too much in favor of this type of activity, and before you could say "que pasa," the club was full of air policemen discretely suggesting that perhaps it would be wiser if we left the bar until another day. Admittedly, we had gotten a little out-of-hand. There were several games that thickheaded fighter pilots used to play to amuse themselves. One of them was "Dead Bug." How this ever got started, I'll never know, but it was an established part of the lifestyle at the O Club bar. The rules were not too complicated. All you had to do was shout "Dead Bug!" As a self-respecting aviator, you were obliged to fall to the floor at once, with your hands and feet up in the air. The last one to hit the floor bought the drinks for the whole bar! Good motivation to be quick. However, at $.50 per drink, and even at the low wages our masters paid us, it didn't drive us to bankruptcy even if we lost several rounds. Another favorite pastime was "MiG Sweep." One squadron would link hands and run (yes, run!) from one end of the bar to the other, knocking everything in their path out of the way. Yeah, it was fun, but it did cause a lot of damage and, on occasion, some busted bones. The Thai bartender would dutifully keep track of all the damage, and miraculously the next day, an itemized bill would be presented to the squadron. A collection was taken up, and sure enough, we would be back in the good graces of the O Club gods again. It doesn't take much to keep fighter pilots happy; they're a lot like little kids.

Anyway, on this particular New Year's Eve, we outdid ourselves and were eventually escorted out of the Club. By then, I don't think we were capable of much resistance. I remember mouthing a few dynamic oaths and well-chosen phrases, then slinking/lurching off to my room. Thus ended 1967 and my introduction to combat. It was not quite what I'd expected, but in many respects was more. Had I made the world safe for democracy? Not quite . . . maybe next year. Such were the thoughts that raced through my hungover head on New Year's Day, 1968. I took a long shower, girded my loins, and resolved to change the world for the better in the coming year.

CHAPTER 7

"You're OK!" "No, I'm Not!"

I had begun to settle in. It was January 4, 1968, and I'd been at Ubon for almost a month and was near the end of my checkout phase. Tonight would be my twelfth mission—a night two-ship flight against the Ho Chi Minh Trail. The trail was a series of interconnected dirt roads that allowed the North Vietnamese to move their supplies from Hanoi, all the way down to South Vietnam. Since trucks and supply vehicles were much easier to see during daylight hours, most of their activity took place at night. There were three other squadrons at Ubon, and I was assigned to the world-famous, highly respected, 433 TFS, Satan's Angels. We all took our share of the night missions, but we didn't specialize in it like the 497th did. Night ground attack was a dangerous business, and most pilots preferred to fly during the day. You got shot at more in daylight, but at least you could see where you were going.

I'd flown seven night combat missions up to this point, and they had all been relatively uneventful. We were to work with a FAC call sign: "Nail," in the portion of southern Laos where the Ho Chi Minh Trail came out of Mu Gia Pass in North Vietnam and snaked through Laos before going back into South Vietnam near Khe Sanh. As a major trans-shipment point, it was well defended. My back-seater was Capt. Jim Chastain. Captain John Hamm was the flight lead. We completed the usual premission details and were soon airborne and headed for our rendezvous with the FAC, airborne over Laos in an O-2. About 20 minutes later, we made contact with Nail, and he briefed us on our target for the night.

We turned off all exterior navigation lights. I'd dimmed the front cockpit lights as much as I dared. I could still read my instruments, but just barely. This allowed my night vision to adjust to the darkness so I could see outside better. Nail described the target and marked it with some ground flares. Then he told us where to bomb in relation to the flares. As the wingman, I orbited high and stayed clear of the flight leader as he prepared to attack the target. Lead dropped his bombs, and we reversed positions. He held high, while I descended to strike the target. In this way, we avoided a potential collision. I saw Lead's bombs hit, and was amazed at the amount of flak that was fired at him.

Nail called me, "Two, if you have the target in sight, you're cleared in."

John Hamm, the flight lead, responded, "I'm clear above you."

I saw the target area clearly, because at least three 37-mm antiaircraft guns shot at Lead on his first pass, and fires still burned on the ground.

I hit the mike button on the throttle, "Two, target in sight. In from the west." I then pulled almost inverted into a 45-degree dive-bomb pass and rolled out with the gun-sight pipper just short of the target. It was a good dive-bomb pass. If I reached my precomputed bomb release altitude with the planned airspeed and proper dive angle, I would hit the target. No trick for a showdog! Some sixth sense told me I needed to be careful, but the thought passed quickly.

As we tried to destroy targets on the ground, the people down there did their best to hinder our success. The antiaircraft fire was often intense, and the fear of getting hit made it difficult to focus on meeting the required parameters for accurate dive-bombing. We didn't have navigation lights on, but if there was any illumination, such as from the moon, they might spot us. On this night, the moon was minimal. Often, the gunners just fired a barrage over the approach path and hoped we'd run into some of the shells. I was aware of all this as I watched the pipper track up to the bomb release point.

So far, so good. The FAC had given me the winds, as best he knew, so I offset the bomb release point slightly into the wind to compensate. Almost there . . . dive angle okay . . . airspeed right on, almost at pickle altitude . . . Now! I hit the bomb release button on the stick with my right thumb, and felt the bombs leave the airplane . . . thunk, thunk! I immediately started a high G pullout and began to jink. Now the guns were really shooting! More than on John's pass!

What happened next is as vivid now as it was at that moment. I do a rolling pull-up to the right. I want to get away from these big blobs of fire as they come toward me. I'm scared, but can't help staring at the flak. It mesmerizes in a detached, bizarre, kind of way. I know the gunners are trying to kill me, but head-on, it all looks like a lot of slow-motion baseballs, on fire, heading toward us. As the blobs get close, they seem to speed up, and "swoosh" over the top of the canopy. They seem inches away. I can't imagine living more than a few more seconds. The shells seem so close, and they are everywhere! Guns on the left side are also firing furiously, and the whole spectacle to the side looks like a water hose that shoots out curved blobs of fire as the gunners try to hit us. I count at least five gun sites shooting. Some of the shells explode, and are getting closer to my plane. And I'm only looking at some of them! For every tracer I see, there are several more rounds between that I don't see but that are equally deadly. I've got to get away from this stuff!

I look over my left shoulder and watch in terror, as each exploding shell seems to be closer. I jink wildly, so that I don't get hit. The bursts are getting closer, and I'm really scared. It is very nerve wracking, and my concern with the flak diverts my attention from what I should be doing—maintaining control of this fighter.

At last, we're clear of the worst if it. I still jink though, just to be sure. A shell has just exploded at my seven o'clock low position, but it's no danger. I look back in the cockpit as I abruptly roll the wings level from my right hand rolling pullout. I'm horrified at what I see! The attitude indicator shows us in a very steep climb—at least 60 degrees, maybe closer to 75 or more, although wings level. The needle on the airspeed indicator is rapidly decreasing, going through 150 knots at a horrendous rate! All I can see are stars in front of the canopy. I'm in an unusual attitude! And in an F-4—an airplane that doesn't tolerate high angles of attack and adverse yaw very well without going into what is known as a post-stall gyration.

I can't focus! Mentally or visually! We are in very serious trouble and will likely get killed if something isn't done quickly, but I feel as if I've never been in an airplane before! I can't read the instruments. I feel like I'm yawing, spinning, and rolling, all at the same time. I'm aware of a sound, similar to a vacuum cleaner, but that's all. If Jim is talking to me, I can't hear him. I sort of feel conscious, but not quite. The sensation is similar to waking up from a deep, dreamy sleep, or coming out of anesthesia; a feeling of utter helplessness and total mental confusion. Time passes . . . I have no idea of the length. It seems like slow motion. Ever so slowly, I realize I'm in an airplane, an F-4! Did I get in a spin? If so, at night, the main recourse is to eject. My hand gropes for the D-ring on the seat between my legs. If I pull it, we will both be ejected. I'm not even sure if that's the right thing to do. I have no idea how high we are.

It seems like forever, but now I can start to read the instruments. I see that we are straight and level at about 10,000 feet above the terrain as the airspeed creeps back up past 200 knots. We are flying! I can hardly believe it. I hear Jim from the backseat say, "You're okay!" I emphatically respond, "No, I'm not!" But things are getting better. I can see the instruments, and I'm more aware of my surroundings. I have never experienced anything like this in an airplane before, and am absolutely shaken.

But I still have some problems to overcome. The last thing I remembered before all this happened was seeing stars as I looked through the front windscreen of the canopy. There is no discernable horizon. Even though the instruments indicate we are in level flight, and regaining airspeed, I still think I'm looking at stars. I feel a tremendous urge to push the nose down, since I'm convinced we are still in a steep climb! If I put my face right in front of the ADI (attitude director indicator), then the feeling subsides. As soon as I sit back in the ejection seat, I feel like I'm still climbing steeply, and the urge to lower the nose returns. The feeling is so strong that it's hard to believe the instruments. I can't tell any difference between the stars and fires on the ground.

About this time, the flight lead, John Hamm, calls, "Two, what's your position?" I haven't said a word on the radio since I rolled in. I have the presence of mind to say, "Standby Lead, I'm having problems." I look at the navigation instruments and see that we were headed into North Vietnam, and we definitely don't want to go there. It takes all my concentration to make a simple 30-degree bank turn to head back to Laos. This is normally about as simple as a left turn at an intersection when driving. I have experienced vertigo/spatial disorientation on many occasions, but never to this extent. Now I am reduced to a very scared pilot, over enemy territory, forced to use every bit of my instrument-flying skills just to make a simple 30 degrees of bank, level turn of about 180 degrees. It is a very humbling experience, and I question how this night will end.

Suddenly, as if in answer to my prayers, another airplane that was bombing another target nearby drops an airborne flare. Whammo! All of a sudden, I have a visual horizon and I can see where the ground and the sky are. It is absolutely amazing. That quickly, my vertigo disappears.

I call John, "Two's okay. I'm a few miles east, heading back to the target and climbing to Base plus five," which means I'll be at 5,000 feet above a coded base altitude that changes every day.

We continue with the mission. It is like night and day now (no pun intended). I'm back in control of the situation—as it should be.

I knew immediately what had happened. You spend much time and effort in pilot training to learn how to fly on instruments. It's often the phase that causes students the most grief because there are two main problems: First, you have to learn complicated procedures that must be flown very precisely. But the most important thing you must learn is to totally ignore whatever physical sensations you feel and maintain control strictly by what the instruments tell you. Nonpilots are tempted to say, "Of course," at this point.Wish it were so simple. When there is no visible horizon, such as when flying at night or in weather, your body plays tricks on you because of vertigo, or spatial disorientation. We are able to maintain our sense of balance and equilibrium through a very complex sensory mechanism located in the inner ear. There are tiny hairs within the inner ear, which can detect minute accelerations up, down, and sideways. But there's a problem. If the rate of movement is less than 15 degrees per second and there is no visual horizon to corroborate the sensation, our inner-ear mechanism often cannot detect the motion, or may perceive it as something else. Worse, a sudden movement can give you an entirely false sensation. For example, an abrupt acceleration may convince you that you are in a climb when you are not. You have to learn to ignore these normal sensations and believe your instruments. Night flying is very similar to flying in clouds because there is often no visual reference to substantiate or disprove the sensations. For these reasons, a pilot is taught to make very slow, small, and precise motions to prevent or minimize false sensations, which can be almost overpowering at times. An extreme form of this experience is known as Coriolis Vertigo. It is very rare because the fluid in two of the semicircular canals of the ear, 90 degrees opposed to each other, must be in motion at the same instant. It produces an extreme sensory overload, and with no visual horizon to overcome the sensation, you become violently disoriented. I had never experienced it, and most pilots never will. I tried to demonstrate it to students in pilot training but was never successful. When I abruptly looked back in the cockpit after staring at the flak at seven o'clock low, I had apparently also rolled the wings to the left at the same time. This combination of movements was enough to induce inner-ear fluid motion in two geometric planes simultaneously. The only reason the plane was still flying when I recovered was because of habit and training; I had instinctively neutralized the controls, which prevented a stall, or worse. During the 15 or so seconds I was disoriented, I had absolutely no control. There was no great skill or airmanship on my part whatsoever. This is why night ground attack is so dangerous. You violate all the procedures designed to minimize vertigo, and I had just done exactly that.

By now, the gunners in the target area were well aware of our presence. Lead rolled in on another target marked by Nail and really got shot at pretty bad. The FAC wanted to know if I saw where the guns were. "Was the sky blue? The Pope Catholic?" How could I miss them? He cleared me in to attack the gun sites that just fired at the flight lead. As I screwed up my courage and rolled in, I selected the switches for rockets on the armament panel. By now, the guns directly in front had begun to fire at me. I saw about three separate gun sites and prepared to fire all three pods of 2.75-inch rockets (nineteen rockets per pod). I mashed the pickle button on top of the control stick. Instead of all three pods firing at once, each pod fired its contents in a slow-motion, ripple-fire mode.

It took several seconds for each pod to empty. "So what?" Well, the problem is that the gunners can't see you very well at night. To a large extent, they are guessing where you are, or where you are going to be. I just solved their problem for them! They now knew exactly where I was, and shot up, and in front of my projected flight path. Several other gun sites opened up as well! I could see the tracer's arc toward me like a proverbial water hose. I pulled up, hard, and to the right. Somehow, I had to keep myself from running into those tracers marching toward me. As I climbed and turned, I had performed a barrel roll! Jim, in a rather excited voice, said from the backseat, "You're inverted!" After my vertigo episode, Jim was understandably concerned. When I responded, "It's OK, I know what I'm doing this time!" that seemed to calm him down. We outmaneuvered the guns, and my rockets found their target and knocked out several gun sites. By now we were out of gas and headed for home. Slowly, my breathing and pulse started to return to normal.

Only later, as we debriefed the mission, did Jim realize how acutely disoriented I had been. As I said, this was my twelfth mission, and I think it validated the theory that if you survived the first fifteen missions, then you had a reasonable chance to survive the rest of the tour. It was also one of the most humbling experiences of my flying career and absolutely one of the most terrifying, because of the feeling of utter helplessness. It probably only lasted about 15 seconds, but it seemed like forever at the time. I faced many other stressful situations, but at least I knew what was taking place. In this case, I didn't, and the experience is still as vivid in my mind now as it was 38 years ago.

CHAPTER 8

A Typical Mission

So what was a typical mission like? It's a bit hard to explain because from a pilot's perspective, there were three different wars in Southeast Asia at the time. First, there was the "In Country War," which is what the public is most familiar with today. This was fought in South Vietnam and involved many close air-support missions to assist American and South Vietnamese forces that often were in direct contact with the Viet Cong or North Vietnamese enemy. In many cases, our forces would have been wiped out if the air strikes had not saved the day. Often, these planes would have to drop bombs or strafe within feet of friendly forces. It was that critical. The battle for Khe Sanh was a good example. I once had a neighbor who knew I'd been a fighter pilot in the war, who would thank me with tears in his eyes, for saving his life during a battle he'd been involved in. I was honored, but had to admit that I had flown very few missions in the south and hadn't been responsible for his longevity. Nonetheless, it was a proud moment to be a fighter pilot.

The second type of air war was that flown over Laos. Although a "secret war," because both the United States and North Vietnam had signed agreements that declared Laos a neutral nation, it was an open secret and a vicious war nonetheless. It seldom involved troops in contact with the enemy, unless it was a search and rescue mission to try to save a downed crewman. The missions were attempts to interdict enemy supply lines, through which the material of war flowed to the Viet Cong in South Vietnam. Some of these routes were well established, and heavily defended, often *very* heavily defended. They were also difficult and, in some cases, impossible to see. Since there were also friendly villagers and sensitive areas near some of these targets in Laos, a FAC had to clear us in on each pass in that country. They were far more familiar with the area than we were since they flew in the same area during every mission. We might be on a mission to Hanoi one day and then fly in southern Laos the next. It was

51

quite possible that we might not be in a particular target area for several weeks or more.

And then, there was the air campaign over North Vietnam, which was known as "Rolling Thunder." This was the most intense and dangerous. To some extent, the air war in southern Laos and lower North Vietnam overlapped since the supply routes ran through both countries. The farther north you went in North Vietnam, the more dangerous the mission became.

There was no hard requirement for a FAC in North Vietnam. The entire area was considered hostile. To improve effectiveness, we did use what became known as "Fast FACs," and the F-100 Misty FAC program was the most notable one of my tour. The principle was the same as that of the FACs in Laos and South Vietnam, but the "Mistys" used a two-place F-100 for survivability. We'd already proved that slower aircraft could not survive in areas that had intense defenses. Most of what is now known as the Ho Chi Minh Trail was a series of crude dirt roadways and river-crossing areas in both Laos and North Vietnam. There were no autobahns in that part of the world. From the air, it all looked like one huge, impenetrable expanse of jungle. The triple jungle canopy was often so thick that we carried 100 feet of nylon tape in our parachute harness so we could rappel to the ground if we bailed out and became stuck in the trees. The dense jungle also made it very difficult to detect targets on the ground, and this is what the North Vietnamese and Pathet Lao used to their advantage to conceal supplies. The number of bombs and rockets dropped on these targets was astronomical, and some of the heavily bombed areas looked like the surface of the moon—no vegetation for miles. That also meant they were most likely well defended.

The closer we got to the source of supplies, and the further north we flew, the heavier were the defenses. This was the most dangerous air war, which included the high-threat targets clustered in the northern areas of North Vietnam, particularly in the Hanoi and Haiphong areas. When we went to one of these targets, it was treated as a very dangerous mission indeed. We went as part of a strike package, which consisted of aircraft such as the EB-66, which would jam and spoof the North Vietnamese radar with electronic emitters. F-105 "Wild Weasels" went ahead of the strike force to tempt the enemy to launch SAMs. The Weasels could detect this with their sophisticated equipment and if a SAM was fired, they would launch a Shrike missile, which, under ideal conditions, could home in on the source of the emission and blast it into a bazillion pieces, or at least force it off the air long enough for the strike force to hit the target. It was a very dangerous mission, and I was grateful that my earlier attempt to be a Weasel had been turned down! One or two MiG CAPs would either be ahead of the strike force or off to the side. Their task was to intercept any MiGs that might attempt to shoot down the fighter-bombers in the strike force. From the MiG pilot's perspective, he was successful if he forced the fighter-bombers to jettison their ordinance to defend themselves. Those bombs wouldn't hit the target. If the target were well defended, there might even be a flight of four, whose sole mission was to bomb the guns around the target and suppress the flak seconds before the bombers rolled in on the main target. And, of course, the main part of the strike force consisted of the F-4s or F-105s that had been assigned to bomb a specific target such as an airfield, railroad, power plant, or any other high-value target. The entire strike package meant that thirty-six to forty-eight airplanes were converging on the target within seconds of each other. On top of this, it was an absolute necessity to air refuel because of the loads and distances involved. Prestrike for sure, and, perhaps, poststrike refueling was often necessary. This involved four to six tankers on preestablished "tracks" over Laos or the Gulf of Tonkin. The whole force refueled at the same time so they could drop off to-gether and form the strike package, or large formation. It was one of the most complex operations I have ever seen. Because of the political sensitivities, all targets within a 30-mile ring of Hanoi had to be approved by the Joint Chiefs of Staff before we could take off, and this go-ahead often didn't happen until we were in the mission briefing. When I went on one of these missions, I felt as though it was a major big deal. There was an intense excitement and sense of fear at the same time.

But despite the vast differences between the missions, there were some com-mon threads. We usually found out what mission we would be on the afternoon before. If it were a low-threat target, I didn't worry too much and got a reason-able night's sleep. On the other hand, a Route Package VI mission to Phuc Yen Airfield near Hanoi was guaranteed to induce thoughts about my own mortality. I would have a very restless night in that instance. As a friend of mine once re-marked about flying combat, "It doesn't bother me too much. I can sometimes go almost 5 minutes without thinking about it." And that, pretty much, was my experience. It was hard to erase it from my thoughts, but at the same time I found that I developed a very fatalistic attitude about it. As I mentioned before, the first few missions have an air of unreality about them. It is almost like watching your-self in a war movie. You have met the "monster" and survived your first missions. Others may not have had such a benign experience. I've known people who were shot down on their first five missions, sometimes on their first mission. Said one such survivor after he was picked up, "One down and ninety-nine to go. It's going to be a long war!"

So, I can only relate my thoughts and experiences. In my case, after several missions, I'd had a few close calls and seen a few airplanes shot down. Flak, especially at night, is an unsettling experience, particularly as I saw tracer's zip over my canopy during dive-bomb passes. Over time, your certainty that you'll survive this whole business is called into question. I recall that I reached a point where I thought I'd used all my luck. It just didn't seem possible that I could do this indefinitely and not get hit. When a SAM blew up 500 feet underneath me one day, it accelerated this line of thought. I'm sure it sounds strange, but I remember a point when I wanted to get hit! Nothing bloody or messy, of course, but enough to drive the odds back to zero again. Maybe a couple of 23-mm holes in the wing, or something like that—not a major calamity.

That said, we didn't wander around with a morbid "Woe is I" kind of attitude. My term for it was "resigned acceptance." Of course I hoped it wouldn't happen, but I felt there was a better than even chance that it might. I don't believe I was unique in this aspect. A casual observer might never have detected this attitude if he were to observe the pilots as they went about their day-to-day business. "Stiff upper lip," as the Brits would say, "just carry on." Or, as another friend would quip, "If you can't take a joke, you shouldn't have signed up!" For the most part, we all kept these thoughts to ourselves. I never saw anyone refuse to fly in spite of whatever fears they may have harbored within themselves. The worst disgrace, the absolute worst disgrace, would be to be deemed not worthy by your peers. So I pushed these fears to the back of my mind as best I could.

The big missions to the Hanoi area took off early in the morning or afternoon, and the entire mission would take 3 or more hours. Those flights would start to brief at 2:00 AM or 9:00 AM to allow adequate time for all the premission planning and a detailed update plus the coordination with the other wings that were not at Ubon, but would be on the mission. As I said, it was a very complicated endeavor.

For a typical mission in Laos or lower North Vietnam, we would start to prepare about 2 or 3 hours before the scheduled takeoff time. First, we plotted the route on maps and determined how we would approach the target and discussed any special tactics that would be employed. The order that assigned us to the target also listed the ordinance that was on each airplane. Most of the time it was the same, although for some missions it was significantly different. For example, on night missions, one aircraft might have more flares and a different mix of bombs or rockets. This was also true if the type target were not known, such as an armed reconnaissance mission, where we searched for whatever target we could find. Once we knew the bomb load, we computed the release parameters and gun-sight settings that would allow us to drop the weapons on the target. At this stage of the war, late 1967 and on, we had determined that the tactics used early in the conflict were not effective. We suffered too many losses. When "Rolling Thunder" began, the USAF believed that we could go in at low altitude, very fast, and then pop up and roll in on the target to minimize exposure to antiaircraft fire. It's axiomatic that the closer to the target you are when you drop the bombs, the more accurate you will be. Alas, we soon learned that the sheer number of guns on the ground meant that you would be in the effective range of the antiaircraft fire most of the time during your actual attack. The losses were unacceptable. So we switched tactics, approached the target, and released the ordinance at much higher altitudes. We'd discovered that the probability of getting hit went up about 80 percent when we went below 4,500 feet in the target area. No, we weren't as accurate, and it was harder to acquire the target, but it was a reasonable trade-off given the circumstances.

Once we had the flight planned and weapons computations completed, we checked the intelligence folders for the latest data on the target area. Often there were photos taken by reconnaissance aircraft. Sometimes they were quite current, but sometimes they were rather dated. The big strikes near Hanoi usually had recent photos. We would study those in great detail so that we could recognize the target, since we would have just a few seconds in the area. Once all that was completed, it was off to the intelligence brief, which was held in a large room, adjacent to the planning area.

If the strikes were in the same general area of Laos, or the lower part of North Vietnam, then several flights would brief at once, since a lot of the information was common to all the targets. The intelligence officer would give the latest information available. Some of it applied to the war in general, but most of it was specific to the mission area assigned that day. Of particular interest was any information on aircraft that had been shot down. It was not uncommon for a crewman to come up on the survival radio a day or two after they went down. If it were at all feasible, a massive effort would be launched to try to rescue them. Sometimes we knew where the downed crew was, but the rescue forces might have been unable to complete the rescue. If we could hear the survivor on the radio, he might still be alive and perhaps could be rescued. In most cases, if they weren't picked up within a day or two after they were shot down, the odds on a successful rescue were pretty slim. At that point the survivor was likely dead or had been captured. We all realized that one of us might be the subject of this briefing someday, which gave it an added sense of urgency. Often, a "safe area" was briefed. This was an area where friendly forces (U.S. Special Forces, or certain tribesmen in Laos) operated. There was a code word for each area, and the theory was that if you could evade in that area, these forces would try to rescue you from the ground. I was always rather skeptical about how realistic this was, but strange things happened in Laos. Finally, any specific info about the immediate targets was discussed and any questions would be answered. If the target just involved a four-ship flight, the update lasted about 15 minutes or so, and the detailed briefing by the flight leader was often done in the same room.

The situation for the large missions near the Hanoi area was quite a bit different. For one thing, there were many more crews involved, and the detailed preparation that would precede the actual mission brief was more intensive. Sometimes, each separate flight had to consult with adjacent flights on the mission details. There was a definite added sense of urgency—these weren't "milk runs." A typical mission for these strikes might consist of two MiG CAP flights, a flak suppression flight, a Wild Weasel flight, and perhaps four flights that would bomb the target. On these missions, it was also standard practice for a fifth crew to brief with each flight as an "airborne spare." They would take off with the flight and fly with them to the tanker. If anyone in that flight had to abort their mission prior to the drop-off from the tanker, the spare would refuel and take their place. If no one aborted, the spare would return to Ubon or sometimes join up with another spare and proceed on an alternate mission. You never ever went on a combat mission by yourself. The F-4 was a great aerodyne, but it was also very complicated, and system failures were not uncommon. There were some systems that had to be operable for a trip to Hanoi—electronic counter-measure pods, radar, missiles, and, of course, basic aircraft functions. Most of the time, the spares weren't needed, but on occasion they had to fill the gap.

The briefing for these missions would often fill the entire room. Sometimes the Wing Commander, Vice Commander, or Director of Operations would be there, especially if it were a high-value target. There was always a sense of foreboding at these briefings. As I looked around the room, I realized that some of these people might not be here for the debriefing 6 or so hours later. It might even be me. It didn't happen all the time, but there were enough times when it did that I could never dismiss it from my mind.

On the "big" missions, there was a detailed briefing after the intelligence portion. These missions always had a mission commander who was a senior, very experienced, pilot. He was responsible for the entire strike force, an awesome job. Experience meant more than rank here. Often it would be a senior Captain who had the most experience. It was an absolute test of leadership, and the stakes were too high to allow someone who didn't have an excellent grasp of the situation to lead the show. With that many airplanes in a small expanse of sky, the force couldn't be turned around on a dime. It took a lot of "thinking ahead of the airplane," and they had to live with the results. It was not a simple task.

In that case, after the overall strike-force briefing, the individual flights went to their squadron areas and went over their individual flight procedures. Again, the purpose was to make sure that, as far as was possible, there were no questions left unanswered. We tried to plan for every eventuality and at least have a method to deal with the unexpected. Clausewitz called it the "fog of war" and he was exactly right. No matter how well we planned, there were always unexpected things that popped up and required an immediate response. As far as possible, we tried to anticipate what they might be. After that, there might be time to get a quick snack, but that was rare. Regardless of whether it was a big strike package, or a four-ship to Package I, there came a point when all the premission tasks had been done, and you still had a few minutes before it was time to "suit up" and go to the airplanes. This was the part I hated the most. You were alone with your thoughts, and there wasn't much conversation.

In some respects, I often felt like a condemned man about to meet his fate. Call that negative thinking if you will, but I sometimes felt that way, especially on the difficult missions. I didn't talk about it, and maybe it wasn't obvious to my squadron mates, but this lull was always a difficult time for me. To calm my fears, I reviewed in my head all the tasks I would have to do on the mission: switch settings, rejoin procedures, emergency procedures, radio frequencies, call signs, and so on. I tried to anticipate anything that might give me an edge in the combat that would take place in a few hours. It also helped take my mind off my fears. At last, even that ordeal was over, and it was time to "suit up."

There was one vital step before we suited up, and that was to hit the latrines. The F-4 had no bathroom, so you would not be able to take care of nature's functions until you landed. Once that was done, it was just a few steps to the Personal Equipment room.

The 433rd Tactical Fighter Squadron (Satan's Angels) had the PE room located just off the lounge where we had a perpetual coffee machine and a few snacks. Since the war was a 24-hour affair, it was busy all the time. As you entered the room, there were long racks that held the parachute harnesses, survival vests, and G-suits, with an individual wooden locker for each crew member above that. The individual lockers held all your personal stuff: gun belt and .38-caliber pistol, survival knives, and whatever other items you might have. Before each mission, you had to "sanitize" yourself, as it was so eloquently phrased. What that meant was you had to remove any items that could give the enemy personal information. There were just a few items we were allowed to carry: a Geneva ID card, which was supposed to mean we would fall under the protocols agreed to at the Geneva Convention for the treatment of POWs; and our military ID card, which had our name, rank, and serial number. Everything of a personal nature was to be left in our lockers until we returned. Our flying suits had no patches on them, although we did have a leather patch with wings and our name sewn over the left breast pocket. I wasn't totally scrupulous in this regard. I always carried a rosary that my Irish grandmother had given me, a prayer to St. Joseph, and a St. Christopher medal. What could they do to me? Send me on a mission to Hanoi? Other than that, I followed the rules.

This was the "suiting up" process, and at least for me, it was a very ritualistic affair. At first I didn't realize it, but after a few missions I found that I tended to do it the same way every time. If it had worked for the previous missions, why tempt fate? First I would "sanitize" and leave all the personal stuff in my locker. Next was the G-suit. This apparel looked like a cowboy's "chaps," and it covered your lower legs and abdomen with a hose on the left that would plug into the cockpit. I also carried a survival radio and an extra battery in the pocket, and there was another survival knife sewn onto the back of the G-suit as well. Next came the Matt Dillon business. I strapped on the pistol, survival knife, and gun belt. The bottom of the holster for the .38-caliber pistol had a leather strap, which I tied around my thigh. The old gunfighters in the West used to do this so they could "draw" faster, but in our case, it was so the holster would not flail around in the violent slipstream if we had to eject. Even though I was left-handed, I had to wear mine on my right side, so it wouldn't interfere with the drag chute handle on the F-4. We carried several rounds of ammo in the pistol belt, but a lot of it consisted of tracers to signal with, if necessary. Next came the all-important survival vest. This thing looked like a fly-fisherman's vest, and had several well-designed pockets that held an incredible amount of critical gear that would become your lifeline if you were shot down. The most important item from my viewpoint was the survival radio. This broadcast a tone on the emergency frequency that could not be mistaken for anything else. When you heard that, somebody was in dire trouble. We always tested these before every mission, and there was quite a bit of noise as everyone pulled out the antenna to activate the "beeper." We also had another radio in the survival kit that was part of the ejection seat. We could talk and receive on the handheld radio, which was crucial to a successful rescue. The vest also held a first aid kit, compass, extra ammunition, a small flare gun with several rounds, a couple orange-smoke dispensers (which could be seen in the dense jungle at the critical last stages of the rescue), language pamphlets with emergency phrases, maps, and the "blood chit." This last item was a silk map with messages in several languages that stated the U.S. Government would reward anyone with gold who helped the person shot down return to U.S. control. As far as I know, it was never used, although I was aware of one incident where the North Vietnamese discussed it with the rescue forces, but to no avail. The pilot was still captured. Almost finished, the parachute harness came next. The actual parachute was located in the Martin-Baker ejection seat, and this harness had fittings that connected to the parachute riser cords. When you ejected, a very elaborate system would extract you from the seat, and the para-chute would deploy. Next, you put on your camouflaged helmet and tested the oxygen mask to make sure there were no leaks and to insure the microphone worked in the mask. Most pilots also wore a kneeboard, which held cards with the mission data as well as maps. Now you were ready to "step" and proceed to the airplane. I went through this ritual in the same exact way, every mission. It had worked before, so I didn't want to anger the ritual gods. Superstition at its finest.

The squadron had a few bread van trucks with seats along the sides that we used to ride out to the planes. Since the planes were all in individual revetments for protection, we wouldn't see our other flight members again until we started to taxi out. We faced each other in these converted bread vans, and self-conscious banter would fill most of the ride, as we all tried to convey an attitude of business as usual, or, as Alfred E. Newman of the "Mad" comic series used to say, "What, me worry?" One by one, we'd arrive at our airplanes, pick up our gear, and get off the truck to be greeted by the airplane crew chief. If all went well, we would see each other in the same truck a few hours later as we were picked up to debrief the mission.

The F-4 Phantom was a complicated airplane, with its myriad of systems. Later, in the Pentagon, I would hear the statement that 37 hours of maintenance was required for every 1 hour of flight. I was not shocked. While the airplane was most advanced for its day, the electronics were often tube type, not transistor, and required much adjustment. The crew chief was responsible for the overall condition of the airplane, and to do this, he relied on specialists in hydraulics, avionics, armaments, ejection seats, and a host of other disciplines. The maintenance crews had often been up all night to insure that the airplanes were ready to go when we arrived. The crew chief had all the aircraft forms and would brief us on the history of write-ups and how they had been corrected. For those not familiar with aviation, many times a discrepancy would be written up, and try as they might, the ground crew often could not duplicate the problem. The best that could be done was to detail how they had tried to solve the problem and make the pilot aware of it, should it occur again. If we had any doubts or questions about the status of the airplane, it was our last chance to get them resolved. Now you might think that because of all the apprehension that I alluded to earlier, that pilots would seize on any opportunity to find something wrong with the airplane so they could abort the mission and not lose face. In fact, I think the opposite was true. Although everyone had their fears, the prospect of being thought a coward and letting your peers down was a bigger motivator. I suspect that many pilots took airplanes with minor problems and figured they could cope with them in the air. Obviously, no one would go without radios, for example, but then the airplane would not have been put on the schedule if an item that serious had not been fixed. My impression over my entire tour was that the maintainers, or "Phantom Phyxers" as they were sometimes known by, did an excellent job, often under very adverse conditions, such as the monsoon rains.

Once the forms were checked, I would preflight the airplane and weapons while the GIB would start to set up the inertial navigation system. I relaxed a bit at this point. I was busy and had many things to do, which kept my mind off whatever fears I had conjured up. It was also something over which I had some control, which made me feel better. That completed, it was time to climb into the beast. The crew chief would help me get strapped in (it's rather cramped, and some of the straps are hard to reach). When I was done, he'd climb down and remove the ladder from the cockpit. I'd put my helmet on and check in with the back-seater to make sure we could talk to each other; then we would begin our checklists. This didn't take too long, and soon, 30 minutes before the scheduled takeoff time, it was time to start engines. When both engines were started, we continued our checklists and tested all the systems on the airplane. The GIB had a very large number of checks to perform on the radar and other weapon systems, and if there were a problem, you wanted to find it at this point. If you did discover a problem and had to abort the airplane, there sometimes was a spare, but it was rare that it was configured with the proper armament load for the mission. Even if it were, the entire preflight process had to be completed and there seldom was enough time. If there were no way to make it, then the designated airborne spare went in your place on the large missions. Soon the flight leader would call for the flight to check in on the radio, and we all taxied to the end of the runway for a "last chance" check and to arm the weapons. In the warm, humid Southeast Asia sun, we were often soaked with sweat by this point.

That completed, we took off. The heavy loads and narrow runway at Ubon dictated that we take off singly, and then join up in formation right after takeoff. If it were a large strike, then the first flight, the mission commander, would circle back and fly over the runway as the last flights took off. This made it easier for the trailing flights to rejoin the entire formation. You were now on your way! I must admit that even now, years later, I can still hear Wagner's "Ride of the Valkyries" in my mind. It was without exaggeration an exciting, intense experience, and I felt as if I were a definite player in a major operation.

If this was a lower North Vietnam or Laos mission, we proceeded to the target. In the case of the large strikes in the more northern parts of North Vietnam, we formed up with the other flights involved and proceeded to the tanker "anchors," or preestablished areas where the KC-135 tankers would orbit for aerial refueling. The F-4 (and F-105 as well) burned huge amounts of fuel with a full load of bombs and external drop tanks. The idea was to insure we had as much fuel as possible before we flew into this high-threat area. The tankers would drop us off as far as they could, without exposing themselves to danger, since they were unarmed and would have been quite vulnerable. Strikes to most targets in Laos and lower North Vietnam didn't require tankers and would take about 20 to 30 minutes to reach.

Regardless of the type of mission, there came the point where you reached the target and had to roll in and attack it. A common question is, "What does it feel like?" First of all, I have to say that the war in the air is a somewhat impersonal, antiseptic, mechanical kind of event. You don't hear the bombs or rockets explode. There's an enemy down there, but you seldom saw them. In my case, I never saw an actual person, just a target, or gun sites that fired back at me. On occasion, you might see a truck or a small boat in a river. You *knew* the enemy was there because there would be quite a few guns shooting at you. This was the worst part. Once you had rolled into your dive-bomb or rocket attack you became vulnerable. If you flew perpendicular to the gun, it was difficult for the gunner to estimate the necessary lead angle because of the large angular rotation. When you dove down toward the guns, you weren't moving through a large angular distance . . . to the gunner; you just got bigger! They now also knew what you were after for a target. If they put enough lead up in the sky, *even without aiming*, there was a good chance that you would run into it. So, they would often just barrage fire over the target. In spite of the sophisticated MiG fighters and SAMs, over 80 percent of the aircraft shot down in the Vietnam War (a whopping total of 3,322 aircraft of all types) were downed by antiaircraft fire.

We did not minimize this threat. We jinked, sometimes violently, just as we rolled in, but during the actual dive the airplane had to be stable. We pickled our bombs around 6,500 feet above the target and started a 5G pull up, and jinked all the time. We wanted to get out of the effective range of the guns as soon as possible and not have a predictable flight path. This was where you always expected to get hit—right in the belly, when you were low and vulnerable. If it were a low-threat target, we would go up and make another pass but would vary the roll-in point and try not to be predictable. Over the targets near Hanoi, you never did—it was "one pass, and haul ass" unless you had a sublimated death wish. What I've just described was often not true of missions in South Vietnam, since, in many cases, they were in close contact with the enemy and the defenses were far less intense. But in our type of air war, it was a higher-altitude, impersonal affair.

If all went well, we escaped unscathed, joined up with our flight, and headed back to Ubon. As we left the high-threat targets, I would often say to myself with a huge sigh of relief, "Whew! I survived that!" My mouth would often be so dry that it was difficult to talk. But as soon as I completed that thought I would realize that I would have to do it again and again and again in the days to come.

As the flight rejoined, every flight member would check the others over for battle damage as they came aboard. I seldom saw any battle damage. Either we didn't get hit, or the hit was so bad that the aircraft was lost and the crew either killed or forced to eject. There didn't seem to be much between those two extremes. Your results may vary, but that was my experience. We would then head home to Ubon. For the targets in Laos and lower North Vietnam that was about half an hour away, but the far north targets sometimes required poststrike refueling. Often you were in an afterburner more than you'd planned and burned more fuel than expected. We always had a "Bingo" fuel, which meant we had to leave the area when we reached that point. However, the enemy often would not accommodate us and we might be very short of fuel. On the way back, we checked in with the control agencies (airborne command posts) and passed on our mission results with code words. Sometimes, if we had fuel and some ordinance remaining, we might be diverted to help with a rescue mission if someone had been shot down, but the norm was to head straight back. This sometimes caused problems because a large number of planes would all return at the same time. Some might have battle damage or malfunctions, but everyone was short on fuel, and Ubon had only one runway. The air traffic controllers had their hands full in bad weather when the large strikes returned. Since the runway was narrow and crowned (higher in the middle than on the sides), we would make approach end engagements with the tailhook if it rained hard. This further complicated matters, but was a wise move. The F-4 had a bad tendency to hydroplane on a wet runway, which means that the tires would not make contact with the runway and you would lose directional control and have no braking capability. We would lower the hook, fly an approach 5 miles behind the aircraft in front of us, and snag the arresting wire just after touchdown. It was a very violent stop and I developed a greater appreciation for our naval brothers! While the barrier could be reset very quickly for any following aircraft, if an aircraft got tangled in the arresting wire, that would cause a problem, because the nearest divert base was quite a distance away. If the weather were good, we just entered the normal overhead pattern, pitched out, and landed.

If all went well, we landed, popped the drag chute, rolled to the end of the runway, jettisoned the drag chute, and pulled into the dearm area. Not a small matter, since, on occasion, a bomb would not drop, or be hung by one lug—a definite safety hazard, but easily remedied once the ground crew safed everything up. Once that was accomplished, we taxied to the same revetment we started the mission from. It was a good feeling!

Once the airplane was parked, the familiar bread truck would show up to take us to the maintenance debriefing area. This was a large complex right next to the flight line and was the hub of the airplane fixer's world. It was pretty crowded, since several crews would all debrief at once. We filled out the forms, talked things over with the maintenance types and tech reps, and tried to describe what went wrong, with as much detail as possible—after all, *you* might get this airplane next time! As I mentioned, the F-4 was a complex creature, so this process might take 20 minutes or so.

Then it was off to the squadron Personal Equipment area to get rid of all the stuff we wore. We reversed the process that we'd just gone through a few hours earlier to our tremendous relief. There was one difference that I never forgot. In plain sight, near a desk in the area, was a bottle of "Mission Whiskey"—it was always a fifth of J.W. Dant bourbon. It was the same as any bottle in a liquor store except for one detail. Along the side of the bottle, a line had been drawn. You could take as much as you wanted, but you had to initial the level of the bottle when you finished. I never asked, but assumed that the flight surgeon checked who consumed how much to gauge the level of stress among the crews. At that point, I had graduated to martinis, but I do remember having a "belt" on occasion, and putting my initials on the bottle.

Then we would head to the intelligence area, where we had planned the mission, to be debriefed. Most of the debriefing was a series of standard questions, which would form part of the premission briefing for the next missions. If anything unusual had happened, such as an airplane shot down, or an unusual missile launch, then that was covered in greater depth. More than one crew was rescued several days after being shot down. Finally, even that part of the mission was over.

Then we would go back to the squadron area to either take care of miscellaneous paperwork or see what the schedule for the next day held. Most pilots and navigators had some sort of additional duties necessary to run the squadron smoothly. By now, you were pretty tired, especially on the long missions to the far north. I never flew two missions in one day. They were long days, and, one by one, they blurred into one another, since it was a 24 hours a day, 7 days a week flight schedule. I still remember the sign in the dining room of the Officer's Club, "Today is Sunday. Take your malaria pill!" And the next day, the process repeated itself. The squadrons tried to make sure that you didn't fly more than 7 days in a row without some sort of a break, which often involved some sort of ground duty that needed to be done by an aircrew.

This didn't leave a lot of time to sightsee. People used to ask me, "What did you see of Thailand?" I had to answer, "Not very much." I saw very little of the area around the base, except when I flew over it. A few times a month I would get into town, which was a few miles from the base, for dinner and some local sightseeing. But that was about it. Most of our life revolved around the process I described above. I could relax after a mission at the Club, but never totally—the next day's mission was always at the back of my mind, no matter what I might do to divert my attention. The missions added up, the weeks turned into months, and, eventually, at least for most of us, it appeared that we might finish this thing after all . . . we hoped.

CHAPTER 9

MiGs

"Fighter Pilot." Just the name evokes images of a swirling battle between two airplanes that continues until one emerges victorious. Indeed, fighter pilots like to think of themselves as "masters of the calculated risk." Whatever else they may do, in their own minds they are training for that one brief moment when they are the victor in actual aerial combat and shoot down their opponent. Indeed, if they do it five times or more, they will be known as an "ace." There is no higher honor in the fighter pilot world. Nothing else equals the respect of their peers if they attain this difficult status...not rank, not money. This deadly contest of skill requires sound flying ability, physical capabilities (not the least of which is endurance), and training. But most important is the ability to visualize in three dimensions and make decisions quickly. Few come upon these attributes naturally. It is also unmerciful. While there might have been some instances of chivalry in the early days of World War I, there is no such thing in today's aerial combat. Airplanes are often shot down without either combatant ever seeing their opponent. Long-range radar and missiles take care of that. But missiles are often not the panacea they were once thought to be. If the magic weapons don't score a hit, then the engagement progresses to the swirling dog-fight that first appeared in World War I. Many of the maneuvers are the same; they just happen faster.

The opposing aircraft will have advantages in certain areas. Maybe one air-plane has better weapons. Perhaps one is more maneuverable. The variables are many, but the fighter pilot's job is to maximize his pluses and exploit the enemy's weaknesses. It all happens very quickly and can be very violent. The airplane is often flown to the maximum of its capabilities, since anything less will most likely result in your opponent obtaining an advantage, which can often lead to your demise. It's the most intense flying a pilot will probably ever do.

During the time I was at Ubon, the threat from enemy aircraft was significant. Early in the war, the North Vietnamese did not pose much of an air threat, but that situation changed after the "Rolling Thunder" bombing campaign began in earnest. True, our primary mission was to interdict the supplies flowing to the south, and one way to do that was to go after the high-value targets in North Vietnam where the flow originated. However, one of the first things you learn in the Air Force is the doctrine that none of these other missions are possible without control of the air. Simply stated, you need to be able to operate in enemy airspace without sustaining an unacceptable loss rate. Lack of control of the air almost stopped the U.S. bombing campaign in Germany during World War II until long-range fighter escorts like the P-51 were developed that could escort the bombers all the way to the target.

Both the F-4 and the F-105 bore the brunt of the USAF bombing attacks in North Vietnam. When you have a full load of bombs and external fuel tanks on board and you've just refueled from the tanker, you are not a very maneuverable fighter. If you were on a strike mission to a major target in the Hanoi area, your task was to get those bombs on the target. If an enemy fighter attacked, there was no choice but to jettison the bombs and extra fuel tanks to defend yourself. The North Vietnamese succeeded in that case because the bombs never got to the target. All that effort was wasted. To prevent that, most of the large strikes in North Vietnam had a MiG CAP flight that flew near the bomb-laden F-4Ds and F-105s to keep the enemy from being able to attack them. The MiG CAP airplanes had a full load of air-to-air missiles, an external 20-mm gun pod, and external tanks. If the MiGs came up, the tanks were immediately jettisoned, and they accelerated to enter the fight at a high-energy state. Ubon, the base where I was stationed, touted itself as "the largest supplier of used MiG parts in the world," since they had shot down the largest number of MiGs. It was written on a sign over the entrance to the Wing Headquarters and we were all quite proud of the fact. It gave us a vicarious feeling of victory.

My first engagement against an enemy aircraft was somewhat similar to my first combat mission. I wondered what I would do when the moment presented itself. Shortly after I arrived at Ubon, I finished my fifteen-mission indoctrination program flying against targets in Laos and southern North Vietnam. Gradually, I learned the vital lessons needed to keep me alive in the far more hostile skies near Hanoi. But air combat was not one of those things. All the strikes in Laos and the southern route packages were ground attack sorties... there were no MiGs to be concerned about. Soon, I was on the schedule for the big missions to the far north. Would the chance to actually tangle with a MiG present itself? I asked myself the question with both a sense of anticipation and fear.

In 1968, there were two main types of enemy aircraft that we might encounter. Both were MiGs, the acronym being derived from the Soviet design works of Mikoyen/Gurevevich. The MiG 17 was an updated version of the MiG 15 that had fought against the F-86 Sabers during the Korean War. It had an afterburner; increased wingspan, and a somewhat redesigned tail. It was far more maneuverable than any of our fighters, since it had a very light wing loading (or a light load compared to its wing surface). It did not have the sophisticated radar and weapon systems that the F-4 had, or the power. The other aircraft was a MiG 21, a more modern supersonic fighter that was also more maneuverable than the F-4 at certain altitudes. An air battle, in essence, is about the management of energy. Both opponents enter the fray with a certain amount of energy. Hard maneuvering drastically depletes this valuable resource, since it takes a high level of energy to sustain a high G turn. Altitude is a form of energy because you can dive down and convert altitude to airspeed. With high excess airspeed you can zoom up and trade the airspeed for altitude, or use it to pull more G's and thus tighten your turn rate. Whoever does a better job of managing this energy will generally emerge the victor. When you're out of energy and ideas, you're dead meat. The danger for an F-4 pilot was if they got into a level-turning fight with a MiG at medium altitude, the MiG had the advantage in that area.

Suddenly we received a call from our EC-121 radar plane that provided us with airborne radar coverage from over Laos or the Gulf of Tonkin. These aircraft were converted Lockheed Constellations that had very advanced radar and intelligence gathering capabilities added. In some cases, they had translators on board that would relay the conversations between the MiG pilots and their controllers on the ground. Since the Rules of Engagement stated that we had to visually identify the suspected enemy aircraft before we could fire a missile, this almost guaranteed a close-in, maneuvering fight. There was one exception: if one of the EC-121 aircraft or Navy picket ships in the Gulf of Tonkin declared the aircraft hostile, then we could lock on with our radar and fire missiles at the "bandit" without ever seeing him. "Rivet Top," the callsign of the radar plane, told us that a MiG 21 was headed back to Hanoi at approximately our altitude, crossing from left to right, about 30 miles from our position, and declared him a "hostile." If we could get a lock-on and achieve the proper missile parameters, we could launch a Sparrow air-to-air missile at the MiG. It was happening!

Our four-ship flight turned toward the target and jettisoned the empty 370-gallon drop tanks in case we got into a hard turning fight. Our missiles were already armed. The back-seaters frantically searched on their radars for the MiG. Finding another aircraft with the F-4 radar was not a simple task. Elevation of the antenna was critical, especially if the target was below you. The target information passed to us by the radar plane was very general in nature. It's difficult to describe the excitement at this point. Once the tanks are jettisoned, a fight is imminent. You are aware, at least intellectually, that in a few moments you may very well be fighting for your life. You are also aware that you may possibly kill someone. But that's more in the nature of an abstraction. You tend not to think of the other airplane as a person, but as a "target," or an "airplane." If you don't get him, he'll get you. So whatever misgivings you may feel, get resolved very quickly, in your favor. It's a moment of incredible excitement. Every part of your being is alert.

As we headed toward the MiG, it was hard to believe that this was happening. I was number four in our flight, which would most likely mean that I wouldn't get a shot. I was a wingman, and a wingman's task is to protect his leader, and make sure no MiG got into a firing position on him if he were pursuing a target. We even had a radio call for it: "padlocked." If the leader made that call, it meant that he was strictly looking at the target and was not checking his six o'clock position. He was depending on you, the wingman, for that vital task. Normally, in a flight of four, the leader would be the shooter if he acquired the target either visually or on radar. The element leader (number three) was generally the secondary shooter, who would most likely be the next one to fire if the leader either didn't acquire the target or had a weapon malfunction. The role of the wingmen in both cases was to insure their leaders were "clear," and that no enemy was about to achieve a firing position on them. Flight leaders were the more experienced members in a squadron, and thus were the most qualified to lead the attack. However, these tactics weren't cast in stone. An air battle can progress from a well-ordered plan to a swirling mass of airplanes where flight members become separated in a few seconds. If the wingmen achieved contact with the enemy first, then they would often become the "shooters." These tactics were later refined based on the Navy's experience with their "Loose Deuce" system, where two fighters alternated in attacking the enemy until one was in the best position to achieve a kill. The excitement was reaching a fever pitch as we raced toward the MiG 21 that was headed to Hanoi.

Suddenly . . . my back-seater had a lock-on! He had scanned the area called out by our radar surveillance plane, identified a target on our radar, then proceeded to lock on to it. When you first identify a target on radar, you can see its position relative to you, but it doesn't give your radar missile any information that it needs in order to be launched. To do that, you have to "lock on" to the radar blip, at which time the radar stops scanning the entire area and strictly tracks the target of interest. When that happens, the entire radar display changes completely. The F-4 radar showed a long vertical line with the target appearing as a blip along the line. A contracting circle and a small dot appear, and the pilot's task is to put the small dot in the circle, which will insure a proper collision course is flown. The rate of overtake is also displayed, so you can tell whether you are closing on the target or if it is pulling away from you. In this case, the MiG was crossing left to right, about our altitude, and roughly 15 to 20 miles away. The aiming dot was almost centered, and it wouldn't take much to accomplish the proper collision course, as we were closing on the target with about 100 knots of overtake. The blip that represented the target had to move down the vertical range line about an inch in order to be within the maximum range of the Sparrow missile. If the collision course dot was centered and the target was in range, I could fire two Sparrow missiles, which would track the target and hopefully score a hit! Why two missiles? The probability of a hit was higher. I called out to the flight lead that we had a radar contact. A few seconds went by, and no one else in the flight had a radar contact, much less a lock-on. At this point, I recall being incredibly excited. If a few more seconds went by and no one else in the flight got a radar contact, or acquired the target visually, I would probably be given the lead, and my element lead would fall back on my wing and cover me while I became the "shooter." I felt as though I was seconds away from downing an enemy MiG! Glory was about to come my way, and I would be the envy of all my peers!

Our flight of four was headed northeast, and the MiG was making a beeline to Hanoi in a southwesterly direction. Roughly 20 miles now separated us. Since no one else even had a radar contact, I expected to be told to assume the shooting position any second. It was a surreal experience—everything that I had imagined about being a successful fighter pilot in combat was coming true.

Suddenly, the MiG's direction changed abruptly, and not to our advantage. He had made a hard 135-degree turn to the left and was headed for the Chinese border! His ground control radars must have picked up our flight of four racing toward him and warned him of our impending attack. The MiGs could land at bases on the Chinese side, but we were forbidden to go within 10 miles of the border so as not to give the Chinese any cause for entering the war. This was another one of the maddening Rules of Engagement. Now, the positive overtake that I had on the target a few seconds ago was a negative value—he was leaving us in the race for the Chinese border. Was my chance for fame and glory being denied me? I still did not have the target visually, although a few seconds earlier, I had expected to acquire him momentarily.

At this point, the flight leader wisely called for a fuel check. Most of us were near "Bingo," which is the fuel required to safely return to Ubon or Udorn if we left right now. In order to overtake the MiG, we would have had to use afterburner, which drastically increases fuel consumption. We were also getting rather close to the Chinese border. Glory was slipping from my grasp with each passing second. We were almost to the limits of our fuel, and if we went into afterburner to catch the MiG fleeing for his safety across the border, we would surely run out of fuel. Glory is nice, but survival is better, even in my fevered state. A few more seconds passed and then the flight lead made the only decision he could reasonably make and called for the flight to break it off. We turned around and started to depart the area. We were pretty far into extremely hostile territory, and if we had been jumped by MiGs or anything unplanned had happened, we most likely would not have made it safely back to Ubon. So near, and yet so far! I had come extremely close to shooting down an enemy aircraft just a few seconds ago. I remember feeling very disappointed and frustrated. I had come so close. But now we were headed away from the MiG, and any chance of shooting him down had just evaporated. I can still recall the searing disappointment that I felt at that instant. The intoxicating thrill of the hunter about to down his quarry had ended as quickly as it had begun.

A few missions later, the gods of war decided to broaden my experience a bit more. This time, I was one of the bomb-laden F-4s that were part of the strike force headed to a Combat Sky Spot target near Hanoi. As I recall, it was a troop barracks area that massed the North Vietnamese soldiers and then sent them south. This was the monsoon season in Southeast Asia, which meant that the target would be obscured by rain clouds, which would preclude normal dive-bombing tactics. The Air Force had gone to great lengths to establish a navigation and radar site on top of a very prominent mountain peak in northern Laos (Phou Pha Thi), about 120 miles from Hanoi. The site served two functions: First, it provided a TACAN (Tactical Air Navigation) site, which allowed aircraft to obtain an accurate bearing and distance from the site, or Channel 97, as it was known. This feature was used on all the missions north, since there were no other navigation aids in the area, and the aircraft inertial navigation systems were not that accurate. However, in the last several months, a special radar site had been installed, as well. This system was a modification of the radar bomb scoring system that Strategic Air Command has used for many years to see how accurate their crews would have been as they bombed simulated targets all over the United States. It had been modified so that specially equipped F-4s and F-105s could be tracked and directed to a target, and was known as Combat Sky Spot. With the bomb ballistics programmed into the radar site's computers, the radar operator would direct the flight to a point in space that was the bomb release point for the particular bomb load. When the lead aircraft arrived at the point, the radar controller on the mountaintop in Laos would give the command to drop the bombs, and all the wingmen flying off the leader would drop their load simultaneously. Obviously, the accuracy was not as great as if the Air Force's finest had dive-bombed the target, but it did allow attacks in the Hanoi area during the bad weather times, which could last for several weeks during the monsoon season.

What was all the more remarkable about the site was that it was in the middle of enemy Pathet Lao and North Vietnamese territory. The sheer inaccessibility of the location was what allowed them to operate with such impunity. Alas, a few weeks after this incident, enemy forces overran it and several radar operators were killed despite efforts to protect it. This bombing tactic was not without risk. We had to be able to see a SAM in order to outmaneuver it, which meant that we needed at least 10,000 feet from the tops of the cloud layer to the altitude at which we were flying. In theory, this would give us time to evade the missile if we saw it. Since the SAM would be supersonic by the time, it punched up through the clouds; it didn't allow a lot of time to react. We still flew in a formation that optimized the electronic jamming pods, which shielded us somewhat from the enemy radars, but it was an awkward and difficult formation to fly and spread us somewhat far apart. If MiGs were airborne and above us, the flight was high-lighted against the layer of clouds below, which made it easier for them to spot our position. It wasn't the most accurate way to bomb. The wide separation of each flight member from the leader cut down on the effectiveness. But it was better than nothing.

So, that's where I found myself on a February afternoon in 1968, only this time I wasn't one of the lucky MiG CAP pilots, but was carrying a full load of bombs and fuel tanks as one of the Combat Sky Spot strike pilots. The bad weather posed problems for the MiG pilots who defended the Hanoi area as well, so we didn't expect to see a large number of them, if any. As we briefed for the mission, it didn't look too bad although it was in an extremely hostile area. SAMs would probably be the biggest threat, although radar-directed flak could shoot up through the clouds with great ease. On balance, we didn't expect it to be a milk run, but we also didn't anticipate it would be a toe curler either. Reasonably optimistic, we launched, hit the tankers over Laos, contacted the secret radar site at Channel 97, and started toward Hanoi.

I'd been on similar missions before in the lower parts of North Vietnam, and a few in the more heavily defended north. As we headed toward Hanoi ("Bulls Eye" or "Downtown" was our more common term), we turned on the ECM pods, turned off the TACAN navaid so as to not emit signals, armed the missiles and bombs, and tried to maintain radio discipline. This last item, radio discipline, was an extremely important matter. In fact, your life might depend upon it. At any moment, there could be over 100 people capable of keying a radio transmitter to say something. One of the vagaries of the UHF radios that we used was that if two people transmitted at the same time, they would interfere with each other, and the nearest transmitter would cancel out the one farthest away. Normally, this is a minor annoyance, but if someone told you to "Break!" be-cause there's a MiG on your tail about to fire, you'd rather hear that than some inane comment from your wingman. You kept your mouth shut unless it was of major importance. As we got closer to Hanoi, the radar homing and warning gear became more active. This device could detect when enemy radars were looking at us and gave an indication of the type of threat and the direction and magni-tude of the threat. You got an aural tone in your headset, and soon learned to distinguish the different types of potential harm. Perhaps the most dreaded sound was the "rattlesnake" tone. It sounded exactly like a rattlesnake, and if it increased in pitch and intensity, that meant the SAM radar site had switched from low-pulse repetition frequency to high. This allowed them to see us more clearly and meant a missile launch was imminent. If they launched a missile, and the booster had dropped away so that the radar site could guide the missile, you got a flashing "Launch" light. This was an absolute "no shit" message that meant *you* were probably the intended target of the missile. You didn't want to be listening to noncritical radio chatter at this juncture. There's also a phenomenon known as temporal distortion to deal with. I had not heard of this term until I returned to the States, but in essence it means you can only deal with so much. When under a great deal of stress, you break your world into chunks of time that you can manage. There's a great deal going on, and in spite of the best efforts, there are all sorts of radio calls, some frantic. The radar warning gear is making all sorts of obscene noises, and your back-seater may be talking to you. You're trying to remember the myriad of switch settings that you have to go through to set up the weapons. All the preflight instructions that the flight lead briefed before the mission are running through your mind. You're checking the navigation and very carefully monitoring the fuel. You look for SAMs and MiGs. There are seemingly a million things going through your brain. So much so that time seems to slow down. Everything seems to be in slow motion. Apparently, it's the body's way of dealing with overwhelming stress. It happened to me on at least three occasions that I can recall. We used to carry small Panasonic tape recorders with us on some of the missions. They would record all the comments made over the radios, as well as any intercom chatter between the front and back seat. Often, when I listened to these tapes after a mission, I was astounded by what I had missed! On the mission, I had concentrated on what could kill me in the next few seconds, and had missed many other events that were taking place around me at the same time. Sitting in the comfortable debriefing area, and relaxed, it was easy to hear—not so, when under high stress.

Such was my frame of mind as we passed over Channel 97, accelerated, and took up our heading toward the target. We must have been about 70 miles or so from the target when we got the first call. Red Crown, a Navy radar picket ship in the Gulf of Tonkin, called out that MiGs had just taken off from Phuc Yen Airfield near Hanoi. I can still remember the radio call today word for word, "This is Red Crown on Guard! Bandits! Bandits! Airborne Phuc Yen, Two Six Zero from Bulls Eye!" This was followed by a few other cryptic calls of increasing intensity. As I turned the pure flame of my intellect to the situation, I realized that the MiGs were headed toward us. We were the only strike force inbound to Hanoi at that time. Yes, we had the usual "package," which included MiG CAP and Iron Hand support, and their purpose was to deal with the MiGs and SAMs so that we could hit the target. But we were the sluggish ones bogged down with bombs and forced to fly straight and level during our bomb drop. If we were jumped, it would be difficult to defend ourselves. Although utterly fearless, I was becoming concerned. After all, from the MiG's point of view, *we* were the ones they were after, not the MiG CAP fighters. We were the ones that would be dropping the bombs. More bandit calls! Each higher in pitch and speech rate! By now, I was *very* concerned, to put it mildly. As on all missions like this, I had already raised the safety switches on the tank and bomb pylon jettison switches so that I could "clean the wings," as we used to say, meaning, get rid of all the tanks and anything hanging on the wings to increase our maneuverability. Of course, you didn't want to do this unless absolutely necessary because the entire mission would be for naught if the bombs didn't get to the assigned target. You might have to go back the next day and do the same thing . . . *better to get it over with!* The MiGs often climbed high, passed their target, and then turned and dove down below and behind the strike force, where it was difficult to spot them. If they fired a heat-seeking missile, you had no choice but to violently turn into the missile to try to defeat it. If there were time, you might have to "clean the wings." The radio calls from Red Crown were getting more intense, and the range between the MiGs and the strike force was rapidly dwindling. I will never forget the next few seconds. Suddenly, Red Crown screamed, "You're merged!" This meant that our radar blip and the MiG blip had come together. We were in the same horizontal chunk of sky, but the radar controller was looking at a two-dimensional view of the world, and couldn't tell what altitude either one of us was at. I skidded and yawed the airplane as I had never done before. If there was a MiG below me in the vulnerable six o'clock low position, where I couldn't see him, I wanted to know! Everyone searched the sky for any glint of an aircraft. The back-seaters were frantically searching with their radars—nothing! The collective pulse rate must have been well over a bazillion! The strike force droned on. Lord Tennyson's poem "The Charge of the Light Brigade" came to my mind, with its talk of cannons on both sides and the valiant six hundred riding into the Valley of Death. Not a comforting thought. Nothing! No one saw a thing! For whatever reason, apparently the MiGs didn't see anything either, or perhaps they had a malfunction of some sort, but no one in the entire strike flight saw any enemy aircraft. The radar picket ship also lost contact with the MiGs. We continued on, dropped the bombs, did the usual massive in-place break, and headed back to Ubon—mission accomplished.

Since they never attacked us, I can only assume they didn't see us either, which is not as remarkable as it may sound. It's a big sky, and if they were 20,000 feet or more above us, they might not have acquired us. Possibly, they were below us, maybe in the weather, although that's unlikely since we could have picked them up on radar and launched a missile at them. More than likely, they took off, climbed in afterburner, and missed us. Low on fuel, they might have had to head back to Phuc Yen in a hurry. Whatever the reason, I had experienced what it is like to be the "hunted" rather than the "hunter." While I had tended to look at the MiG in my first engagement as simply a target, or a technical problem to be solved, I now understood what it felt like to be at the other end of the spear. It changes your perspective.

There is one more episode to relate. It was in mid- to late-February 1968, and again I was one of the envied MiG CAP pilots. Envied in the sense that there was less of a chance of getting hit by flak or a SAM missile if on a MiG CAP mission. For those assigned to bomb the target, the enemy could generally tell what our intentions were, and the bombers would get the lion's share of attention from the North Vietnamese gunners and SAM operators. The CAP flights, on the other hand, were unpredictable. They usually would accompany the strike flight near the target, then break off and pick them up as the force left the immediate target area. Flying into the teeth of a bazillion guns and SAMs is not a lot of fun, so most of the crews preferred the MiG CAP missions. It also meant that they might get a chance to shoot down one of the North Vietnamese MiGs, which further increased the mission's desirability. Ah, glory!

On this mission, we were a flight of four and were cruising at a pretty high Mach number (airspeed in relation to the speed of sound), about 30 to 40 miles south of Hanoi. We cruised at a high speed so we would have high energy if we entered an air battle, especially if "bounced" from behind. We would need the energy to outfly our opponent. The formation we flew at the time was called "fluid four" and was difficult to fly. The wingman's job was to keep within a 45-degree cone extending back from the leader to no more than 2,500 feet. This sounds pretty simple, but when the leader has his throttle set at a high-power setting, say 94 percent, it doesn't leave the wingmen much power to play with. You can minimize the extra power required by cutting inside the leader's turn radius, and if slightly higher, you can enter a gentle dive to gain a few knots of airspeed. If the leader maneuvers violently, it's very hard to stay with him. Wingmen always burn more fuel than the leaders because of this necessity to constantly maneuver to stay in position. Fall back too far, and there is no recourse but to light the afterburners, which increases fuel consumption. It took a lot of concentration to fly a good "fighting wing" position.

Again, Red Crown sounded the clarion call on Guard (the emergency radio channel), "Red Crown on Guard . . . bogey sour, heading to Bullseye, angels high, 090 from Bulls Eye, 40." This cryptic transmission meant that an unidentified airplane (possibly hostile) was returning to Hanoi, either low on fuel or with some possible malfunction. The target was east of Hanoi (Bulls Eye), about 40 miles, and was at reasonably high altitude. The collective heart rate of our flight increased dramatically.

We had a new flight leader, Al Borchik, who was also getting his check to be a qualified flight lead in Route Package VIA, the area near Hanoi. He had been to the area many times, but this was his first as a flight lead. We had been heading south-southwest when we received the call from Red Crown. We weren't sure what type of target it was, or if it was a hostile one. At any rate, he was about 20 to 30 miles northeast of our present position. I was to the left of the flight lead and slightly lower than he was. I had been having difficulty keeping up with him, and being lower didn't help. In order for me to get to his altitude, I needed to climb, and that reduced airspeed, which meant that I probably needed to use the afterburner to keep up and regain altitude. Fuel is life, and you didn't want to do that if you didn't have to. Just at that moment, we accelerated and started a left turn to intercept the target that had just been called out. Great, I thought, now I could cut inside Lead's turn and close the distance and gain some altitude without having to increase fuel consumption by using the burner. I also needed to cross to the other side, so I could keep the other members of the flight in sight who had just crossed over. Everyone was excited, and I felt the same rush of adrenalin that I described on my first encounter. Maybe today would be the day I got a MiG!

Just as I was crossing behind the flight leader, he called over the radio, "Skin the tanks!" Suddenly, two huge 370-gallon wing tanks zipped right by, and just missed me. It seemed as if we missed them by a few feet, but then, I was more than a little excited. At the same moment, I reached down and brushed the toggle switch to jettison my tanks with my left hand. I'd already had the safety cap pushed up, so I could do this in a hurry.

There was a loud noise, and I felt a really hefty jolt to our airplane. Since we were well within the SAM threat area near Hanoi, my first thought was that a SAM had hit us, or that one had detonated pretty close below us. As if the possible MiG engagement wasn't enough excitement! I looked down at the airspeed indicator. We were doing Mach 1.2, or 20 percent faster than the speed of sound. The flight manual had a limitation of 550 knots and subsonic to jettison the tanks. We were well in excess of that, which explained the noise and jolt that we experienced. Still in one piece, we pressed on.

No one in the flight had acquired a visual or radar contact yet, but suddenly, at one o'clock high, you could see a high, thin white contrail. Since the radar picket ship had stated the bogey was "sour," I thought that perhaps it had been hit in a previous engagement and was headed back to Hanoi with a fuel or hydraulic leak. Still couldn't see the airplane—too far away. The missiles were armed; we knew generally where the bogey was, and in a few more moments we might actually be firing missiles at it, if we could positively identify it. Fighter pilots call this, "having your fangs out," and we most certainly did. Suddenly, another voice was on Guard, "Don't shoot, don't shoot! It's me, a Navy RF-4!" I may not have the transmission exactly verbatim, but the intent was crystal clear. We were about to attack a Navy RF-4 that was on a reconnaissance mission—one of our own! The

Navy normally operated on the Gulf of Tonkin side of North Vietnam, and the Air Force took the western side. Hence the Hanoi/Haiphong area was broken into Route Package VI Alpha (Air Force side) and Bravo (Navy side). Great effort was expended by both the Air Force and the Navy to keep the various flights and strikes deconflicted, but on occasion, mistakes were made. This was one of those times. There weren't supposed to be any friendly aircraft operating where we were flying on our mission, so we assumed that the "bogey" was most likely hostile. In this case, the Rules of Engagement served us well, or we could have accidentally shot down a fellow aviator. Once again, we had a fuel check, saw that we were pretty near "Bingo," and headed back to the poststrike tankers and then back to Ubon. It was my first encounter with something that has come to be known as "friendly fire." While it may seem inexplicable that U.S. forces sometimes shoot down one of their own, it drove home to me just how easy it was to get in a situation where this could happen. Those were the only MiG encounters I had during my entire combat tour. The gods of war smiled . . . we all lived to fight another day.

CHAPTER 10

The Threat Unseen

I sometimes wonder why I'm still here to be able to write this, as well as enjoy the many other things that I derive pleasure from. It could have been otherwise, and on several occasions, almost was. What separates those of us who survived from those who were not so fortunate? I've pondered these questions for years, and am no closer to an answer than when I started.

Case in point: What was my greatest fear when I flew missions? Well, I had several, but to get hit by a SAM was right near the top of the list. It was big. It was fast. And if it was locked on to me, and I didn't see the "flying telephone pole" soon enough, I would probably get hit. The warhead on the SA-2 SAM was equivalent to a 300-pound bomb, which was more than adequate to bring a plane down. To make matters worse, the warhead also contained a system of rods that expanded outward in the shape of a cone as the warhead exploded, which meant that even if it didn't hit me, it could still cause tremendous damage if it went off in close proximity. It was a potent weapon, and I never went to the far north without thoughts of SAMs in the forefront of my consciousness. My fear was that one day, there'd be a big flash of light, perhaps a loud explosion, and that would be it for McC. Maybe I would have seen it coming, maybe not. Even if I somehow survived all that and was able to eject, it was still a major problem. If a SAM shot me down, it meant I was in a very heavily defended area, probably pretty close to Hanoi. The chance of a successful rescue was nil. The general rule of thumb was that if you went down within a 40-mile ring around Hanoi, there was not much anybody could do for you. You'd just have to sit out the war as a POW, and hope to survive the experience. The two fears combined did not make for restful nights.

So, what to do? How could I avoid an untimely demise? I tried to learn as much as I could about the enemy systems so I would know what I was up against. Our intelligence section had quite a bit of study material, and I spent a lot of time there. On this particular day in March 1968, I didn't think it would be too big a problem because I'd be on a MiG CAP mission and the SAMs would be most concerned with the bombers in the strike force. With just missiles and the gun and no bombs, we'd be a lot more maneuverable if we did have to out-maneuver a SAM. We had our ECM jamming pods, but they wouldn't be as effective for us MIG CAP types, since we wouldn't be in the optimum "pod" formation. Unfortunately, the strike force that we were to protect was another radar bombing mission above a solid overcast, since Hanoi was still in the grip of the monsoon weather. The strike force would have at least 10,000 feet clearance from the cloud deck below if the forecast were accurate, which was the bare minimum for a mission like this. In theory, this would allow us enough time to see the SAM as it came up through the clouds below, but it was cutting it pretty close. It didn't leave a lot of time to outmaneuver the SAM. There would be an F-105 Wild Weasel flight from Korat Air Base as part of the strike force, whose task was to take out SAMs, or at least keep the enemy radar off the air, which was almost as good. The North Vietnamese were fast learners—if they saw what looked like an airplane about to launch a Shrike antiradiation missile at them, they'd turn off their radar so as not to be a target. As long as the radar was off, the SAM couldn't be launched or guided. So, either way, we were happy citizens. Nobody badmouthed the Weasels!

We finished the briefings, cranked up, and soon were airborne and headed into North Vietnam from the west. This was a large mission with two MiG CAP flights, one on either side of the strike force. I was flying the number four position in our flight. We started to approach the target area from the northwest, and soon the radio chatter began to increase. This would be a busy day! Our MiG CAP flight was in "fluid four" formation, which allowed us to keep each other in sight and intercept any MiGs that might come up and try to knock down any of the bombers. One of the main problems with the "fluid four" formation we flew was that it was difficult for the wingmen to stay in the proper position. I would often quip afterward, "By the time you learned how to do it properly, you were ready to lead the flight." The main problem was that the leader flew at a very high Mach number in order to have as much energy as possible if we got into a fight. This was sound philosophy, but difficult for a relatively inexperienced wingman (which I was) to do, since you didn't have a lot of excess power available to main-tain the proper position. Sure, you could tap the afterburner, but that burned up fuel at a prodigious rate, and fuel was life in a very real sense. You spent con-siderable effort to maintain the correct position on your leader. We were about 30 miles from the target, when the chatter increased dramatically!

Rivet Top, the special EC-121 radar surveillance plane that could pick up enemy-aircraft threats, called out MiGs headed toward the "force." The RHAW (Radar Homing and Warning) receiver also began to make all sorts of noises and showed corresponding threat strobes on the small indicator that was mounted on top of the right front cockpit. This marvelous piece of equipment, quite advanced for its day, could separate the radar signals it received, and give you an indication of what type of threat was looking at you—air-air, antiaircraft radar, or the dreaded SAMs. It used a different audio tone for each threat and illuminated the appropriate light in the display. A strobe showed the direction and relative intensity of that particular threat. The audio pitch increased as the pulse repetition frequency of the SAM guidance radar increased. Their radar used a long pulse to search for a target, but once they found something, they shortened the radar pulse to get better definition. We called it the "rattlesnake tone" because that's what it sounded like. Quiet at first, but then it increased in pitch and frequency. This was not a sound you wanted to hear. If they launched the missile, the booster fell off after a few seconds, and a transponder, or electronic beacon, activated, and this is how they guided the missile to the target. When that happened, you got a very distinctive, high-pitched tone in your headset, and a "Launch" light that flashed on the threat indicator. More than likely, *you* were the object of their affection! Not always, since sometimes other aircraft would receive the signal as well, but, statistically, you probably were the target. You didn't want to see this light come on.

This all sounds pretty straightforward if there's just one SAM site that had locked on to you, but in the Hanoi area there were often multiple sites up at the same time. I looked at my threat scope, and there were all sorts of strobes. I can't even remember how many—too many to count. A cacophony of noise, and all of it sounded very urgent. Antiaircraft radars, SAM radars, and on top of everything else, the airborne radar plane was calling off MiGs in our immediate area. While we fighter pilots love to brag about our multitasking abilities, there is a limit. You can only absorb so much. Did I mention that the radio chatter had also increased a bazillion fold? I frantically looked for MiGs in our six o'clock position. I'd drop the wing and hold top rudder and look down, and below—a favorite place for the MiG to attack. Nothing! I looked in the cockpit at the RHAW scope—at least four SAM strobes ahead, in addition to the antiaircraft Fansong radars looking at us, and all were in high Pulse Repetition Frequency (PRF), or high definition mode—*and* the launch light was on! I anxiously looked for the threats. Nothing!

Suddenly, I heard what I thought was either a "SAM break!" or a "MiG break!" call in a very excited voice, but without any mention of a call sign. A word about radio discipline. It was very important to use the proper radio phraseology and limit radio calls to those absolutely necessary. A "break" call, in air combat, meant that you had about 3 seconds to live unless you executed a high G maneuver at maximum performance, in order to evade a missile or gun attack. You can imagine the pandemonium among thirty-six plus airplanes if someone yells "Break!" over the radio with no particular call sign. Is it meant for you?

There's not a lot of time to discuss it, and you might be dead if you don't do it. In my case, I just heard the first part of the sentence, "Break . . ." If there was more to the call, I didn't hear it. Because of all the MiG calls, I assumed it might be a MiG sneaking up in our vulnerable six o'clock position. The F-4 was a great airplane, but the visibility at six o'clock low was terrible. I did another quarter roll to the left and stomped on the right rudder to keep us going in the same direction, as I frantically looked for a MiG.

As soon as I did this, I saw an explosion immediately behind us! It looked as if an airplane had blown up, and I distinctly remember the huge, orange brown fireball, mingled with black smoke. To this day, I can still remember my thoughts: did one of the other MiG CAP flights shoot down a MiG? Did somebody in our strike force just get hit? I could see all of my flight, and they were okay. It's hard to convey just how chaotic this part of the battle can get, and how many things are going on, all at the same time. You focus your attention on the things that can kill you in the next few seconds, and then switch your attention to the next most immediate threat. Your mind is racing a 1,000 miles a minute, and even that doesn't seem adequate to comprehend what's going on all around you. I wasn't sure what I had just seen, but it didn't seem to be an immediate threat, so I switched my focus back to the strike force.

A few minutes later, the bombers in the strike force had dropped their bombs and done an in-place break to turn 180 degrees and get out of this high-threat target area as fast as they could. We received no more MiG calls, as we covered the strike force on their way out, and the RHAW threat warning equipment became silent as we left the Hanoi area at 9 miles/minute. Soon, we were clear of the danger, and prepared to poststrike refuel for the trip back to Ubon. This particular point in these missions remains one of my most vivid memories. I could hardly talk. My mouth would be so dry that it was difficult to speak. Clever lad that I am, I thought I could solve this problem by drinking water on the way in, just after we dropped off the tanker. We always carried a bottle of water in our G-suit pockets, since it's extremely dry in a pressurized cockpit and you can easily get dehydrated (we were years ahead of the California water bottle crowd). It didn't help; I could still barely talk. Once we were safely clear, my initial reaction was usually, "Whew! I survived that. Lucky me!" But then my next thought would be, "But I've got to do it again in the next few days." I always found this juxtaposition from the relative sanctuary of our base in Thailand to the mayhem over the target area, especially the area around Hanoi, to be very unsettling. It just had an aura of unreality about it. I realize my brethren in South Vietnam, at bases like DaNang Air Base, which were often under mortar and rocket attack, might not have felt this way, but to me it was a surreal experience, and one that I found more difficult to cope with than the initial fears about how I would react to combat. The constant change of extremes was never something I got used to.

The flight back was uneventful, and soon we were on the ground and were picked up by the crew van to go to maintenance and then intelligence debrief. It was at this point that I learned what had happened on our mission. As my element leader got in the van, he looked rather shaken. His first words were something like: "I thought they got you!" Apparently, the Launch light that I had seen was correct—a SAM had locked on to me, and it had exploded about 500 feet below my F-4! It had been launched directly ahead of me, along with several others. In a sense, this was fortunate, since the warhead had apparently been proximity fuzed and was set to explode when it got within 500 feet or so of the target, in this case, me. When the missile explodes, the warhead fragments *ahead* of the flight path, which meant that since I was headed in the opposite direction, I missed all of the missile fragments. Had it been launched from behind me, there would have been an almost 100 percent probability I would have been brought down by the explosion. The frantic call I had heard on the radio had been from my flight. They hadn't seen the SAM until almost the point when it exploded. When I looked back and saw an explosion that I thought was an airplane, it was actually the SAM that almost got me. I never saw it. I never knew it was a SAM until I landed back at Ubon.

So why is it that I can sit and relate this tale today, and others weren't so fortunate? I have no idea, but it's one of the reasons why the end of the movie "Saving Private Ryan" is so difficult for me to watch. There is, I assure you, a certain sense of guilt, mingled with thanks at my good fortune.

The Officers' Club at Ubon. We ate most of our meals here and the bar was always open. It was not unusual to have breakfast early in the morning, and others were just having a drink after a mission. It was a 24-hour war. (Courtesy Mike McCarthy)

This is what it looks like from the fighter cockpit when you refuel. (Courtesy Mike McCarthy)

These F-4Ds are en route to North Vietnam for a MiG Combat Air Patrol mission. (Courtesy Mike McCarthy)

Captain Whit Swain debriefs a mission. All the mission planning and debriefings took place in this area. (Courtesy Mike McCarthy)

General Westmoreland, Commander of the Military Assistance Command Vietnam, visits Ubon Air Base in the spring of 1968. (Courtesy Mike McCarthy)

Going Home. Lieutenant Dick Jonas, after he just completed his 100 missions over North Vietnam. Dick was a talented singer and songwriter and was our official balladeer. (Courtesy Mike McCarthy)

Not all missions ended well. This airplane crashed during a monsoon storm. Miraculously, both pilots survived and finished their tour. (Courtesy Mike McCarthy)

To get this patch you had to fly one mission North of the Red River in North Vietnam. I was quite proud of this when I received it. (Courtesy Mike McCarthy)

Major Al Borchik finishes his 100. (Courtesy Mike McCarthy)

This is the alert area where Dean St. Pierre and I were on alert. The Australian Avon Sabres provided air defense for the base. (Courtesy Mike McCarthy)

The author, toward the end of his combat tour. (Courtesy Mike McCarthy)

Roman 2 was my wingman that was shot down over North Vietnam and spent the night there. In this picture, they have just returned to Ubon after their successful rescue the next day. Left to right: Lt. Col Ralph Gibson, 433rd Tactical Fighter Squadron Commander, Lt. Chuck Mosley, Aircraft Commander, Lt. Don Hallenbeck, GIB. When we left them that night, I never thought I'd see them again, at least until the war was over. (Courtesy Don Hallenbeck)

The author receives the Distinguished Flying Cross at 7th Air Force Headquarters in Saigon in late 1968 from Colonel Daniels. (Courtesy Mike McCarthy)

This is really a short runway! Final approach to the USS Coral Sea as copilot in an S2F. This was a pleasant respite from mundane duties at 7th Air Force Headquarters and greatly increased my respect for our naval aviation brethren! (Courtesy Mike McCarthy)

The end of my war and the start of a new life. My mother and I in Syracuse, New York, after the Christmas and New Year holidays, as I leave for instructor duties at Homestead AFB, Florida. (Courtesy Mike McCarthy)

One of the happiest 2 years of my life. Flying the Canadian CF-104 Starfighter as a USAF exchange officer with the Canadian Armed Forces at Cold Lake, Alberta, Canada. (Courtesy Mike McCarthy)

Ubon Royal Thai Air Base in 1968. The single runway separated the Australian area at the bottom of the picture from the USAF and Thai area at the top. The town of Ubon was just a short distance from the left of the photo. (Courtesy Mike McCarthy)

Headquarters of 7th Air Force at Tan Son Nhut Air Base in Saigon was where the air war in Vietnam was run. I spent my last 4 months here. (Courtesy Mike McCarthy)

The successful rescue of Roman 2 A&B was discussed in detail at a Combat Search and Rescue Conference at Nellis AFB in May 2006. Left to right: The author, Don Hallenbeck, George Marrett (an A-1 pilot who knocked out several gun sites so they could be rescued), and Chuck Mosley. (Courtesy Mike McCarthy)

CHAPTER 11

The Ops Clerk Kid

I have a clear image of him today in my mind's eye. I'm starting my F-4D Phantom II as we prepare to go on a morning mission, but for a change, it's not one of our squadron airplanes. This one belongs to the 497 TFS, the Night Fighters. Normally, we flew airplanes that were assigned to the world-famous, highly respected 433rd Tactical Fighter Squadron, known as Satan's Angels. But the war was a 24-hour-a-day operation, and the job of the Wing Maintenance was to do whatever they had to do to meet the flying schedule. So, sometimes you flew airplanes from a different squadron. Such was the case on this day. The 433rd airplanes were parked in a revetted area that was in the middle of the flight line. The 497th was pretty close to our squadron Ops building, no more that a few 100 feet away. As I looked up toward our squadron, I could see our operations clerk on the porch outside the squadron, watching the morning missions as they prepared to take off.

Now this is an intense operation that will catch the attention of even the most casual passerby. On a typical mission to one of the more heavily defended targets, it would not be unusual for twenty-four to thirty-six airplanes to all take off within minutes of each other. Once airborne, they would join up in formation and proceed to the tankers for prestrike refueling, and then to the target. The F-4 wasn't called "Double Ugly" for nothing—armed with bombs and tanks, it was a pretty imposing piece of machinery. You knew that something big was about to happen to somebody, somewhere.

If it were a mission to one of the more dangerous targets, then it was also a time of nervousness for the crews involved. I found this preflight and start sequence to have somewhat of a calming influence. The worst part, for me, was after the premission briefing. Once that was completed, we just waited around to go out to the airplanes. That left 20 to 30 minutes to contemplate what was going to happen in the next 3 to 4 hours.

Would I still be alive this afternoon? Would I get hit and have to cope with some major emergency? Would I have to eject? Would I be one of the lucky ones and be picked up, or would I be captured by the North Vietnamese, or worse, the Pathet Lao, who would be inclined to torture and kill me, since I would be more of a liability than an asset to them. If captured, would I be able to conduct myself with honor? These and similar thoughts would run through my mind. I was resigned to the fact that I might be killed. What most concerned me was the thought of being captured. I remembered the quote from one of my high school English reading assignments, Shakespeare's *Julius Caesar*: "Cowards die a thousand times before their deaths, the valiant taste of death but once." Either I was a first-class coward, or the author of that sentence never had to go to some of the targets we went to! At any rate, once I got to the airplane and started the preflight and cockpit checks, I would settle down. Here was something I could control, a known routine and a well-practiced set of procedures. At least I had some control of the process, and it always calmed me down.

On this particular day, I was very busy and focused as I completed my tasks. Halfway through my cockpit checks, I glanced up and saw the Ops Clerk as he stood on our squadron porch and watched the strike force prepare to take off.

What I'm about to say is supposition, since I never talked to him about it, and he never said anything to me to indicate what his thoughts were. But I'll bet four martinis that I'm "spot on" when I describe what I think was going through his mind. The ops clerk posted all the flying schedules on the big Plexiglas board in the squadron, and made sure that all countless details necessary for the squadron to function smoothly were taken care of. He'd be there when we all came back from a mission and would hear all the talk, sometimes boisterous, sometimes shaken and depressed, before we went off to intelligence to debrief the mission. He'd hear all the BS, gossip, and rumor that would take place around the ops desk during the day and night. He'd taken care of all our records, so he knew who we were, and what our backgrounds were like. He'd often drive us out to the airplanes, and then pick us up in the squadron van when we returned. So he saw much of our world, but *not* what took place once we left the confines of our base at Ubon—and that's what I think was going through his mind as he watched us prepare to go into combat.

I have a theory. I believe that combat for a man is like the birth of a baby is for a woman. Those who have never experienced it will always wonder, in some way, what it was like, and how they would have reacted. Perhaps that doesn't say much for the evolution of humankind, but if you haven't done it, there's always that question in your mind. My father was a flight surgeon at Lemoore Army Airfield during World War II. He spent the entire war at that pilot training base, and to some extent, felt unfulfilled that he had never seen anything of combat. After the war, his doctor friends would wax eloquent about their combat exploits but he would grow strangely silent during those conversations. It's not my intent to glorify war, or encourage everyone to run off to their recruiter and sign up for the current or next war, but I do think this feeling exists at some level within most men. That's what I think the Kid was thinking about. I think he was imagining what it would be like if *he* were there in that airplane, starting up and preparing to take off for his moment of truth. It *is* pretty exciting to watch this aerial armada prepare to do battle. Look how everyone was quite taken with the movie *Top Gun* a few years ago. They were up there with "Iceman" and "Maverick," vicariously experiencing combat! Just like the Kid was trying to project himself into our situation. There was no doubt in my mind, as I saw him watch us, that he would have given anything to trade places with one of us. It would have been the thrill of a lifetime, an incredible rush and adventure, all at once.

What he never realized was that I was envious of him. He had every expectation that he would go to lunch in about 4 hours. He wasn't worried if he would be alive by nightfall. He didn't have to concern himself with the possibility of torture before the day was over. And he knew that this sort of existence would continue until he'd been there a year, at which time he then would be reassigned out of the combat zone. I can only speak for myself, but there were times when I wished that something would go wrong with the airplane so that I could abort the mission in good faith. The amazing thing was that very few ever did! The airplanes were well maintained, but no matter how scared you were, the thought of being seen as a coward, and of letting your squadron mates down, was enough to keep you from finding reasons to abort. Of course, certain things, like an engine out, would always cause you to have to cancel out of the mission. It was for that reason that on the big missions, where it was crucial to have a flight of four for mutual support, flights always took off with an air spare. The spare would go with the flight to the tanker, and if anyone aborted, he'd take their place but it didn't happen often. Such were my thoughts as I observed the ops clerk watch us.

I never forgot the irony of that moment, and in many respects, it's probably a good metaphor for how most noncombatants feel about war. It sure looks pretty exciting, adventurous, and stimulating, but it has its downsides, as those who have experienced it will usually attest. Moral: All those who think that war is the solution for all the world's ills might feel a bit differently about it if they had actually experienced the nature of combat at some point in their lives. I have no idea whatever happened to our ops clerk. I'd love to run into him someday to see what really went through his mind that particular day. But I think I know.

CHAPTER 12

Lead's Hit!

Getting assigned to a target in Laos was not usually the high point of your day. The main reason was that it did nothing to get you home, other than mark that another day had passed. The missions were not "counters," in the sense that they did not count toward the magic 100 missions over North Vietnam that would complete a combat tour. Missions over Laos didn't count. To add insult to injury, some of these Laos missions could be pretty scary, all on their own. True, there were no SAMs or MiGs in Laos, at least during the time that I was there, but they had an incredible number of antiaircraft guns to protect their supply routes. In my case, I probably came closer to "buying it" over Laos than on high-risk missions to the dreaded North. But the Laotian missions had to be flown. So the squadrons split the load between the "counters" and the "noncounters" as best they could. Later, after the April 1968 bombing halt of targets in the far north and very restrictive rules for the southern portion of North Vietnam, most of the targets were in Laos, and therefore noncounters. The tour length gradually evolved to 1 year, since there was little likelihood that anyone could accumulate 100 missions over North Vietnam.

On March 21, 1968, I was assigned to lead a flight of two to make contact with a FAC in southern Laos and hit whatever targets he had for us. While I wasn't overjoyed, it didn't look as if this was going to be the worst mission in the world, either. Little did I know that this mission would turn out to be one of the most bizarre of my tour—memorable in many strange ways. We briefed all the standard items, suited up, and took off.

Captain Rick Bennett was my wingman, and it was a pleasure to fly with him. He was one of my checkout pilots during my initial fifteen-mission orientation phase when I arrived at Ubon and had been a back-seater before this second tour at Ubon, so he was very experienced and had a pleasant personality as well. The initial part of the flight was uneventful. The area where we were supposed to contact the FAC was not far away, 20 to 30 minutes at the most. We arrived at the designated point and attempted to make radio contact. This was a straightforward procedure and usually took a few minutes. But this was not going to be a normal day.

Several attempts to contact the FAC met with no success. We tried to contact the ABCCC (Airborne Command Control and Communications) airplane, a C-130 that was on station to act as a liaison between the major Air Force Headquarters as a communication relay. Most of the time this was a smooth, seamless operation. You contacted the FAC and got the target brief, he cleared you in, gave you your Bomb Damage Assessment, and home you went. We couldn't do any of that until we made contact with the FAC, and now, after a 30-minute delay, we were getting low on fuel. If there had been a tanker available, we could have refueled and tried again to find our FAC. The ABCCC airplane wasn't sure what had happened either. Sometimes the FAC got busy, particularly if an airplane had been shot down, and the rescue forces were being mobilized to attempt to rescue the crew, but we knew of no shoot downs this morning. Finally, fuel became critical. We still had a full load of bombs, but no clearance to drop them in Laos.

What to do? I came up with the idea that we should divert to DaNang Air Base in South Vietnam because it was the closest. The thought was to refuel, check in with 7th Air Force Headquarters, get an update on the FAC situation, then take off and try it all again. We proceeded southeast to DaNang.

Landing with a full load of bombs was not often done in an F-4. It lengthened the landing roll and increased the danger should a tire blow. The beast was very heavy. Usually, when we landed, we had consumed most of the fuel and only had about 2,000 pounds remaining, but our bomb load that day was twelve 500-pound bombs, which added another 6,000 pounds to our landing weight. The bombs are not armed until dropped from the airplane, but they are an added risk if anything goes awry during the landing. However, skilled aviators that we were, all went well, and we landed at DaNang to refuel and see whether we could still complete the original mission.

DaNang was quite a contrast to our base at Ubon in Thailand. For one thing, there was an active war going on all around the base. We didn't have to worry about such unpleasantries in Thailand, where the nearest actual combat was across the border in Laos. Frequent rocket and mortar attacks were not uncommon at this base on the eastern coast of South Vietnam, and not far from the border with North Vietnam. Conditions were more primitive and sparse at DaNang. Ubon, on the other hand, was like a regular stateside base with all the amenities. It was quite a treat for pilots from bases like DaNang to divert to Ubon, where, for a short time, they could enjoy a lot of pleasures that we often took for granted. This was my first time at the base, and a quick look around confirmed that Ubon was without doubt a more enjoyable place to be.

We refueled quickly and made phone calls to the appropriate command posts to see whether we could straighten out the problem with our missing FAC. We were assured that either the original FAC or his replacement would be available for us when we reached the target area. We copied down all the radio frequencies, rendezvous points, and general target description (which wasn't much) and prepared to sally forth for another attempt—hopefully more successful than the first!

Once more, we strapped on the mighty Phantoms, went through our preflight checks, and started to taxi out for takeoff from DaNang. Strange event number one was landing with a full bomb load; I had never done that before. However, the next experience was almost surreal. As our flight of two taxied out to the runway, we passed a Pan American Airways 707 parked on the ramp. This was how the majority of people arrived and left Vietnam, and I suppose for those stationed at DaNang, it was a pretty routine sight.

But not for me. To see a large 707 jet, with the very American words "Pan American" written along the fuselage and the prominent logo emblazoned on the tail, was a jolting reminder of the United States suddenly right in front of me after many months of flying combat. Several stewardesses stood in the open doorways, resplendent in their nice, tight-fitting blue uniforms, and waved at us as we taxied by them about 200 feet away. They acted like a bunch of schoolgirls at an air show. They waved, pointed, and shouted something at us, which we couldn't possibly hear because of the noise. I have never gotten over that juxtaposition. In the next hour, we might encounter heavy flak, we would drop bombs on somebody or something, and perhaps, one or both of us might not even be of this realm anymore. And yet, to these stewardesses, it was just an interesting sight, passing by for their amusement. Perhaps they realized the seriousness of the situation, but it didn't appear that way to me. In another hour or so, they would take on a new load of passengers and fly off to normalcy. Dumbfounded, we waved back, taxied onto the active runway, and took off for our second attempt to hit our target. Strange event number two!

The weather in the target area hadn't improved much from our earlier visit. It was overcast at 14,000 feet, which didn't give us as much clearance between the hilltops in the target area as we would have liked. It took us a while to wind our way around the cloud buildups, and we spent some more time trying to contact the elusive FAC. Fuel was again starting to become a problem. Finally, the FAC came up on the frequency. That was the good news. The bad news was that he had been in this particular area for several hours and reported that he had seen 3,000 rounds or so of heavy antiaircraft fire. Not so good—that's a lot, and who knows how much he didn't see?

I had to admire these guys. There they were, in their little Cessna O-2 airplanes, and the only armament they had were white phosphorus rockets to mark targets for guys like us. The target area, a place called Ban La Boy Ford, was on the Laotian side of the border between North Vietnam and Laos, just a bit south of Mu Gia Pass. It was a major part of the Ho Chi Minh Trail, and appropriately defended, since so much of the resupply effort to South Vietnam came through there. I had flown over the area when I first started flying missions and remembered it as a dense, green jungle. It wasn't now. After repeated bombing, it looked more like the dark side of the moon. The vegetation and trees had been destroyed and all that was left were bomb craters and dirt for a 2- to 3-mile area around the river crossing. This mission was not going the way I had hoped.

I could tell by the FAC's uncertain voice over the radio that he was not looking forward to marking the target for our flight. Often, the gunners would not shoot at the FACs because they didn't want to give away their position. They knew that the FAC could get fighters on the scene in a few minutes, and they didn't want that to happen. However, once the FAC found a target and directed fighters against it, there was no reason not to shoot at them. Such was the case today. I had been to the general area several times, and since I felt rather magnanimous that day, I told him there was no need to mark the target for us. If he could just describe where he wanted the ordnance delivered, that would be sufficient. I also mentioned that we were short of fuel and would drop all our bombs in one pass. I suspect his pulse rate dropped 100 points as soon as I said that. He gave a quick description of where to drop the bombs and, in a very relieved voice, cleared us in to attack the target.

Because of the clouds, I was lower than I wanted to be as I started the roll-in, and was also slow (a relative term: I was around 400 knots), since I was trying to conserve fuel as the FAC described the target. My roll-in technique was some-what violent because I used negative G to present an unpredictable pattern to any gunner that didn't think I was such a neat guy. The negative G pushover usually required a high G pull to get back to the flight path that I needed to achieve a good dive-bomb pass. I went through my world-famous, highly re-spected roll-in, and put the pipper just short of a tree line that the FAC had described. Supposedly, there were some trucks or supplies hidden at the edge of this bombed-out area. Airspeed: a little slow, dive angle: good, 45 degrees, and I was coming up on the release altitude.

One of the great things about the F-4D was a system known as "Dive Toss." As I rolled in, the back-seater locked on to the ground return with the radar. I then had to put the pipper on the target and press the pickle button. As soon as I did that, the slant range was fed into the airplane's on-board computer, and it took into account all the requirements needed to drop a successful bomb. This was great because I didn't have to manually fly the aircraft to exactly the right pa-rameters for bomb release. Once I'd designated the target by putting the pipper on it and pressed the pickle button on the stick, I could start my pullout. The

computer then would compute when conditions were optimum for bomb release and drop the bombs during the pullout. This was shit hot because I could
pull out early and the computer did the rest. In most cases, the system was more
accurate than manual dive-bombing, especially in high-threat areas, since all
those tracers over the canopy tended to ruin my concentration. I watched the
pipper move up to the target, and as soon as it was over the right spot, I punched
the pickle button and started a pull-up.

In rapid succession, I felt the "thumps" as the Mark 82, 500-pound bombs
dropped off the airplane. I looked down and noticed that the right inboard bomb
pylon light was still on, which meant that at least one bomb was still on the pylon.
A glance at the airspeed indicator showed 420 knots, which was *way* too slow for
such a threat area. I'd bled off a lot of speed during the lower-than-normal jinking
roll-in to the target and had to do something to regain it. This was not a place for a
leisure departure from the area. I selected afterburner on both engines, and
started to jink in earnest. Since we were again short of fuel, I was reluctant to burn
the extra gas, but my survival instinct quickly overcame my concern.

Wham! There was a violent shudder that shook the entire airplane and
knocked my feet off the rudder pedals. I thought I'd been hit in the belly of the
F-4 by a 37mm or higher caliber antiaircraft shell. I had never experienced a jolt
that severe in the airplane, so it had to be something bad . . . really bad. If that
were true, then I'd probably start losing hydraulic fluid pretty soon, which would
mean I could no longer control the airplane and would be forced to eject right
over the target I had just bombed. My worst nightmare was coming true.

This will sound strange, but my immediate reaction when I felt the jolt was,
This can't be happening to a nice guy like me. My disbelief lasted only a second
and was replaced with absolute stark, sheer terror. There was little chance of
evasion. The immediate target area was all bombed out, and it was right near
major supply routes. I had not seen any flak, but could think of nothing else that
would cause that severe a disturbance. I quickly looked down at the hydraulic
gauges, which were all rapidly oscillating. I was convinced we would have to
eject in seconds.

I had given this possibility quite a bit of thought. I had two plans: If shot down
over North Vietnam, I would try to evade—I wasn't going to be able to shoot my
way out. If captured, I would just have to attempt to survive the POW experience. But at least the North Vietnamese Army took prisoners. If I were shot down
over Laos, I had a quite different plan. If not rescued quickly, I didn't see much
hope. Prisoners were a luxury the Pathet Lao and North Vietnamese couldn't
afford. They just tortured and killed them. As a Catholic, I couldn't rationalize
suicide. My plan was to charge them if capture were imminent. I was unlikely to
succeed, but they would have to kill me to get me.

I shouted on the radio, "Lead's Hit! Lead's Hit! I'm heading for the karst!" The karst was a series of most-inhospitable-looking limestone-rock outcroppings that were about 5 miles away and actually in North Vietnam. Now, normally, when you think of a parachute landing, you want a nice, flat, soft place so you don't get banged up too bad. Not so in combat. We were more concerned about the enemy getting to us, and the more inhospitable the better if it kept them away. Mike Suhy, my back-seater, asked, "What's the matter?" "What happened?" I told him we might have been hit in the belly and had some bombs still on the right side of the airplane. By now, we had reached about 10,000 feet, and the airplane felt pretty normal, which amazed me.

Rick Bennett had rolled in right after me, dropped his bombs, and was now racing to rejoin on me to see how badly I had been hit. About the time I leveled off at 10,000 feet, he was coming up underneath me to check for battle damage. Rick moved in closer and said, "I don't see anything. You look okay." I couldn't believe it! Rick had good eyes. I knew he wasn't blind—*why hadn't he seen anything*? I looked back down at the hydraulic gauges. They were all steady. I sheepishly asked Rick to look again—there had to be something! Now I started to feel a little foolish. Had I lost it? Was I so scared that I was imagining things? I couldn't believe there wasn't a massive hole in the belly. Rick crossed under and behind me to the other side of my airplane. After what seemed like eons, he came back up on the radio, "Okay, I see it now. You're missing about four tail feathers from the nozzles of your right afterburner section. You've also got a bomb hung by one lug on the right pylon." Now I began to realize what had happened.

During takeoff at Ubon, I had noticed that the right afterburner was slow to light. Enough to be noticeable, but since it eventually lit, I thought little more about it and pressed on. If it hadn't lit in a few more seconds, we would have had to abort the takeoff, but it was only a few seconds' delay. When I pulled off the target, I was slower than normal, which also meant that not as much air flowed through the engine. When you select afterburner, you dump raw fuel into the section of the engine aft of the turbine. An igniter, similar to a spark plug, ignites all this new fuel with the already superheated air and provides a tremendous increase in thrust, almost double. What had happened was that the igniter in the right afterburner section was faulty and didn't ignite the raw fuel that was injected. All my jinking had most likely aggravated the situation, and, as a result, the raw fuel had pooled in the afterburner section. The hot turbine exhaust section had finally ignited it, and that was the jolt that I had felt. The resulting overpressure had been pretty severe and that's what had blown the exhaust nozzles off of the afterburner section. A relatively minor problem compared to what I had originally thought it was. Thank you, Lord! The fluctuating hydraulic pressure—what caused that? I did! I had never looked down at the hydraulic gauges when I was jinking. You needed to have your head out of the cockpit to see any threats so you could avoid them. Had I looked while I was moving the controls rapidly in many directions, I would have noticed the same thing. Once I quit jinking, all was normal.

Thoroughly relieved and now really short of fuel, we headed back to Ubon and an uneventful landing, hung bomb notwithstanding. Sure enough, the maintenance folks did discover that the afterburner igniter was bad. The nozzles were replaced, and the airplane flew again the next day, no worse for its adventure!

In retrospect, it was a bizarre mission that even had some comical aspects, but it certainly didn't feel that way at the time. I was absolutely convinced for a few moments that perhaps my time had come to an end. I was quite skeptical when Rick Bennett said that he could see no damage. I desperately wanted to believe it, but it was hard to reconcile his statement with the violent thump I had felt a few moments earlier. As one of my heroes, Winston Churchill, once said, "There is nothing so exhilarating as to be shot at without result!" I quite savored my martini that night at the club.

CHAPTER 13

It's Sunday!

A trip to Hanoi was always a heart-acceleration experience, but one particular Sunday stands out in vivid detail, perhaps because it was a Sunday.

The strike that day was to be against North Vietnamese Army barracks, southwest of the center of Hanoi. Since it was just a week after St. Patrick's Day, the luck of the Irish was with me, and I was number two in the MiG CAP flight. My brethren who were scheduled to "haul the iron" didn't feel quite so blessed. As these strikes went, it was a small one. We were the only MiG CAP flight, and we didn't even have an "Iron Hand" SAM suppression flight with us, since there were only two flights of F-4s that would actually bomb the target. The scheduled target wasn't anticipated to be that well defended. Not at all like the Paul Doumer Bridge that crossed the Red River, or one of the major airfields. Nonetheless, I was thankful that I was a "Capper," rather than a "bomber." The mission commander, Major Ron Iberg, would lead the strike flights that would drop the bombs. Ron was a pretty steady kind of guy, a good stick who had a lot of interceptor experience. One of the worst aspects of being a mission commander was to make the call to either press on to the target, or abort the mission. It was often a tough call, and there wasn't a lot of time to mull over all the variables. It was most difficult to turn a large number of airplanes around in a heavily defended area, and, of course, no one wanted to be tagged as someone who didn't have the "right stuff," so there was always a lot of pressure on the mission commander.

The mission planning and briefing was normal, and pretty straightforward. Our CAP flight would be about a minute ahead of the strike flight. At our speeds of 540 knots plus, this equated to about 10 miles. Weather was the main concern. It had been pretty bad in the Hanoi area for the past several weeks, but had started to clear up. Cloud cover wasn't forecast to be too bad, but visibility was a big concern. We wouldn't know for sure until we arrived in the target area. We briefed that our MiG CAP flight would pull a bit ahead of the strike flight, descend to their altitude (normally we'd be higher to be better positioned to engage any potential MiGs), check out the visibility, and call it back to Ron. We'd then pull up to a higher altitude and turn 45 degrees from the flight path of the bombers. After a minute, we'd make a 90-degree turn back toward the bombers and pick them up just after they'd dropped their bombs and made a max performance 180-degree turn to get out of the target area as quick as they could. We'd be able to cover them as they left the target should any enemy aircraft come up to challenge us. There was nothing unusual about any of this, so we completed the briefings, made the usual nervous bladder stop in the men's room, suited up, and went to the airplanes. Although I didn't give much thought to it at the time, my MiG CAP flight lead mentioned that we might do some armed recce near the Dien Bien Phu area, depending on how things went after our main mission. This was unusual, but I was intrigued by the idea, since Dien Bien Phu was the site of the tragic French defeat that caused them to lose the French Indo-China War. I had read Bernard Fall's book, *Hell in a Very Small Place*, which was about the battle, and thought that it might be interesting to actually see the site. As the Chinese saying goes, "Be careful what you wish for, you might get it."

Start, taxi, take off, and join up were all normal. The entire force hit the KC-135 tankers and topped off before we headed into North Vietnam. You could never have too much fuel over that place. After we crossed into North Vietnam, we could see why the weatherman had been such a pessimist. At around 25,000 feet, it was reasonably clear, and there were no significant clouds. But below that, it was really hazy—miserably hazy. The kind of brown, smoky haze that limits your visibility to a few miles, and definitely the kind of haze that makes it very difficult to see a SAM that's just been launched. You needed to see the SAM to avoid the thing.

Soon, we were almost at the target. Our MiG CAP flight descended into the murk to around 18,000 feet, which is where the bombers would be. Since they knew the weather would not be good enough for dive-bombing, the plan was for them to use a technique called Radar Offset Bombing, in which they would use their own radar to identify a known ground return and then fly to a predetermined point that was offset from that. If they all dropped the bombs at that point, they should hit the target. The ballistics and bomb range of the bomb load they carried determined the offset point, and it was not something that could be easily changed. The mission commander was understandably nervous behind us and kept asking what the weather was. This was a tough call. Nobody wants to be known as a wimp. You could see straight down okay, but forward visibility was pretty limited, maybe 3 miles at best. In that part of Southeast Asia, there is a lot of rice-field burning at that time of year to prepare for the new crops and that was most likely the cause of most of the haze.

We received another call from the mission commander for weather status. My flight lead gave a rather vague radio call in response. Something along the lines of, "Well, it's sorta so-so." Not really a go or no-go call at all. The poor mission commander, about a minute or two behind us, was no better off than if we had said nothing and, in fact, might have been lulled into a false sense of confidence. The good news was that everyone in the bomber flight had functioning electronic countermeasure jamming pods—they were going to need them. The bad news was that the time to make an abort decision had now passed, since they were about 25 to 30 miles from the target. At this point, the best thing to do was press on and hope for the best. A large, unwieldy, in-place break a few miles short of the target would be just as dangerous as doing it over the target, and the target would remain untouched.

After this nondescript weather report, our four-ship MiG CAP flight lead climbed out of the murk and took us back up to 25,000 feet, where it was clear. We turned 45 degrees to the left of the target run-in course in the direction of a possible MiG attack. This way we would offset from the fighter-bombers and pick them up on their way out. We had no sooner headed outbound when the Radar Homing and Warning Gear became active with all kinds of unpleasant and dangerous sounds. Each type of threat, antiaircraft radar, SAMs, or airborne tracking radar, emitted a different sound and gave a strobe on a small screen that indicated the direction and relative strength of the threat. The strobes all emanated from the target area and rapidly increased in number and volume. As we started to turn back toward the strike force, I found it hard to grasp what I saw! SAMs were exploding all over the place near the target area! I thought, "They shouldn't be doing this—it's Sunday!" Granted that didn't make a lot of sense, but that was my thought nevertheless. I had never seen that many SAMs all at once before.

Since the entire strike force was on the same frequency, I could hear the bombers frantically asking if anyone had seen a launch, since they had plenty of indications that multiple SAM launches were taking place. The jamming pods were good, but, believe me, it's very hard to put your full faith and trust in them if you think a SAM is about to hit you any moment and you still can't see it visually! In order for the jamming pods to give the best protection, you *had* to keep the wings level, or the coverage would be disrupted. I used to have an audio tape of this mission that has long since disappeared, and you could clearly hear the two flight leads yelling for pilots to keep the wings level, or it would just make things worse! It was absolutely good advice, but I could certainly sympathize with the strike pilots' terror and fear of not seeing a SAM in time to avoid it. My heart was in my mouth at what had unfolded in front of me, and I wasn't even in the worst of it!

At last, I heard Ron, call out, "Standby, Ready, Pickle . . . NOW!" That command was the signal to drop the bombs, and all planes pickled their bombs at the same instant. This was followed by, "In-place break . . . NOW!" They had dropped their bombs and were in the process of doing an in-place, max performance, hard turn to get out of there as fast as the F-4 could! This may sound simple, but wingmen often got thrown out of position since, in line-abreast formation, you are belly-up to your leader for part of the turn and could lose sight. You then had to rapidly get back into pod formation with *somebody—anybody*! Once you were out of the area, you could form up with your original flight, if necessary. Miraculously, no one had been hit, in spite of the fact that 37 SAMs had been launched at them, as I later learned from the Intell folks. Our flight picked up the strike force, and in a matter of minutes, we had all egressed the target area. It was hard to believe our good fortune. If you'd seen and heard it as it happened, you wouldn't have believed it could have such a happy ending.

Once we were out of the immediate target area, we quickly checked each other over for battle damage, did a fuel check, and proceeded to head back to Ubon. All except for my MiG CAP flight leader and myself. Lead sent the rest of the flight back home, and the two of us headed off in the general direction of Dien Bien Phu. The reason for our detour is still unclear. We didn't have much in the way of ordnance, just air-to-air missiles, so we would not be able to shoot up much on the ground, even if we found a target.

Dien Bien Phu is almost at the western border between North Vietnam and Laos. It's a small valley surrounded by mountains, which, as the French found out, severely limited their ability to maneuver. I mean, it's a really small valley. We didn't see anything of note, and, as far as I know, we didn't get shot at, either. Normally, we didn't go up there as a two-ship, unless we had a definite purpose, and to this day, I'm not clear what our purpose might have been. Maybe 7th Air Force Headquarters tasked him and he didn't share the rationale with us. Sometimes, we'd fly over an area where someone had been shot down to see whether they came up on the radio. Maybe that was it. We didn't see anything unusual, and Lead finally turned back southeast. "Whew," I said to myself!

At this point, I developed a love affair with my fuel gauge. I'm an avowed "fuel enthusiast." I'd been short of gas too many times not to be concerned about what might happen if the gauge went to "0." It's bad any time, but over North Vietnam or Laos . . . it's really bad! On every mission, there was a planned "Bingo fuel," which meant that when you got to that level, you had just enough to get to one of several airfields. Actually, we had a couple of different "Bingos." One was enough to get to Udorn, right on the border of Laos and Thailand, in a pinch. The most common one was adequate to get us back to our home base at Ubon. At this point, I was below both numbers. I was not bashful and let my flight lead know about this, which was standard practice. We had overstayed our time. Wingmen always burn more fuel than flight leaders because they have to jockey the throttle to stay in proper position. Usually, there's not much difference between the two, but at this moment, every little pound of fuel was critical. I confess to obscene thoughts directed at my flight lead during this period.

Maybe it was just an opportunity to see whether Irish luck had any foundation in fact. At this point, Lead got on the radio and started calling for a KC-135 tanker to come toward our position as quickly as possible. We were still pretty far north, and the tanker lads had specific directives that limited where they could go. After all, they were utterly defenseless if jumped by MiGs or shot at by SAMs or AAA. They were just big, flying gas tanks in the sky, with no defensive capabilities. In the past, there had been times when tensions ran pretty high because the fighters were low on fuel, but the tankers would not violate their directives and come any further north.

We were hurting! We jettisoned the empty tanks and pylons off the airplanes to get rid of excess drag, and climbed to higher altitude where fuel consumption was less. Finally, Invert, the Ground Control Intercept (GCI) radar site in Thailand, gave us a vector to a tanker.

God bless these guys! I know they came way further north than they were supposed to and exposed themselves to danger. Minimum fuel in the F-4 is around 2,250 pounds. A "fuel level low" light comes on at that point. I'd been looking at it for some time. Finally, we had a "Tally-Ho" on the tanker, which meant we had a visual contact and could proceed to join on it to get our fuel. Lead, graciously, cleared me in first—I had about 500–700 pounds at that point and he was a little better off. I plugged in within 13 picoseconds, and started taking precious fuel. We had to keep swapping positions, or Lead would flame out. I took only about 500 pounds of fuel; then he would plug in and take a small amount. We'd then switch positions and, gradually, each of us was able to take on more fuel each time. Finally, many sweat-drenched moments later, we had both taken on enough fuel to get back to Ubon. We thanked the tanker and headed back to Ubon. I never met those tanker guys and, to this day, have no idea who they were. One of them might have even been my future brother-in-law for all I know. Whoever you were, you have my profound thanks. You probably didn't know who we were either. But, if you're reading this, and it rings a bell, know that you have my immense gratitude.

Finally, after all the pulse-pounding events of the day, the tires gave their familiar thump as we once more made contact with the runway at Ubon. We dearmed, shut down, and went through maintenance and Intell debriefing. Surprisingly, our flight lead didn't have much to say. If there were harsh words exchanged between the mission commander and our MiG Cap lead, we junior officers didn't hear them. Perhaps there should have been. He later went on to do great things, and maybe it was just one of those days. We all had them. As the old saying goes, "When you're hot, you're hot; when you're not, you're not." Some days are better than others. At the time, I didn't think too much about it. During a period of atypical and bizarre events, it was just one more.

CHAPTER 14

A Very Memorable Mission

As I related at the beginning of this book, I had major concerns about the flak suppression mission that I had been scheduled to fly against Phuc Yen Airfield, northwest of Hanoi, on April 1, 1968. I had learned that I was on the schedule late the day before, and it made for a restless night. I tossed, turned, and worried about tomorrow's strike to this difficult target for quite some time. I finally accepted that there was nothing more I could do and drifted off to sleep. At least I got a few hours before the dreaded alarm clock went off at precisely 2:00 AM. The time had come. The mission I was more worried about than any of the others I had flown was about to take place.

I took a shower, shaved, and got dressed. Odd thing, I never used a deodorant or aftershave whenever I flew a mission. My thought was that if I were ever shot down, I might get captured if they could smell me. It wasn't totally silent at this early hour, because some of the night mission crews were coming back, but still, it was pretty quiet. I could hear a few guys going through the same ritual as I. Each squadron was located in the same "hootch" area, so I recognized some who would also be going on the mission. They weren't much more talkative than I was. Somebody had a squadron truck that we piled into and drove to Wing Headquarters for the mission planning and briefing. In many respects, I felt like a condemned man going to the gallows. Events were happening that I couldn't stop.

We got to the squadron, grabbed a cup of coffee, and then went to intelligence to plan for the mission. To get this many airplanes on one target simultaneously, we couldn't come from all points on the compass, which pretty well dictated our arrival route. The fighter wings had learned from bitter experience that flying in low and then popping up to roll in on the target just exposed us to more flak, so an attack from a medium altitude was pretty much the standard tactic. Yes, we gave up an element of surprise and became somewhat predictable, but the alternatives were worse. This mission would not be a surprise like Pearl Harbor, and we all knew that. We just wanted to get in there as quickly as possible, do our business, and get out. Later, we found out that the North Vietnamese even had agents near the base at Ubon who would radio our takeoff times and flight data up the line as we took off on a mission. We weren't going to fool anyone.

The back-seaters started computing the navigation legs and the fuel consumption. We front-seaters studied the target photos and tried to identify where the guns would be when we rolled in on our targets. This was not as simple as it sounds. Frequently, the photos were old and often not of good quality. They might show some areas very well, but not others. This was pretty important because we had only a few seconds to take all this in and figure out what to do. On the run-in to the target, most of our attention was on flying formation and looking out for MiGs, SAMs, and flak. The flight leader had an incredibly difficult job in that he had to do the same things plus get the entire flight of four to the roll-in point where we could make the attack. Otherwise, the whole effort was for naught. This part of the planning was quiet—not much talking except for murmurs from the back-seaters as they asked other flights for certain vital pieces of information. I concentrated on looking at the photos of Phuc Yen Airfield to see whether I could pinpoint where the flak sites were. The intelligence types had circled and annotated them. Since there were only four of us who were concerned about these sites, we developed a plan on how we would attack them by splitting them up among ourselves.

Occasionally, as I had often done in the past, I looked up at a large photo that was hanging on the wall, just as you walked into the intelligence area. It showed a panoramic shot of a reconnaissance RF-4 taken by the wingman, and consisted of about five frames. In the first one, you can see a SA-2 coming up at the RF-4 from about his five or seven o'clock position. The crew probably never saw it. In the second or third frame, the SAM explodes just beneath the recce Phantom and sends shrapnel into the airplane, which causes a massive explosion. The last two frames show the RF-4 broken in two, and engulfed in flames. Although we didn't know it at the time, the crew ejected and was captured. I didn't learn this until after the war, but the front-seater, Major Atterbury, managed to escape from Hanoi briefly. Unfortunately, he was recaptured relatively quickly (it was hard for a six-foot-tall Caucasian to walk around North Vietnam unnoticed) and was beaten to death after his recapture. The back-seater survived his captivity. I guess it was good to have pictures like that up there to remind us of the hostile environment we were about to go into, but it certainly didn't give a warm, fuzzy feeling about what lay ahead during our normal workday. Finally, we had done all we could do in this phase. It was now about 3:30 AM—time for the mission intelligence briefing.

All those who were going on the Phuc Yen Airfield strike filed into the large, mahogany briefing room right next to the mission planning area. There were probably about fifty of us altogether, including the air spares. We weren't all from the same squadron. Some I knew; others I didn't. Within each four-ship flight, we were all from the same squadron, for the wing schedulers seldom, if ever, put a stranger in there. But the aircraft that would bomb the target often were from one of the other squadrons. The F-105 Wild Weasel SAM suppression flights were always from either Korat or Takhli Air Bases, also in Thailand. After this generalized briefing, we would have to get on the secure telephone and coordinate certain key items with them, such as rejoin points, emergency procedures, and other details. The secure phone worked by breaking up our conversations and then reassembling them, similar to the Internet e-mail system today. But it was primitive, and it sounded like the person on the other end was really drunk—difficult to understand, but at least we could talk in plain English.

The young intelligence captain who gave the mission briefing walked up on the stage, and the room immediately quieted. Our lives might depend on what he was about to tell us. I remember looking around the room. It was possible that some of these people were not going to be here this afternoon—it had happened before. Would I be one of them? I tried to think positive thoughts, but they were not easy to conjure up.

The briefing started. General target description, enemy defenses, number and location of SAM sites, weather data, radio frequencies, latest intelligence on the activity in the area—that sort of thing. I distinctly remember the briefer stating, "Gentlemen, latest intelligence shows guns in the vicinity to be at least 1,000." This was a major strike to the North Vietnamese, and it would not be a walk in the park. Safe areas were briefed. These were areas where friendly Laotians, CIA, or Special Forces were supposed to be operating and, if possible, would try to rescue us if we could make it there. There were special code words of the day and numerous other details that were disseminated. We always briefed a primary and secondary alternate target in case the weather or some other problem prevented us from attacking the main target. But today the weather was clear and visibility unlimited, so there wasn't any doubt in my mind that we were going to hit Phuc Yen Airfield. I wrote all the data down on my kneepad so I could refer to it during flight. Much of it I just memorized, because there wouldn't be time to look at it during the mission. The whole process took 30 to 45 minutes and covered the mission as a whole. Once we finished that portion, we went back to our individual squadrons and had our own flight briefings, which were more specific, and clarified our own, individual responsibilities.

The object was to leave as little to chance as possible. The unforeseen might happen, but we tried to minimize it. It was now about 4:00 AM as we went to the 433rd Tactical Fighter Squadron (Satan's Angels) briefing room. I grabbed another cup of coffee and a quick snack. Then the leader of our flak suppression flight briefed how we would accomplish our mission that day. I had very mixed emotions at this point. On the one hand, I would be part of something important and participate in a major strike against an important target. Everything I had trained for and dreamed about was coming true from a professional military standpoint. I must admit that I felt quite proud to be a "player." On the other hand, this was not going to be like a routine gunnery-training mission back in the States.

I thought about my family. It wasn't until years later, when I was a parent myself, that I realized what my poor mother must have gone through. My father had died years earlier, and I was the only son. At least I knew what was going on. She could only read the newspaper headlines that often described air losses over North Vietnam and wonder if I were one of them. I was so consumed with my own concerns that I didn't realize the depth of her anguish.

I was also involved in an "on-again, off-again" relationship with a woman whom I had been engaged to, but had broken it off because, intuitively, I knew something wasn't right. We had started up again by mail correspondence, as improbable as that may seem. It wasn't realistic, but at the time I'd convinced myself otherwise. It was bizarre: on the one hand I didn't want to think much about the future—just survive 1 day at a time. On the other hand, I longed for something permanent and someone to love; so I made myself believe things were better than they really were. In retrospect, it wasn't very realistic, but that didn't stop my idealistic fantasies.

I thought about all these things as we finished our individual flight briefing. Finally, it was over, and we had about 20 minutes before we received the "execute order" from 7th Air Force Headquarters. Since all targets within a 30-mile radius of Hanoi had to be approved by the JCS (Joint Chiefs of Staff), that sometimes didn't happen until nearly the time we were ready to walk out the door to the airplanes.

The clock ticked, my stomach churned, but still, nothing happened. This was the worst time. You were alone with your fears, and there was nothing anyone could say or do that would make the situation any better. After about a half hour of this, the jocks were really getting antsy. I could pretend to be nonchalant for a bit, but it's hard to do it for an extended period. Normally, about the point when I couldn't stand it any more, the time to suit up came, and the necessary actions occupied my consciousness. Things kind of took care of themselves—at least we had something to do other than think about what was ahead. As we waited, I tried to fill the time by going over and over in my mind the myriad details of the flight.

I tried to think positively, and imagine exactly all the procedures I had to perform if the mission went perfectly. When I finished, I'd start again.

Still, the clock ticked, and nothing happened.

We couldn't afford to delay much longer, or the intricate mission timing and tanker rendezvous would be screwed up. This was about the point where we were assigned our alternate target and, if necessary, even changed the bomb load to accommodate that target. None of this was happening.

By now, we were about an hour past our scheduled takeoff time—something was drastically different. Finally, the mission leaders went to Intelligence and the Wing Commander's office, a few doors down from our squadron area. About 10 minutes went by and suddenly they returned. The mission was cancelled! Not just our flak suppression flight at Phuc Yen Airfield, but everything! Initially, we dolts assumed that we would be going on the alternate mission. But, no! *Everything* was cancelled! This made no sense. The weather was about as good as it would get and would stay that way for several days. We *always* went to our alternate target. Why the change? No one had an answer.

We milled around, not really sure of what to do next. This was all very strange, and had never happened before. My initial reaction was one of incredible relief. For reasons that are still hard to understand even today, I had an overwhelming foreboding of doom. I was convinced that something would happen to me on this mission and it probably would not be good. I had never taken a hit in all my prior sixty-six missions, and was starting to feel that I had used all my luck at a prodigious rate—it couldn't continue forever. However, that reaction was tempered with the thought that if I didn't do this mission today, I would have to do it in the next couple of days. The weather was good and was forecast to stay that way, which meant that our squadron would just keep being assigned to targets like this for the foreseeable future. Maybe it was better to just get it out of the way and meet my fate, whatever it was. We hung around for about an hour until it became obvious that the cancellation was real, and we definitely weren't going "Downtown" this fine day. With nothing to do, and very tired, we all dispersed. I went back to my hootch to catch a bit of sleep. By now, it was about 8:00 AM.

I hit my bed and immediately fell asleep—total oblivion. Not exactly the "sleep of the just," but a sound sleep nonetheless. I awoke a few hours later, somewhat bewildered, since this whole morning was most unusual. I flipped on the radio, so I could pick up the Armed Forces radio station that broadcast in English. The first thing I heard was the voice of President Johnson, and it was obviously something out of the ordinary. He announced: "I shall not seek and I will not accept the nomination of my party as your president." This was a bolt out of the blue! But there was more! He also announced that there would be no bombing north of the 20th Parallel (the upper part of North Vietnam). Now it became clear—that's why the missions were cancelled! The speech was given in

Washington at 9:00 in the evening on March 31, 1968, which was 9:00 AM our time on April 1, a day ahead due to the International Date Line. Since we would have been airborne at the time of the speech, the missions had been scrubbed so we wouldn't violate the halt the president was announcing.

The atmosphere around Ubon changed dramatically. Pilots openly made comments like, "Now we can survive," "I can finish my tour," and "There's hope!" I think this was the first time I had ever heard these thoughts expressed candidly, and it surprised me. They weren't saying anything I hadn't thought of myself, but it was the first time I had heard the fears discussed in such a frank manner. It was quite a revelation. Previously, we just didn't say things like that— since it was not becoming of real fighter pilots. It was like a blanket of fear had just been lifted from the entire base. Now that the weather had improved, the likelihood of flying most of my missions in the Hanoi area was a very real possibility. And, the more missions I flew in that area, the more my odds of getting hit went up. Now—all that had changed significantly. Since it was April 1 in our part of the world, more than one jock thought it might be an April Fool's joke, and a cruel one at that. We had become a cynical lot.

But it wasn't. That really was the president we had heard on the radio, and he really did institute a bombing halt for the far-north targets.

I never went on the mission that I was so concerned about, although I would fly another fifty-eight missions after that. Ironically, the euphoria was somewhat illusory. From that point, until I finished my combat tour in August, we had a higher loss rate than when we flew to targets in the Hanoi area. There were probably a couple of reasons for the turnabout. Since the North Vietnamese knew we would not attack targets in the Hanoi area, many of those defenses most likely moved south to areas that we still attacked, including targets in Laos. The other possibility might have been complacency. When we went to the Hanoi area, we treated it like a high-threat area and didn't make multiple passes, go in at low altitudes, or use other risky procedures. Prior to the halt, we could sometimes get away with those tactics in the lower parts of North Vietnam and Laos, and that thinking might have influenced some of the crews. At any rate, the losses went up.

Never have I been impacted by a major national event in such an immediate manner. Even today, whenever I hear that speech or read about it, I can remember with incredible clarity exactly how I felt on that morning. Maybe I would have come away unscathed. I have always maintained that good things happen to you when you're Irish. But I'll never know, and often wonder why I was so afraid of that one particular mission, and what would have happened if the president hadn't decided, at that particular moment, to forgo the presidency and institute a bombing halt. I still wonder.

CHAPTER 15

Sydney

After a while, you just got burned out. I thought I could cope okay and that I could handle everything, "no sweat," but deep down in my pancreas I knew that it had become more difficult. That's why they had R&R (Rest & Recuperation). And it was a wonderful thing. We were allowed one "official" R&R during our tour. This meant that the Air Force paid my way from Ubon to a destination I chose. The squadrons were good about letting us off for a few days if space were available on one of the many transport airplanes that came to Ubon every day. The ride was free, but it was always a bit of a dicey operation to get back. I've never been a great fan of "Space Available." It's wonderful if you have enough time, but not so hot if you have to be somewhere at a specific time. That's why R&R was so great! All the travel was part of the package, and we didn't have to worry about it. It was easy to get to places like Hong Kong, but I was holding out for Sydney, Australia. The numbers of slots were more limited, but it sounded better than some of the other choices like Hong Kong, Tokyo, and Hawaii (very popular among the married types). We had an Australian squadron of F-86s stationed across from us at Ubon, and I had met several of them. On top of that, Australia supported the war and had sent troops to Vietnam. The luck of the Irish prevailed, and Australia it was. I was ecstatic. At the end of April 1968, I started off for Sydney and didn't get back until the second week of May.

First stop was Bangkok. That part of the trip required that I hop on the regular C-130 flight that came through every day. No problem, there was always plenty of room. At this point, I'd flown eighty-three combat missions at Ubon. After the short ride from Don Muong Airport, I stayed overnight at the Chao Phia Hotel, the same one that I'd stayed at on my first night in Bangkok, on the way to the war. As I recall, I didn't really do much that night, since I had an early Tan Son Nhut airport in Saigon the next morning. The hotel was welcome stop and seemed more an Officer's Club than a hotel. I ran people I knew and had a few drinks with them before I called it a night. Bright and early the next day, I was off to Saigon.

This was my first time in Saigon and it impressed me as being on more of a war footing than Thailand. This was not too long after the Tet Offensive, and everyone was more on edge. One of the big shocks was that after the battles that raged all over Saigon, including at the main base at Tan Son Nhut, they discovered that some of the Viet Cong attackers were trusted workers on the base. In one case, the barber that cut the hair of all the officers, to include some of the generals, was found draped over one of the barbed wire fences where he had tried to lay an explosive satchel charge. Some battles were still being fought in certain areas.

Tet was a violent shock, both to the American forces that were in South Vietnam and to the American and foreign public as well. It started to become obvious that all the body count, trucks destroyed, suspected ammunition dumps blown up, and other statistics that were supposed to signal the "light at the end of the tunnel" might perhaps be a wee bit illusory. Militarily, the uprising was swiftly put down, and it cost the Viet Cong and North Vietnamese dearly in lives and equipment lost. But, as a North Vietnamese general mentioned after the war, when reminded of this fact by a former American officer, "Yes, but it is also irrelevant," and in the end, they won the war and the United States lost. The seeds of doubt had been sown and would eventually force our withdrawal from the war. But all that was to come. All I cared about at that moment was to get to Camp Alpha, a small tent city at the air base where I would process out and get on the Pan American 707 that would take me to Sydney. It was hot, sweaty, and noisy, but I didn't care. In a few hours, I would be on my way to a welcome respite.

Finally, all the paperwork was finished, and we boarded the Pan Am bird. I knew that Sydney was a long distance away, but I hadn't grasped quite how far. For starters, we couldn't make it in one leg. We would have to stop in Darwin, on the northeast coast of Australia. It was a long flight—9-plus hours plus the time on the ground at Darwin. As much as I enjoyed myself, my pleasure was nothing compared to some of the Army and Marine soldiers on the airplane with me. Frequently, they had been in the field most of their time in Vietnam. A hot shower was heaven on earth! That was one of the reasons for Camp Alpha, to provide a place for them to clean up and rest before going on the big trip. My existence at Ubon didn't look so bad in comparison. I used to joke that "clean sheets and cold martinis" were part of our Air Force contract. Not all our ground force brethren thought it was as funny as I did.

Darwin was hot and humid when we landed there late in the afternoon. We had a few hours to refuel, and it was a chance for everyone to get something to eat. I had read about Darwin during World War II. The Japanese had almost overrun it, and New Guinea, where several major battles had taken place, was not too far to the east, just across the Coral Sea. I must admit, it wasn't the most attractive place I'd ever seen. Finally, we reboarded the 707 and headed for Sydney. We still had several more hours, and much desert to fly over before we reached our destination. It was a revelation for me to experience the vastness of Australia. Again, it validated how travel broadened one's education.

We flew over more desert than I ever imagined existed and landed in Sydney early in the morning. Even from the air, it reminded me of San Francisco, the city I'd left to join the Great Patriotic War. A war that, at the time, I thought would be over before I could arrive and settle it. By now, we were all pretty tired, but we still had Australian Customs to go through, which was far more stringent than I had imagined it would be. I remember the customs inspector opening a new pack of cigarettes on a few of the troops ahead of me. It struck me as a bit of overkill, and I politely mentioned it to him when I came before him. He was quite pleasant about it, but also mentioned that they had uncovered quite a bit of marijuana the week before, and it was disguised in just that fashion. Suitably chastised, I went through the rest of the process in humble silence.

Once we were through Customs and had retrieved our baggage, we had to go to a special R&R briefing in another room at the Sydney airport. We were all tired, and I must admit that I wasn't too much in the mood for it, but it's one of the main memories of my visit to Australia. It was incredibly well organized, and what I thought would be a "behave yourselves" lecture was really an introduction to Australian hospitality. We were given several numbers to call depending on what we might find of interest. If you wanted to go wallaby hunting, there was a family or group you could call about that. If you just wanted dinner with an Australian family, there was more than an ample list of those. The briefer was quite candid about it all. If you didn't want to spend the entire evening in small talk with a family you'd never met, you didn't have to. They would quite understand if you just ate and ran. I was overwhelmed. I had never run across such hospitality anywhere, and never have since. The list was endless. You could go waterskiing, sightseeing, and take small trips to see the Aborigines, and so on. The Australians truly made you feel as if they were happy to have you as guests in their country and were doing everything possible to make your stay a pleasant one. I have never gotten over the experience to this day.

By now, it was around 10:00 in the morning and I was wiped out. All I wanted to do was get to bed. I'd come down to Australia by myself and didn't know anyone on the flight down. I was tired and just wanted to be by myself and get some sleep. After that, I'd figure out what to do with myself for the next 7 days. I got a cab to downtown Sydney and checked into the Menzes Hotel. This was paradise! It was the middle of May, and Thailand was very hot and humid. It was fall in Sydney! Not being a fan of hot weather, I couldn't have been happier. The hotel was excellent. I took a shower, immediately went to bed, and fell into a deep sleep. I'd wake up when I woke up.

That turned out to be around 6:00 in the evening. This was great. I could do whatever I wanted to, whenever I felt like it. No schedule or briefings to be concerned about. No nasty targets here in Sydney. No night flying over un-friendly terrain. My only vertigo problem would be function of how much I drank, and I didn't even have to worry about that since I wasn't on the schedule to fly tomorrow. As we said back at Ubon, this was "super shit hot!"

I took a long shower, got dressed with the one sport jacket I'd brought with me to Ubon to last the entire time, and began to explore Sydney. I went downstairs and walked out on the street a bit. I hadn't gone too far when I saw what looked like a pleasant bar and walked in. I'd only been inside for a minute or so when a guy came up to me and said, "Hey, you're a Yank, aren't you?" I was not unaware of the strong antiwar feelings back home in the United States, but I was some-what surprised by his comment. I said to myself, "Oh, great. I've only been here a few hours, and I'm probably going to get in a bar fight about America's Vietnam policy." I was wrong. I don't know what it is about Americans, but people throughout the world seem to be able to spot us a mile away. I said, "Yes, I am," and with that, he took me by the shoulder and dragged me to where his "mates" were sitting and introduced me to all of them. They insisted on buying the beer, and, yes, it was Fosters. They seemed genuinely interested in my thoughts and experiences, and we had a very pleasant hour or so. By now, I was getting rather hungry, so I gave my thanks and broke away in search of dinner.

I'd picked up the name of a dinner club and decided to try that. I stood outside the Menzes Hotel and got in the queue for a cab. There was a man and a woman ahead of me who looked to be in their mid- to late-forties. A cab came up, and he turned to me and asked where I was headed. I told him, and he insisted that I join them. I tried to demur and said okay, but only if they were going in the same general direction. As I said, I don't know what it is that causes people to pick out Americans in a heartbeat. As we drove along, it became apparent that their destination was in almost the opposite direction. We talked some more, and it turned out he'd been a Royal Australian Air Force Lancaster bomber pilot and had flown many missions over Germany during the "Big One." At that point, I think he knew better than I did, what I must be feeling. We arrived at my destination, and despite my protestations, he insisted on picking up the cab fare. I was amazed. I'd never seen such hospitality, before or since.

I didn't last too long. A few drinks, some dinner, a liqueur, and I was back in my hotel room early. It had started to dawn on me what a bizarre existence I had been living. Sleep; brief; fly; debrief; get some food, sleep; and then start the whole process all again—day after day after day. Yes, it was a relatively pleasant existence at Ubon compared to what many were experiencing in South Vietnam, but it was still strange. I, at least, could never forget what I was doing, and what I might be doing tomorrow. I never knew whether I was still going to be around after a few hours, especially if it were a rough mission.

As I leisurely woke up the next day, and walked around Sydney, it soon became apparent to me that these people weren't worried about being alive the next day. They probably didn't even think about it as they went about their normal routine. I didn't consider myself a morose, negative person, but then I could never completely forget that I was involved in a major war either.

At the time I was in Sydney, it happened to be ANZAC Day. The term stands for Australian New Zealand Army Corps and initially was meant to commemorate Australian and New Zealand participation in the World War I Battle of Gallipoli. It has since come to honor all military events, similar to our Memorial Day. It was also the anniversary of the Battle of the Coral Sea, which took place on 7–8 May in 1942. This decisive battle was just before the Battle of Midway, which spelled the beginning of the end for the Japanese. It was downhill from that point on. The Coral Sea Battle prevented the Japanese invasion of the Australian mainland during the early stages of that horrific war. Australians were extremely grateful to America, since it was predominantly a U.S. Navy battle and one of the first that was fought strictly by aircraft from the opposing sides. The major surface ships never saw each other. Prior to this battle, the Japanese had marched south pretty much unrestricted, and the Australians had every reason to be concerned about a possible invasion. Maybe that had a bit to do with the incredible hospitality I received when I was there in 1968, or maybe that's the way the Australians always are. Since that time, I've traveled to many different countries but have never experienced that kind of welcome. Unfortunately, Americans are sometimes not all that well received in some countries for a variety of reasons. I certainly couldn't say that about my interlude "Down Under." It's still a pleasant memory, decades later.

The days burned up in a hurry. I didn't do anything exotic, just the normal tourist things. I visited the zoo, took a tour of Sydney Harbor, saw the famous Opera House, and generally enjoyed doing whatever struck my fancy. I'd never been to Australia before, but I didn't have time to venture too far afield from Sydney, so I enjoyed the local sites. It was great to be able to go and do anything I wanted without the need to have to worry about a schedule. I began to realize how tired I was. This was a normal existence. What I was doing, and would go back to doing, was a decidedly abnormal arrangement. Although I had come to Sydney by myself, that didn't particularly bother me. I rather relished being by myself for the brief period, and just relaxing. Most of the married pilots and navigators would use their R&R to meet their wives, usually in Hawaii. If I'd been married, I would have done the same. Many would take a few weeks' leave and actually return to the States to visit their families if they could find a way to arrange transportation. Some of the married types chose not to return Stateside and preferred to keep flying to get their tour over with and then return home.

I've often wondered how I would have reacted if I'd been married and had a family. I don't think I would have handled it well and would have found it difficult to leave and go back to fly combat. When I first went to the war, it was kind of exciting, and, in a sense, I rather looked forward to it, because I didn't really know what it was all about. Even if I'd been married at the time, I think I would have still felt that way. Once having seen combat, however, I was no longer naïve. I was well aware that planes got shot down with great regularity, and there was no guarantee that it might not be me. Leaving for the war zone again wasn't like going on a business trip where you would soon be back in the warm embrace of your family, and everybody would live happily ever after. Some didn't come back, and many families didn't know what happened to their loved ones for many years. For a few guys in the squadron, this was not their first time. Some had been in World War II or Korea. They knew what they were getting into, and, years later, I often wondered how they and their families coped. On the other end of the spectrum were some of the backseat pilots who had completed their first tour as weapon system operators and volunteered to go back for a second tour so they could upgrade to the front seat. Most were single, but not all. Youthful feelings of invulnerability might have helped them to some extent, but in at least a few cases that I was aware of, it could be extremely difficult. I can only relate my own feelings, but after a week of being away from the day-to-day business of flying combat, I didn't have a burning desire to go back. But, back it must be, and after a very pleasant interlude in Sydney I prepared to retrace my steps to Ubon.

We took the same route on the way back, but stayed a bit longer in Saigon because of the aftermath of the Tet Offensive. There were still many large-scale guerilla attacks by the Viet Cong. I was fortunate to stay with a friend from my days at Webb, Maj. Larry Klinestiver, who had a small apartment not too far from Tan Son Nhut Airbase. I spent much of that night in Saigon on the roof of his building as we watched the war that raged around us. It was all very exciting: flares being dropped all over the place, gunships firing tracers at enemy positions, and all this took place within a 5-mile radius from where we were! The next morning all was relatively quiet, but I still recall an A-1 Skyraider dive-bombing a target about a block away. The war looks a little more immediate from that perspective. Things soon quieted down, and I boarded the airplane back to Bangkok; had a brief overnight stay at the Chao Phia, then was back at Ubon the next day.

I was a little the worse for wear, and had picked up a monster cold during my visit to the Southern Hemisphere. I flew one mission, thinking I could tough it out, but that convinced me that I needed to go to the flight surgeon. I was grounded for a few days, but was soon back on the schedule, and flying pretty much every day. I remember the first few flights, which were night missions. I was nervous and jumpy. Every little thing seemed to cause me concern. I was hypercautious and seemed to worry about many things I hadn't thought too much about before. But then, after about a week, all that gradually went away, and I pretty much was back to where I had been before I left for R&R. Again, the abnormal became the normal. I just accepted everything that was involved in flying combat as the normal way of doing things. The fears and concerns were still there, but had been sublimated.

CHAPTER 16

Slippery when Wet

"Into every life, a little rain must fall," goes the old saying, and it was certainly true in Thailand. Heavy rains were quite common during the monsoon season, which generally ran from May to October. I mean reference-standard heavy rains! I hadn't seen rains that heavy and sustained even in Florida, and this would sometimes go on for days at a time. But the war went on 24 hours a day, so there was little to be done about it. We would preflight the airplane in the rain, and get soaking wet in the process. Then we climbed in the Phabulous Phantom, shut the canopy, and hoped to dry out once we got to altitude. Definitely an uncomfortable experience. Takeoff was slightly different in that we took off with 30-second spacing between airplanes, locked on with our radar, and stayed 5 miles in radar trail until we broke out on top of the clouds and could then join up visually in normal formation. We didn't take off unless the weather in the target area was good enough to fly the mission, and often it was okay at the target although it was miserable at Ubon. When the mission was over, we'd return in formation, then split up at the TACAN navigation aid over Ubon and land separately, usually from a precision radar approach, which would safely get us down through the murk.

One day, when the monsoon was in full swing, I was scheduled to lead a two-ship to northern Laos, an area that was known as "Barrel Roll." Since President Johnson had declared the bombing halt of the far northern portions of North Vietnam, we had been flying to this area far more often than we had in the past. It was a strange place. Very beautiful to fly over, and it appeared from the air to be almost totally devoid of any signs of civilization. But populated it was, quite often by the Pathet Lao and the North Vietnamese moving supplies to the South. There were also quite a few Laotians who were allied with the U.S. cause, and Air America, the CIA-run air operation, was all over the place. You never quite knew whom you might be encountering on these missions. Generally, our missions were to support General Vang Pao, who was the leader of the friendly Muong people and fighting with us against the Pathet Lao and the North Vietnamese. Throughout the area were all sorts of small airstrips, called "Lima sites," that the CIA would operate out of. You always kept track of these in case you got hit, since they were relatively safe areas of refuge in an otherwise very hostile environment. Of course, they were just short, dirt strips that the F-4 couldn't land on, but at least there were "friendlies" there, if you bailed out in that area. There was also a bit of historical significance. Burma was to the west of Laos, and this was part of the area where the famed Flying Tigers operated during World War II.

This mission was scheduled to be in the central part of the Laotian panhandle, about 50 miles from the North Vietnamese border. We were given a rendezvous point, a radio frequency to contact the FAC on, and a general description of the target area. There were Muong forces in the area threatened by the Pathet Lao, or North Vietnamese. It wasn't exactly clear which enemy force posed the threat to the Muong. The weather was forecast to be generally good in the target area. Our mission briefing was relatively short, given the paucity of the data, so we finished quickly, preflighted the airplanes, got soaking wet in the process, then took off to the north. On missions like this, I really didn't know exactly what would happen until I made contact with the FAC and got the latest data directly from him. The weather at Ubon was not great, but adequate for us to take off, and the forecast was reasonable for our return. This was no small matter, since the nearest alternate was about 150 miles away, and we were generally short of fuel upon return. Jets burn a tremendous amount of fuel at low altitude, so if I needed to divert, I would have to make that decision early, before we penetrated down to the lower altitudes for the approach.

Gradually, the weather improved as we approached the target area. We were in the clear above the clouds, which gradually dissipated as we headed to our rendezvous point. A few more miles, and everything opened up. We could see the ground clearly, mostly green jungle and the occasional dirt road. It looked deceptively quiet as I switched our flight over to the assigned frequency. After checking my wingman in on the new frequency, I called the FAC. There he was! Right where he was supposed to be. I gave him our position, and he already had us in sight. I looked down, and sure enough, there he was, below us at ten o'clock. But it was a strange airplane, a Donier D0-28, high-wing, twin-engine aircraft designed to operate from short airfields, such as the Lima sites. I had never seen one except in photos. This was certainly different. The voice on the radio was strange also. We were speaking in English, of course, but it certainly didn't sound like John Wayne. The voice had a distinctly foreign accent, which I couldn't place (a linguist I am not). I thought perhaps it might be a Royal Laotian Government observer who might be actually giving us the target briefing, but it sounded more European, not Oriental. I couldn't see any markings on the airplane either, so I suspect it was one of our friends from "The Company," the euphemism for Air America. At any rate, it didn't make much difference; the process was the same no matter who was doing it. The target wasn't supposed to be heavily defended, and the FAC thought there might be some supplies stockpiled some distance off one of the roads. We acknowledged the data, confirmed we had him in sight, and prepared to attack his rocket mark from random directions.

We had enough fuel for several passes, so we dropped our load of 500-pound bombs in pairs. Our FAC with the odd accent would mark the target the first time with a smoke rocket, then give us corrections from where our last bombs had hit. After pulling off on my last pass, I looked down at the weapons panel and noticed that one of the lights was still on for the right inboard pylon. This meant that I still had a bomb on that pylon, which normally carried a total of three bombs. I made another pass to try to get it off, but no luck, the light was still on. When we dropped a bomb, we fired a small propellant charge in the pylon, which in turn opened the bomb shackles and caused a piston to push the bomb away from the airplane. The airflow at high airspeeds could prevent the bomb from separating from the airplane without this added force. Once the bomb was clear of the airplane, it followed a normal free-fall path. Unfortunately, sometimes the bomb shackles didn't completely open, or only one of the two lugs would open properly, in which case the bomb would "hang." It wasn't a great situation, but it wasn't the end of the world either, and we frequently landed with a hung bomb. I needed to be careful, since I didn't want to knock it off on landing. The bomb wouldn't arm until it was quite a distance from the airplane, but I didn't want to put that hypothesis to the test. Our flight got the bomb damage assessment from the FAC with the strange accent who was in the funny airplane and then joined up for the trip back to Ubon.

As soon as we rejoined, we looked each other over for any signs of battle damage. Nothing there; the luck of the Irish apparently still worked. But I did have a hung bomb. The front lug had released, but not the back one, so it was drooping down about 6 inches on the pylon. My concern was that the back lug might have partially released, and the bomb might not be on the pylon very securely. I would have to make one of my truly smooth, masterful landings. What normally happened is that we landed and taxied to the end of the runway dearm area where the weapons crew would safe everything up. At this point, I'd probably landed with five or six hung bombs and had seen many others do the same.

Our glimpse of the sunshine in the target area was to be short lived, however, for the reported weather at Ubon was the same soggy, wet stuff we had left a little over an hour ago. Soon, we were in the clouds in formation as we drove toward the TACAN navigation fix for our instrument approach. We had a unique situation at Ubon in that the runway was rather narrow (125 feet wide, not the normal 150 feet), so we couldn't make formation takeoffs or landings; every airplane had to land singly. It was also crowned or higher at the center than the side, which is never good news when a runway is wet. The last piece of bad news was that the F-4 had a very bad tendency to hydroplane at touchdown speeds, which meant that the tires did not actually contact the concrete, but skimmed along on a thin film of water until the aircraft slowed. The net result of all this was that we would not have good directional control or braking when we landed in heavy rain. But not to worry! The F-4 had one of the heaviest, stoutest tail hooks I had ever seen. Not surprising, since it was originally designed as a Navy shipboard fighter. With a wet runway, it was standard policy at Ubon to split up on the instrument approach, so we arrived on final with 5-mile spacing between aircraft. When we put the gear and flaps down for landing, we also put the tail hook down. There were three arresting wires strung across the runway: the first at approximately 2,000 feet from the touchdown end and another at the midpoint. Finally, if we hadn't snagged either of those, there was the last one, 2,000 feet from the end. If I had to resort to the last one, it would be a real thrill ride. The procedure was to land; then snag the first barrier (a very violent stop to say the least); raise the hook, which we could do in the F-4; then taxi off the runway so the plane behind us would do the same thing. Here's what I mean by an abrupt stop: we went from 150 knots to nothing in about 500 feet! After your first approach-end engagement, you'll never question the necessity of a seat belt again. At this point, I had made about ten approach-end engagements and felt comfortable doing one. No trick for a show dog, right?

I checked in with Ubon Approach Control and got the latest weather—not good. The ceiling was about 300 feet, with a visibility of 1/2 mile in rain, occasionally heavy at times, crosswind from the right of about 12 knots. Not horrible, but not great either. I started down in the penetration, and soon, the Precision Approach Radar picked me up. These guys were great. Their radar could tell them how high or low I was from the glide path and how far left or right of centerline. They would talk us down all the way to touchdown, and the radar was extremely precise. Our minimums were 100 feet ceiling and 1/4 mile visibility, which is actually lower than most airliners can go using the standard Instrument Landing System. We had to fly very precisely, but it would get us down in very bad weather. I had already made them aware that I had a hung 500-pound bomb, and the crash crews were standing by, just in case. With only one runway at Ubon, we didn't have many divert options once we started down in the instrument penetration.

The rain was really coming down hard. The F-4 didn't have windshield wipers (don't laugh, some airplanes do) but could blow hot compressor air over the front part of the windscreen, which helped me see a little better in heavy rain. The air was reasonably smooth, and I was "on course, on glide path" during the approach. Piece of cake! I did notice that I had to crab into the crosswind from my right to stay "on course." I broke out of the clouds about 300 feet, on centerline, and "on speed" at the proper angle of attack, but pointed about 5 degrees off the runway heading to the right because of the crosswind. I applied a slight amount of left rudder and lowered the right wing simultaneously to line the airplane up exactly with the runway centerline. This is a normal crosswind landing procedure. I was looking good! Gear down, flaps down, hook down, on speed, and exactly lined up on the centerline. I touched down about 500 to 800 feet from the approach end of the runway and deployed the drag chute. Just as I touched down I started drifting to the left side of the runway. I frantically punched the nosewheel steering button to correct back to the right—nothing! I hit right brake—nothing! I moved the stick to the right—nothing! I was perfectly lined up with the runway, but I had absolutely no control over the airplane and was slowly drifting to the left side of the runway. My heart was in my mouth. I would go off the left side of the runway *with a hung bomb*, before I could snag the arresting wire, and there didn't appear to be anything I could do to stop it! We're only talking about 1,500 feet of travel down the runway, at most, from touchdown to the arresting wire.

Mercifully, I finally engaged the arresting wire on the extreme left side of the runway, just before I went off the edge, still pointed perfectly parallel with the runway. The hung bomb had not dropped off either, so I breathed one huge sigh of relief. I had never experienced hydroplaning like this before, and it was quite an introductory lesson! Now at 150 knots, this entire event took just seconds, but I never forgot it. I came to a stop; the ground crew gave me the signal to pull up the hook, and I taxied off the runway to make way for my wingman, albeit with a much higher heart rate than I'd had a few seconds ago.

What had happened? It was pretty simple, actually. The normal method of landing in a crosswind (wing down into the wind, and rudder to align with the runway) works fine if the runway is dry. The airplane is actually in a slight skid, but it neutralizes the drift and as soon as the wheels hit; the friction is enough to prevent any further drift, as the wings become level. Unfortunately, when the runway is wet, and the airplane hydroplanes, there is not enough friction to stop the drift when the wings are leveled upon touchdown. There is actually a thin film of water between the tires and the runway. Hydroplaning is a function of speed, and the worst speed for hydroplaning in the F-4 was right around touchdown speed. Gradually, as the plane slows, the weight breaks through the film enough to get some traction. When I leveled the wings just as I touched down, I started drifting in the air mass again. With no friction with the runway to stop me, I just kept drifting, that is, going sideways, until I had slowed somewhat. It didn't make any difference if I were perfectly aligned with the runway; I was still drifting. From that point on, I just landed in a slight crab on a wet runway. It seems awkward compared to the normal method, but the airplane aligns itself and straightens at touchdown.

Humility is an amazing thing. It took only about 3 seconds to go from patting myself on the back for flying a beautiful instrument approach in bad weather, to stark terror when I realized I had no control of this hurtling machine.

CHAPTER 17

Dean St. Pierre

The situation at Ubon in early May 1968 was unusual in that we were on 5-minute alert, which meant that we had to be in the cockpit, all strapped in, ready to take off within 5 minutes if we were scrambled on a mission. The Royal Australian Air Force had a contingent of F-86 Sabres at Ubon which performed this function. There had been some signs of a potential air threat from the North Vietnamese Air Force, and so our base increased its alert status as well and put two F-4s on alert. This was a new situation for our wing, and we had two airplanes all cocked and ready to go at the end of the runway where the Australians sat alert. Our flight had been on alert for an hour, and I was getting uncomfortable in the hot cockpit of the Phantom and began to wonder how much longer we would have to be there.

Captain Dean St. Pierre was my backseat pilot that day, but I really didn't know him very well. I had not flown with him often before this mission; maybe three or four times at the most. He seemed to get along well with the other back-seaters and had somewhat of a laid-back attitude. Dean had arrived months before I did, which meant he was near the end of his tour. Since he'd arrived much earlier, he had his own circle of friends and I had not had many conversations with him. He had never asked me very much about my background, and the same was true on my part. We just didn't travel in the same circle of friends. We'd had some idle chitchat on the intercom as we waited, then lapsed into silence and reverted to the solace of our own thoughts.

Suddenly, the alarm went off at midafternoon and we were scrambled. As we started up, the command post gave us cryptic details of the mission over the radio. It was suspected, but not confirmed, that someone had been shot down in Laos, and we were being launched to provide flak suppression and knock out the enemy guns so that an attempt could be made to recover the crew. As it became clear where we were headed, Dean was quite agitated, and complained very strongly that the mission would not be a "counter." This wasn't the normal intercockpit chatter that goes on between the front and back-seaters. Dean was very upset that this mission would not hasten the completion of his tour and allow him to return home.

A word of explanation: during Operation Rolling Thunder, the normal combat tour for pilots was 100 missions over North Vietnam. South Vietnam and Laos didn't count; hence the term, "counters." When Rolling Thunder first started, this wasn't much of a problem, since most of the missions were over North Vietnam. Missions over Laos probably accounted for only about 10 percent of the crew's total missions. All that changed in April of 1968 when Lyndon Johnson decided not to run for the presidency and declared a bombing halt over the northern half of North Vietnam, although missions over the southern half were still counters. Normally, a crew would complete 100 missions in about 8–9 months. Suddenly all that changed, and a pilot or navigator might not complete 100 counters before they'd been there for 1 year. Everyone would rotate back to the States after 1 year. So, those who had almost 100 missions faced the prospect of combat for a few months longer than had been the case just a short time earlier. So, while the chances of surviving a tour increased, the halt did lengthen the time for those who expected to finish 100 missions. This was the cause of Dean's anger.

I lost my temper with Dean. His comments such as "Shit! It's not going to be a counter, just a damn Search and Rescue mission" hit me the wrong way. At this point in my tour, I had about sixty counters and forty noncounters and most likely would finish my combat tour with less than 100 counters. I'd had several close calls myself, and was no stranger to the dangers of combat. I was shocked. A fellow pilot or navigator might be down in Laos, and if we didn't help him get out, he was either going to be tortured and killed or held captive, although in Laos, the former was the more normal outcome. I don't think I've ever become so angry with anyone in an airplane. I reminded him that he could be the person on the ground and rhetorically asked, "How would you feel if you heard someone say what you just said?" I was so angry; I just told him to "shut up."

We flew the mission is stony silence. He did his tasks and read the required checklist items as expected. I responded, but the entire mission was flown in a rather eerie quietude. Normally, there's a lot of chitchat and intercockpit BS that takes place. I was still mad and shocked at his attitude, and I'm sure he knew it. We dropped our bombs where a FAC directed and headed back to Ubon. The potential downed pilot turned out to be a false alarm. One of the bad things about prolonged combat is that you get a little calloused and burned out after a while. You get rather blasé about things that would normally be very hard to forget. SARs (Search and Rescue missions) became a matter of routine after a while. Sometimes they went on for several days, and if it wasn't someone from your outfit, you

were on to other missions, and that became what you focused on. We each hoped
we wouldn't be the cause of a SAR effort. It was comforting to know that the war
stopped for a short time as every possible effort was expended to attempt to rescue
a downed crew. That was why Dean's comments shocked me so—it wasn't the
normal response. While I didn't know Dean very well, I was still surprised and
angered by his outburst. I wasn't quite sure what to say when we got back on the
ground, and spent quite a bit of the flight back wondering how to handle it.

The landing back at Ubon RTAFB was normal, and nothing unusual
happened during the mission and our return. We landed, taxied back in, and
parked in the revetments. The squadron bus picked us up and took us to the
maintenance debrief area, where we filled out the normal forms and told the
maintenance types what was wrong with the airplane (the F-4 was a great airplane, but it was very complicated and full of tube electronics—the average
maintenance for 1 hour of flight was 37 hours! There was always something to
talk about with the airplane fixers). Dean didn't say much, and neither did I. We
just directed our comments to the maintenance types, who probably didn't
detect anything abnormal. We finished that chore, got back on the squadron
truck, and headed back to the 433rd Tactical Fighter Squadron to get rid of all
our flight gear, then went to the intelligence debrief area next door. There wasn't
much of an unusual nature to debrief, so that didn't take too long. We finished
and went back to the squadron.

It was here that Dean apologized. I could instantly tell that he was quite upset.
He no longer was the wisecracking person that he sometimes tended to be. It
caught me by surprise. He said he was sorry for acting the way he did, but that he
didn't think he would make it through his combat tour, and that's why he reacted
in such a manner. He desperately wanted to get home, and anything that set back
that event was of great concern. This I could identify with. Despite many war
stories to the contrary, my experience was that when you are in combat, and face
your possible demise daily, an overarching concern is to survive. I later found out
that Dean had about ninety-two missions that were counters, at the time of our
mission.

I tried to perk him up with the usual pep talk that the odds were in his favor,
and he would finish up in a few missions; not to worry; everyone felt this way;
he'd be all right; and other banal comments. I sort of believed it, but had my
doubts also. I think we all had a bit of the same fear. But we never talked about it
openly. We would make dark jokes that hinted at our concern, but in my experience, each of us suppressed our deepest fears and emotions. My attitude
toward Dean changed considerably. I wasn't angry anymore, and, all of a sudden,
his emotional outburst made some sense. I'm not bashful about expressing
myself when my Irish gets up, and I felt bad that I had yelled at him so strongly. I
tried to make light of it and cheer him up, but didn't feel as though I did.

As we talked, I remembered another incident a few weeks earlier. Several of us were putting on our personal equipment prior to a mission. The squadron was making some alterations to the area where we had our equipment gear (parachute harness, G-suit, survival vest, pistol, radios, flares, and similar items) as well as personal lockers. Dean's gear had to be moved because of these alterations, and it was relocated a few spaces away, no more than 20 feet from the original location. Dean was visibly upset. He yelled at the personal equipment sergeant and wanted to know why this had been done. The sergeant patiently explained why the relocation was necessary. Dean then proceeded to "suit up" and we went about our mission. I didn't think much about it until later, after the fact.

While the relocation incident may seem like an emotional outburst of a self-centered pilot to those who have never been in combat, I tend to think it wasn't. We became very superstitious. Intellectually, we knew it was foolish, but I tended to follow a very scripted ritual, prior to going on a mission. I didn't want to change whatever had worked for me before—it might bring bad luck. I had done it this way before, and nothing happened to me, so I was loath to change anything. None of us talked about it, but we all did it to some extent. An example: moustaches were big when I arrived at Ubon—probably an attempt to emulate the World War I aces—I'm not sure why. But it was also considered bad luck to shave it off before your tour was over—you might get shot down. There was, of course, no evidence that this was true. I promptly grew one, and, after the novelty wore off, I discovered that it was not much fun to fly with a moustache in the hot, humid Southeast Asian climate . . . you sweated profusely! But I didn't shave it off until I finished my combat tour. Such was the mindset of many of us. I'm sure a layperson would have thought the locker episode to be a bit of an overreaction. But to those of us "of the cloth," it was all quite understandable, and I didn't think much about it at the time.

A few days later, Dean's morbid premonitions came true. He had been scheduled for a night-armed reconnaissance mission in Package I, the lower part of North Vietnam, near Dong Hoi. He was paired with John Crews, a young pilot who had just been upgraded from the back seat to the front seat, after a quick local checkout at our base. The circumstances are unclear as to what exactly happened. Night ground-attack missions were quite common during the air war, which went on 24 hours a day. At Ubon, we even had one squadron that specialized in this type of mission. I never particularly liked night missions, and I certainly wasn't unique in that respect. In retrospect, I don't think they were very effective at all, and we deluded ourselves into thinking that we had caused significant impact to the North Vietnamese.

Night flying was far more dangerous, since you didn't have the obvious advantage of being able to see your surroundings. Vertigo is a major problem for anyone flying at night, or in bad weather. I could speak from terrified experience that the sensations can be almost overpowering. Often you are unaware of a dangerous situation, since everything "feels" all right. We thought this is possibly what happened to Dean and John.

The leader of Dipper flight had illuminated a target with flares and cleared Dipper Two to attack it. John Crews called "in" on the target, and that was the last anyone ever heard from them. The flight lead saw a flash from the CBU-24 cluster bomb, as the explosive cord ignited to split open the two halves of the bomb. This type bomb split into two halves and scattered smaller, hand grenade–size bomblets in a large circle that would cover the target. Dipper Lead then saw the bomblets from the CBU impact the target, as expected. Several seconds later, there was a large impact short of the target. The aircraft hit on the path to the target, not after the target. We don't know what happened, but a logical explanation is that they both may have been looking back over their shoulders to see what damage had been done. Instead of pulling off straight ahead, they might have inadvertently introduced some bank and pulled back in kind of an offset loop. This may sound incomprehensible to the layman, but it was a very real problem. In combat, we never pulled off a target without "jinking" or moving the airplane around, sometimes violently, so we weren't where an antiaircraft gunner had predicted we would be when he fired at us. This necessary maneuver alone was often enough to induce vertigo. To see anything outside at night, we kept the cockpit lights dimmed to a very low level. If we fired rockets at night, or there were large explosions such as flak, we often lost whatever night vision we had. So, the procedure was to have the back-seater monitor the flight instruments very carefully, since it was quite possible that the front-seater might have vertigo and not be aware of it. I had experienced this often myself.

That could explain why they impacted prior to the target. If they had been hit pulling off, they most likely would have hit the ground after the target. But we don't really know, and this hypothesis is speculation. There were no radio calls, and no emergency radio beeper signals, which would indicate that they didn't eject from the airplane. But for whatever reason, Dean's premonition was fulfilled. At the time of his death, I believe he had ninety-four missions—just six short of completing his combat tour. If he'd been lucky, he might have flown those in a few weeks and returned Stateside.

Dean's death had a major impact on me because of the incident we'd had a few days earlier, although I was not that close to him. I recall one of his friends remarking after the event that his wife had written to him every day. I left Ubon shortly after that, and life moved on. But a strange thing happened. Dean is the one name I look for whenever I go to the Vietnam Memorial in Washington. I must admit that the first time I saw it I had a very emotional moment and was glad that I had gone there by myself. In a sense, I think Dean came to personify for me the futility of war, and the tragic aftermath that follows. He was a real person with real thoughts and dreams, and in one brief episode he opened his soul, although it was inadvertent. There are many other names there that I am very familiar with, and I don't mean to minimize their suffering, but Dean is the one that has come to represent the tragedy of the war to me most eloquently. What would he have done in life if this hadn't happened? Would his life have been a success, or would he have had difficult times? We'll never know.

The movie "Saving Private Ryan" came out several years ago, and there was much discussion about how brutal and realistic it was, especially the opening scenes about the troops going ashore at Normandy. But the part that hit me the hardest was the ending. Private Ryan goes back to Normandy as an old man with his family and visits the grave of the character played by Tom Hanks, the man responsible for Pvt. Ryan being alive. Ryan collapses in grief, breaks down, and asks no one in particular, "Did I live a good life?" I think most of us who survived the war ask ourselves the same or a variant of the question. Why did we survive? Did we live our lives in a way that made good use of the time we had, but that those that died didn't? It's a question I ask myself every time I go to the memorial and see Dean's name.

CHAPTER 18

"Shillelagh"

July 5, 1968, began as an absolutely great day! I was finally, after 6 months and 23 days of lending my heroic efforts to the Great Patriotic War, getting my own airplane! Most of the World War II pictures of pilots and airplanes would lead one to believe that all pilots had an individual airplane, that they flew continually. Maybe it was true to some extent then, but that certainly wasn't the case at Ubon. As I mentioned before, the F-4 was a complicated beast, and it took the frequently overworked techs many hours of work to insure that it was ready to fly when needed. So you flew whatever was available to meet the flying schedule. The ground crew could usually crank out the required number of airplanes for the scheduled missions, but it most likely would *not* be your particular machine. Every airplane had the aircraft commander's name on the left front canopy sill, while the weapon systems operator's name was stenciled on the left canopy sill. On the right side, in a similar arrangement, were the crew chief's and assistant crew chief's names. A lot, but not all, airplanes had a name for the airplane stenciled somewhere as well.

I wasn't scheduled to fly that day but was down at the squadron fairly early in the morning anyway, since there were other tasks to be done. It must have been around 8:00 AM or so when one of the maintenance types sought me out to tell me I was getting my own aircraft, and what did I want to name it. This was a normal process as crews finished up their tours and went home. The ground crew would just paint over the old name and put a new one on. The general idea behind it was laudable. If it were at all possible, you would be assigned "your" airplane to fly. Not only did this make you feel like one of the "swells," but you also got pretty familiar with that bird. You would get to know its little idiosyncrasies, and whether it was a problem that was getting worse, or just a trait of that airplane. Contrary to popular opinion, each airplane sometimes flew a bit differently. Maybe it was really stressed during a violent maneuver and got "twisted" a bit. That might make if "feel" just a slight bit different from other airplanes. Sometimes, you could just sense it in your fingertips by how much pressure you had to apply to the stick to do something, or maybe how long it took a certain system to react to an input. One of the worst nightmares for the ground crews were the dreaded "cannot duplicate" malfunctions. A pilot would write up some malfunction after a mission. The ground crew might work on it all night to see whether they could figure out what it was and fix it. Sometimes, try as they might, they just could not create the situation that caused the problem and hence they could not claim to have fixed the malfunction. Normally, when you inspect the maintenance forms prior to flight, you always check the previous write-ups to see what has been done to fix them. With these elusive ones, all the ground crew could say was what they had done, and that they could not duplicate the problem. Maybe it was a fluke, maybe not. There was no way that you or they could tell. When you flew with one of those write-ups, you were always super alert to the first sign of a problem, especially if it was a flight control malfunction. That was really all that could be done. If you flew the same bird often enough, you soon got pretty familiar with its quirks.

So what to name it? I wasn't really prepared for this, but it took me only a few picoseconds to dream up a proper name. "Shillelagh" was what I settled on. What the hell is that, you ask? It's Gaelic for a club, or cudgel, the kind of weapon that many a fine Irishman had used to convince various enemies of the soundness of the Irish way. What better name for an F-4? It was truly a fine weapon of war if there ever was one. With that decided, I went out to the airplane, F-4D serial number 66-7756, to witness the personalization of my very own airplane. What a day! I'd never had an experience like this before.

The ground crew was already out there with the stencils and paint. All our airplanes were painted camouflage, which was a mottled variation of shades of green, brown, and a white underbelly. The 433rd TFS squadron colors were green and yellow, so that worked out pretty well. As I recall, the bottom of the canopy sill or frame was given a yellow background and the letters were in green. For the name of the airplane, "Shillelagh," they had painted the small air scoop, just in front of the main air intake for the engines, a yellow color, and then stenciled a great-looking green shamrock with "Shillelagh" written in green underneath that. It would make any Irishman proud, and it really looked sharp to see our names displayed so prominently at the bottom of the canopy. No longer were we anonymous gunslingers going off to battle; now we were clearly identified. I could already sense the North Vietnamese starting to tremble.

We spent a few more moments in the revetment congratulating each other on how nice it looked, and what a good paint job the crew had done, then it was time to get on with our normal duties. I can't remember exactly what I was doing the rest of that morning, but soon it was lunchtime. I was eager to go to the club for lunch, not so much because I was hungry, but because I wanted to stop by my hootch to get my trusty Pentax 35-mm camera. Since I wasn't expecting the "christening" of my airplane that morning, I didn't have the camera with me and therefore was extremely anxious to get some shots of "Shillelagh" to show that I really was a player in the war—why now, I even had my own airplane!

My room wasn't that far away from the club, so after lunch I just walked over, grabbed the mighty Pentax, and walked back down to the squadron. I checked the flight schedule, and was moderately miffed to find out that "my" airplane was gone. It was being used as part of a two-ship strike in Package I, the lower part of North Vietnam, and would return probably around 4:00 PM. Not to worry. I still had some more work to do in the squadron, which would keep me busy until then. I would just finish that up, and by then "Shillelagh" would be back, and I could get my pictures to send to the folks back home.

Bad news travels fast, even in those days. Late in the afternoon, we learned that "Shillelagh" was no more. Lt. Col. Carl Crumpler and 1st Lt. Mike Burns were flying the airplane and had attacked a North Vietnamese 37-mm gun sight about 20 miles northwest of Dong Hoi. They got hit, apparently during the pullout, when you are most vulnerable. They had been headed west, toward the heavy karst mountains, and since the airplane was still flying okay, that seemed like the safest thing to do—it got you away from the low, flat areas along the coast. Suddenly, it became apparent that all was not well after all. As I recall the story, the crew realized they had a fire (probably hydraulic) and made a 180-degree turn for the coast. If you had to eject, you definitely wanted to do it over the water in the Gulf of Tonkin. As long as you weren't too close to the shoreline, hopefully 5 miles or more "feet wet," you were almost assured of being rescued. The war stopped when someone got shot down, and every effort was made to rescue them if possible, and sometimes even if it wasn't. More than one rescue aircraft had been shot down trying to get a crew out. But, if you came down without any cover, and had large numbers of the enemy around you, the odds went down dramatically.

If you haven't flown over North Vietnam, it's hard to visualize just how small a piece of real estate it really is, especially in the southern part near what used to be the Demilitarized Zone. To the east is the Gulf of Tonkin. The beaches look like what you might find in Florida, and they go inland for about 8 miles. As you go more inland, the terrain gets very mountainous as it approaches the border with Laos. In the area where they were hit, it's only about 25 miles from the border of Laos to the coast. Now granted, the border is not exactly the safest place either, but at least it was mountainous, and if you went down there, you could hope-fully evade until rescued. The water, and therefore safety, looks tantalizingly close—just a few more miles. Unfortunately, the clock ran out for Lieutenant Colonel Crumpler and Lieutenant Burns. They lost all hydraulics, which meant they could no longer control the aircraft and ejected about 6 miles from the coastline, which was so near, but too far. To make matters worse, it's also very flat, with little vegetation in that area, so there are no good areas of concealment. Unfortunately, it also happened late in the afternoon. It takes time to mount a rescue effort because you can't just go in there with a helicopter and pick up the downed crew. For one thing, there are generally many heavy caliber guns in the area, or they wouldn't have been shot down in the first place. To deal with that, you need some jets to knock out the big guns, and then you have to protect the helos with what we called "Sandys," the call sign for the A-1 Skyraiders that would go in low and protect the helicopters. This whole process took much coordination, and, consequently, a lot of time, little of which was available to Crumpler and Burns.

I didn't know either of them very well. Crumpler was 3 days past his 41st birthday, a bit old for a fighter pilot, but not unusual. He'd actually enlisted in the Navy during World War II, but it ended shortly after he came aboard. He was released after the war; went back to college, and came into the Air Force via the AFROTC program and then into pilot training. He'd had a series of Air Defense Command interceptor flying assignments, and had most recently been assisting the Iranian Air Force in their acquisition of F-4s through the Foreign Military Sales Program. Lieutenant Mike Burns was on the opposite end of the spectrum. He was 24, just a few years younger than I was at the time (I was then 27, going on 80). He had recently arrived, and had only flown a few missions before all this happened. I don't think I ever flew with him before he got shot down. I remember him, because he was one of the last of the pilots in the weapon systems operator pipeline. He, of course, wanted to be in the front seat, not riding in the back, but that's where he ended up for his first assignment right out of pilot training, so he would make the best of it.

The day ended on an inauspicious note. It was too late to get the rescue effort started, but they would attempt a recovery at first light the next day, if the downed crew had not been captured. Alas, it was not to be. There was nowhere to hide, and they were picked up, probably not too long after they were shot down—only 6 miles from the coastline—so near, yet a million miles away. Although it didn't seem so at the time, there's a somewhat happy ending to this story. They were captured and spent the rest of the war, until March 14, 1973, as POWs. They were repatriated when the United States finally pulled out of the long war, but had to endure that entire time as unwelcome guests of the North Vietnamese government.

"Shillelagh?" My euphoria over finally having my own airplane was short lived. It's in a bazillion pieces, buried in the Vietnamese coastline, unless it was dug up at the time for scrap metal. Maybe it, or a part of it, is in a war museum in Hanoi, or elsewhere in the war-ravaged country. I never got a picture of it and never saw it again after those few, delirious moments as our names and "Shillelagh" were painted on the bird. I never had another airplane to call my own. It was truly a proud moment, however short lived it might have been. But it could have been worse. I could have been flying it that day.

CHAPTER 19

The Roman 2 Episode

If the title of this chapter sounds slightly familiar, it's possibly because I mentioned it in the introduction to this book. Roman 2 was the call sign of my wingman on one of the more dramatic episodes toward the end of my tour. I never forgot it, and I'm sure my recollection of the incident pales in comparison with theirs.

At this point, on July 7, 1968, I had flown a total of 110 combat missions, sixty-seven of which were over North Vietnam. During this phase of the war, most of the pilots in the squadron could expect a one-year tour, since the likelihood of completing 100 missions over North Vietnam was remote, due to the partial bombing halt that was in effect since April 1, 1968. My combat time was ending as well. I had already been selected to be a weapons planning staff officer at 7th Air Force Headquarters at Tan Son Nhut Airfield in Saigon, and would be leaving Ubon during the first part of August. But that wasn't true for everybody. Some of the crews were fairly close to 100 North Vietnam missions before the bombing halt had gone into effect, and if they could complete the magic 100, they could still complete their tours in less than a year. This is the point in your combat tour where you get rather nervous; at least I did. The end is in sight, and you can imagine actually surviving the experience. Nonetheless, you're fearful that maybe something will still happen, and you might get shot down. Unfortunately, I had seen it happen before. You tried not to dwell on it and took each day as it came, but it was impossible to completely push it from your thoughts.

If I were getting concerned, my wingman for this mission, Chuck Mosley, had every reason to have the "single digit fidgets," a malady brought on by the fact that the number of missions remaining in your combat tour was less than ten. Chuck was one of the first persons I had met from the 8th TAC Fighter Wing on the flight from Bangkok to Ubon when I first arrived in Thailand. Chuck had done well, and had been selected to upgrade to the front seat while still at Ubon. This was quite an honor, since the normal upgrade program in the States took about 6 months. The armed reconnaissance mission in North Vietnam that we were scheduled for on this day would be Chuck's ninety-eighth. At the opposite end of the spectrum was his back-seater, Don Hallenbeck, who had recently arrived at Ubon. This would be his third mission if memory serves. He was so new that I really had not had a chance to get to know him very well.

We were scheduled to fly what is known as an "armed reconnaissance" mission over some of the supply routes in the lower part of North Vietnam, the area known as Route Package I. The North Vietnamese would move most of their supplies down numerous roads (quite a euphemism really, since they were mostly dirt), which would wind in and out of Laos at some locations such as Mu Gia and Ban Kari passes. Eventually, these supplies would find their way to the insurgents in South Vietnam. Usually, they would wait until nightfall before venturing onto the roads, but, occasionally, they tried it in the daylight. There was a fairly major route system in the western part of lower North Vietnam, and that was our assignment today—fly up and down the road, and if we saw anything on it, then go ahead and bomb it. We didn't need a FAC because anyone on those roads would be an enemy. Since the bombing halt had been declared on the far north targets, the North Vietnamese had moved more antiaircraft defenses south, so perhaps they felt somewhat emboldened to travel in daylight. Our losses had actually increased since the bombing halt in April of 1968, mainly for this reason. Our flight would be a two-ship loaded with MK-82 500-pound bombs, and we were scheduled for a late-afternoon takeoff. We did our preflight planning, got the Intell brief, completed our flight briefing, and soon were headed for North Vietnam. Jim Hoffman, a navigator recently assigned to our squadron, was my back-seater, and our call sign for the mission was Roman Lead. Chuck and Don, our wingman, were Roman 2.

Everything was normal for the first part of the mission. We entered North Vietnam about 5 miles north of the Demilitarized Zone, found the road, and proceeded to follow it in a northwest direction. The weather was generally good: a few scattered cumulous clouds, but clear for most of the route. We usually did this type of mission at around 6,000 to 8,000 feet above the terrain. It was a compromise: low enough to be able to see reasonably well, but not low enough to get hit by everybody with a BB gun. Was a truck loaded with supplies a good enough swap for an F-4 and two crew members? The general policy was that it was not.

Even at this altitude, you were still plenty vulnerable. To put the odds more in your favor, you jinked constantly. At half your altitude in seconds, you should be changing position. This approximated the time of flight of any bullets that might be coming your way, sight unseen. If you weren't where they predicted you to be, you wouldn't get hit. It was a pretty straightforward proposition. My own particular technique was to use quite a few negative G's. Besides changing your position, it also allowed the Phabulous Phantom to accelerate more easily, which compensated for the moments when you had to pull a lot of positive G's which added drag, and slowed you down. You had to keep your airspeed up, and this technique seemed to help. Speed was life! The wingman also never flew directly behind the leader he was following. Both airplanes were constantly maneuvering in different geometric planes. We started up the road looking for any targets of opportunity.

After a few minutes, I did see some trucks headed south. I called them out to Chuck and pulled up to roll in on them. The F-4, with its two huge black smoke trails was quite visible from a long way away. Not surprisingly, when I actually rolled in on them, they had pulled off and were hard to spot. I dropped on where I thought they were, but we didn't see any secondary explosions. Chuck rolled in behind me and had similar results. I made another pass, thinking the trucks couldn't have gone too far from where I last saw them, but again had no results. I told Chuck not to roll in, since I wasn't sure where they had gone. We proceeded up the road system toward Mu Gia Pass, a major junction point on the Ho Chi Minh Trail. Seeing nothing, we reversed course and headed back down the road to the southeast, hoping that the trucks we'd seen earlier would resurface, or perhaps we'd find some new ones. I'd already dropped all my bombs, so Chuck was the only one with any ammo left.

We had only gone down the road a few minutes when, lo and behold, there were about five trucks, just in front of me. I called them out to Chuck as I passed over them, and he acknowledged that he had them in sight.

I pulled up in a wide arc to give Chuck plenty of room to set up for his attack. As I started to pull up, I noticed Chuck's F-4 behind and above me in the rearview mirror, about 3,000 feet back. He had pulled up and would roll in shortly. There was a small layer of clouds at around 6,000 feet above the target and I lost sight of him at that point. I continued my climb to 12,000 feet and circled, waiting for Chuck to complete his pass. I heard nothing more on the radio. The clouds had obscured the target from my position, but should not have prevented his attack, since it was a relatively small clump of clouds.

Suddenly, just below the clouds that were covering the target, I saw an F-4 emerge . . . low, way low. There were contrails streaming off the wing tips, which in itself was unusual. Normally, when pulling any amount of G's in a moist atmosphere, the sudden reduction in pressure over the surface of the airplane will cause visible condensation to appear. You can notice the same phenomena on an airliner as it comes in for a landing on a wet, humid day. Usually, you could hardly see an F-4 pulling off a target in the humid, Asian climate. The entire airplane would be covered in vapor during the high G pullout. Also, the F-4 I was looking at was extremely low. Very low! I must have watched it for about 3 seconds and remember thinking to myself, "He's going to hit the ground!" I was absolutely correct.

The next instant, a huge fireball exploded in the jungle. The airplane I had been watching was no more. Not a word had been said on the radio after Chuck acknowledged that he had the target in sight and was setting up to roll in. Jim, my back-seater, was relatively new and commented over the hot microphone, "There go the bombs!" It was my unpleasant task to inform him that those weren't bombs, but our wingman that had just hit the ground.

I almost felt sick. If not physically, then at least emotionally. I had seen this before, but this had a far greater impact on me. Chuck was the first Ubon person I'd met. He was a nice guy, and had almost finished his combat tour. I didn't know Don very well, but he seemed like the typical "All American" kind of person. And now this! I must admit that about this point in my tour, it sometimes became difficult for me to differentiate between who had been shot down, who had completed their tour, and who had been killed. Once they had been there; now they weren't. They tended to blur together. Perhaps that was just my way of dealing with things. I tended to focus on only the immediate, and to try to get through each day.

I circled where Roman 2 had hit the ground, and made a low pass, around 5,000 feet, to see if there was any hope at all. Often, when someone ejected, you'd hear the emergency beeper emit its distinctive, urgent sound, but we had heard nothing. As we flew by the site where the airplane had impacted, there were no signs of parachutes. Nothing . . . just the smoke from the burning F-4 that had, only moments ago, been our wingman. There seemed to be no hope. I was sick of this whole business—the waste of lives and the frustration of not achieving any tangible results despite all the carnage and loss.

The only thing I could think of doing was to climb to around 15,000 feet and call Waterboy, a radar site in South Vietnam, near DaNang, to have them plot my position on their radar. At least we'd know where Chuck and Don had crashed if the war ever ended. Perhaps that knowledge would help in the re-covery of their remains. We were well within range of their radar, so I contacted them and explained that our wingman had just been shot down, and that I was orbiting their position. Would they mark the position for future reference?

Suddenly, Chuck's voice comes up on the Emergency Guard frequency, just as calm and collected as can be! To this day, I'm amazed at how calm he sounded. He coolly related that he had ejected safely, and was on the ground. I couldn't believe it! Within a few seconds, Don Hallenbeck was on the radio as well, sounding far calmer than I felt at that moment. In an attempt to pinpoint his position, I asked him where he was. I'll never forget his response. "Standby, I'm (puff, puff) climbing up a hill!" Don was so new to the squadron that he had not even had a chance to pick up his jungle survival boots. He still had the slick-soled normal flying boot, and was struggling to climb a small hill with very little traction. He'd come down near a mountainous area, which was a good place to be if the North Vietnamese came to look for him.

Whatever misgivings I have about how the war was fought, I will never forget that the war stopped when someone was shot down. Every possible effort was made to rescue downed crews, even if it meant the potential loss of more airplanes in the process. It gave you much strength to know that if it were at all possible to get you out, the effort would be made. I immediately relayed to Waterboy, the radar site, that the two pilots had ejected and were now safely on the ground. This immediately started the very complex rescue process. I became the "on-scene commander" until the official search and rescue forces could arrive on the scene. However, the situation was becoming grim. I was getting close to "Bingo" fuel, which meant I was getting quite low on fuel and would have to depart shortly. It was also becoming dark at an alarming rate.

Everyone worked as quickly as they could. An Airborne Command and Control aircraft, a C-130 loaded with a bazillion radios to communicate with all the different forces, diverted a Misty FAC to our area to see whether they could pinpoint Chuck and Don's position. These aircraft were two-seat F-100Fs that would spend 4 hours or more each day in the lower part of North Vietnam. To say they had the best grasp of the situation in the area was definitely an understatement. They knew the area like the back of their hand and, most importantly, knew exactly where many of the guns were located. Misty 51 soon arrived in the area. Meanwhile, the Airborne Command post was attempting to assemble the actual rescue forces. This was an extremely dangerous task, but it had an incredible success rate despite the problems. "Sandys," A-1 Skyraiders, which were old, propeller-driven, former Navy ground-attack airplanes, were in charge of this mission. These were based at Nakhon Phanom Air Base, just on the border between Thailand and Laos, or at Udorn Air Base, further north in Thailand near the Laotian capitol of Vientiane. The Jolly Green crews flying Sikorsky HH-3 or HH-53 helicopters would perform the actual pickup, and they were also based at both locations. The general process had been worked out pretty well during many actual rescues. The lead Sandy would locate the survivor and determine if they could be picked up safely. If the guns were too much of a threat, the lead Sandy would call in whatever "fast movers" were available to eliminate the guns, if possible. The helicopters would hover in a safe area until the Sandy mission commander felt it was safe enough to proceed with the pickup. When that point in the mission was reached, the A-1 Sandys would escort the helicopters to the survivors for a pickup. Both these tasks were extremely dangerous. The A-1s were well suited to the task, since they could stay on station far longer than the jets. They also were pretty durable and carried a huge amount of weapons. Their big disadvantage was their slow speed, which made them extremely vulnerable to ground fire. Most of the time they were down low where the antiaircraft guns were most effective. Frequently, the guns would remain still until the actual rescue started, then they would open up with a fury. The most harrowing part of the entire process was the helicopter pickup, which required a hover for what seemed like an excruciatingly long time! The chopper would lower a let-down device on a cable right over the downed crewman, who would have to grab it, extend the small petals that acted as a seat, and strap himself onto the cable. Then the rescue crew pulled him in. If the pilot were injured, a Para rescue man, or PJ (Para Jumper) would actually go down and help him. This often resulted in the PJ being left behind to be rescued himself. Once the survivors were aboard, the Jolly Green got out of there as fast as possible, escorted by the A-1 Sandys. My hat's off to these crews. They had one of the most dangerous jobs of the war, and took quite a few losses in the process. I'm not sure I would have had the guts to do what they did on a routine basis.

As the process I described above was starting to unfold, Misty 51 arrived on the scene. I talked him into the general area of the crash site, and he made voice contact with both Chuck and Don on the ground. My fuel gauge in the right corner of the cockpit was going down at an alarming rate. Fortunately, Misty 51 had a reasonable amount of fuel remaining and he could stay in the area a bit longer. It was becoming more and more obvious that it would not be possible to pick them up tonight. Darkness was approaching too rapidly, and helicopters had a difficult time hovering without a visual horizon. The Sandys also could not perform their role well at night. The well-honed rescue process that I described above required daylight, and we were rapidly running out of that. Finally, I had to depart. I asked Misty if there was anything else he needed from me. He didn't, and I turned toward Ubon, sick at heart. I talked to Chuck on the radio and told them I had to leave, but that Misty would coordinate the rest of the rescue effort. It was one of the most poignant moments of the war for me. Chuck responded with, "OK, Mac, I'll see you." At that moment, I never thought I'd see the two of them again. They'd probably either be killed or captured and spend the rest of the war as POWs in the infamous "Hanoi Hilton." They were not in a good part of North Vietnam, and it would be a race against time to get them out.

I listened to Misty on the radio as I headed back. They located both Chuck and Don relatively quickly. Don was reasonably well situated in a rocky karst area. Even if the North Vietnamese knew exactly where he was, it would be difficult to get to him. Chuck was not quite so fortunate. He was relatively close to the wreckage of the airplane, and not as well hidden. Finally, Misty told both Chuck and Don that they would have to stay hidden during the night and come up on the radio when they heard the F-100's afterburner ignite in the morning (it had a huge "boom" when it was selected). The two Misty pilots knew exactly where they were, and would be there in the morning with the rescue force, poised to attempt the rescue at first light (sunrise would be at 0521). There was nothing more to be done.

It was almost dark when I landed at Ubon. Communications were excellent all during my tour there, so as I pulled into my revetment and shut the engines down, the wing commander, Col. Charles Pattillo, and the Red Cross representative were already there. I climbed down and explained the situation. I got into a bit of an argument with the Red Cross person because he wanted to call the families immediately and inform them of the situation. I was incensed, and not in the best of spirits. I thought the call should wait until after tomorrow, in case the rescue was successful. Why put the families through all that anguish needlessly? There was apparently some legal requirement that families be notified immediately, and I lost that argument. The wing commander and the Red Cross guy left, and Jim and I debriefed with maintenance and intelligence and passed on anything that might be useful for the rescue effort tomorrow. We went to the club to get something to eat, and I had several belts of whiskey. It didn't do any good. I still felt like shit. I couldn't stop thinking, "Here I am eating, and having a drink . . . what are Chuck and Don going through? Is there anything I could have done differently to have prevented this from happening?" I went to my hootch and finally fell into a troubled sleep.

Unlike many war stories, this one has a happy ending! I awoke the next morning and was back down at the squadron a little after 7:00 AM. I could hardly believe what I was hearing. Both Chuck and Don had been successfully picked up and were on their way back to Nakhon Phanom. They were OK, both of them! No one in the rescue force had suffered any losses, so it was an incredibly successful rescue. Occasionally, Providence smiles.

Which brings me to the experience I mentioned in the introduction to this book. Thirty-five years later, I'm in a Barnes and Noble bookstore in San Jose during a visit to our daughter, Saint Erin, the Magnificent, and her husband Scott. I came across a book on display, called *Cheating Death*, by George J. Marrett, which is about combat air rescues in North Vietnam and Laos. The author had been number four in the Sandy flight that had resulted in the successful rescue of Roman 2 A&B (Chuck and Don, respectively). As George points out in his excellent book, he *never met* either Chuck or Don, since he landed back at Udorn and the Jolly Green helicopters recovered at Nakhon Phanom, which was closer. I couldn't resist the urge to call him and discuss the episode. He never knew what had happened the previous day, and I had no idea what had taken place during the successful rescue. All I knew was that Chuck and Don were safely back at Ubon, and at that point that was all I needed. A little more research led me to discover the audio tape of both days of the rescue (the URL is http://skyraider.org/skyassn/index.htm). I could hardly believe my ears as I listened to one of the most significant events of my wartime experience — 35 years before! I had no idea the tape even existed. A little more snooping and I discovered that the pilot in the backseat of Misty 51, the two-seat F-100F, where the recording was made, was Dick Rutan—the same one who received much notoriety during his around the world "Voyager" flight. It is indeed a small world. On an even more ironic note, Dick Rutan was shot down near the same area a little over a month later and forced to eject. Fortunately, they made it to the water in the Gulf of Tonkin and were also rescued. As I said, some stories have happy endings.

Self-portrait of the author in an F4E at Homestead Air Force Base. (Courtesy Mike McCarthy)

Outside the 433 TFS: Gerry Horiouchi (obscured by post), Marcus Hurley, my GIB (Guy in Back) most of my tour, and Willy Flood. (Courtesy Mike McCarthy)

End of mission. MiG CAP F4 jettisons drag chute after landing. (Courtesy Mike McCarthy)

Al Borchik finishes his 100th Mission. Bob Jones was his GIB. (Courtesy Mike McCarthy)

Dinner at Ubon O Club. *Left to right:* Frank Zander, Dave Hettinger, Willy Flood, Marcus Hurley. (Courtesy Mike McCarthy)

Debriefing after a mission. *Left to right:* Frank Zander, Gerry Oriuchi, Dick Huskey (head obscured), Marcus Hurley. Intel officer in uniform is unidentified. (Courtesy Mike McCarthy)

Bob Boles and Butch Battista after a MiG kill. Ron Iberg in center of photo. (Courtesy Mike McCarthy)

Typical F4 refueling. This particular photo was of one of the first six F4s delivered to the Korean Air Force in 1969. (Courtesy Mike McCarthy)

The author and Marcus Hurley about to take off on one of the first Walleye TV-guided weapon missions. (The Walleye is the white object behind Hurley.) (Courtesy Mike McCarthy)

"Hoot" Gibson, 433 Squadron Commander, and Dick Crews preflight before a mission. Crews was later killed on a mission with Dean St. Pierre. (Courtesy Mike McCarthy)

The rather inhospitable landscape of North Vietnam. (Courtesy Mike McCarthy)

Typical "100 Mission" party at the Ubon O Club. (Courtesy Mike McCarthy)

After Ubon, I was an Instructor Pilot in the Replacement Training Unit at Homestead AFB and flew the new F4E Phantom. (Courtesy Mike McCarthy)

A Navy F4B about to be launched from the aircraft carrier *Coral Sea* during my visit to the carrier while I was stationed at 7th Air Force Headquarters in Saigon. Definitely a short runway! (Courtesy Mike McCarthy)

The King of Thailand's airplane during a visit to Ubon in 1968. (Courtesy Mike McCarthy)

F4s taxi back in after returning from a MiG CAP mission. (Courtesy Mike McCarthy)

The author (right) and Scott Stovin during a stopover at Hickam AFB (Hawaii) during the ferry of the first six F4s to the Korean Air Force. Scott was an instructor at Webb and later had to eject over North Vietnam when a bomb exploded under his F4 as it was released. Fortunately, he was recovered and was later assigned to Hickam AFB. (Courtesy Mike McCarthy)

F4D landing at Homestead AFB. Later, we converted to the newer F4E, which had an internal gun. (Courtesy Mike McCarthy)

An F4E from Homestead AFB en route to the gunnery range. (Courtesy Mike McCarthy)

Bob Boles and Butch Battista land back at Ubon after shooting down a MiG over North Vietnam. (Courtesy Mike McCarthy)

An air strike on Laos as seen from an O-2 Forward Air Controller airplane. (Courtesy Mike McCarthy)

Saigon during the Second Tet Offensive in May 1968. Flares are the large bright spots and tracers from gunships are in the lower left corner. (Courtesy Mike McCarthy)

The author preparing to return to Thailand after Combat Stage, an air-to-air missile enhancement program at Clark Air Base in the Philippines. (Courtesy Mike McCarthy)

A CIA Pilatus Porter airplane at Ubon. The building is the rear of the 8th TFW. (Courtesy Mike McCarthy)

Return of a MiG CAP flight after de-arming. (Courtesy Mike McCarthy)

The Captains McCarthy. My wife, Linda, was a nurse and also a captain in the USAF until we left for our Canadian Air Force exchange assignment. Although we hadn't met at the time, she was an Air Force Nurse at the 20th Casualty Staging Flight, Tachikawa Air Base (Japan) from 1967–69. (Courtesy Mike McCarthy)

CHAPTER 20

Good Bye Ubon

Eventually, there is an end to everything, and my combat tour in Southeast Asia was no exception. On August 3, 1968, I flew my last combat mission against a target in the lower part of North Vietnam that was so insignificant that I can't clearly remember the details today. I don't recall any flak, and nothing untoward happened during the mission. After all this time, it was almost anticlimactic.

By this time, the significance previously associated with the end of a combat tour had diminished quite a bit. Since April 1, 1968, fewer and fewer crews finished their tour after 100 missions over North Vietnam. The normal tour was now a year from the time you arrived "in country." 7th Air Force, the major USAF command in Saigon that ran the air war in Southeast Asia, had an urgent need for a fighter pilot to be a weapons planner at their headquarters, and I had been selected, since I'd be in the theatre for almost a year anyway. I would only be there 4 months, and then I'd be going back to the States. I already had my assignment: I'd be an F-4 instructor pilot at Homestead AFB, just south of Miami, exactly the same place where I'd checked out in the airplane prior to coming to Ubon. I'd also gone to college at the University of Miami, just up the road, so I was going back to an area that I was already very familiar with. In a turbulent time, there was comfort in returning to the known.

As I write this, I'm amazed that I remember so little about my last mission. It was over, and I recall being very tired. My recollection was that we were becoming locked into a war of attrition, and I shed no tears that my participation was ending. Still it was a bittersweet moment. On the one hand, it was incredibly exciting, a real "adrenalin rush." I have never experienced, on a sustained basis, anything remotely similar. The camaraderie, the sense of participation in a shared danger, and the sense of mission are things not easily forgotten. I had met the monster of combat, and I knew what it was and how I had reacted. If I hadn't done this, I always would have wondered. On the other hand, I had an incredible sense of frustration and to some extent sadness. I had seen no great victories during my tour at Ubon. No islands were taken, no new airfields were constructed, no major battles had been won, and no areas had been conquered. John Wayne had more victories in "The Big One." At the end of the day, there were no successes to show for all the effort and sacrifices. Granted, Khe Sanh survived, but even it was eventually given up after that. The Tet Offensive inflicted massive casualties on the enemy, but not enough to deter them from their objectives. The days just blurred, one into another, and my concern was to survive each one. The noble cause that I once thought I was part of was nowhere to be found. It had long since vanished. I wouldn't have expressed it quite this way at the time, but the general sense of unease and ambivalence toward the war was beginning to make itself felt, at least with me. I would miss the people; the excitement; the sheer magnitude of the effort; the sense of being able to perform a difficult, complicated flying mission; but I wouldn't miss the grinding nature of a struggle without end that the war had turned into for the United States. It would be nice to know when you woke up in the morning that the odds were good that you'd still be around for dinner that night.

I must digress a bit, and talk about what was going on in my personal life during this period. I alluded to it a bit earlier; when I arrived at Ubon, I had no romantic, emotional attachments. I had been engaged to a woman for a few years, but had also broken off the engagement twice, for various reasons. Deep down in my pancreas, perhaps I knew that this was a relationship that was not destined to come to the altar. However, breaking off a relationship and totally dismissing it from your mind and emotions are two different things. The situation was somewhat complicated by the fact that she was my sister's roommate, which meant that our relations were not totally severed.

Out of the blue, I received a letter from her a few months after I'd arrived at Ubon. Suffice to say that although I'd convinced myself that the here and now is what I had to be concerned about, there was a strong desire to rekindle a deep, emotional relationship. I answered the letter, and after a while, it was as if all the problems of the past had been swept away, and our romance started to blossom again, or at least I thought it had. One letter led to another, and soon, things almost seemed to be back where they were before I had broken off the engagement, shortly before I received my assignment to check out in the F-4 at Homestead AFB. The letters increased in frequency and intensity, and when my tour at Ubon was about to end, we'd made arrangements to meet in Hawaii and, possibly, even be married. Communications were not what they are today, and all this planning had taken place through letters. We had not spoken with each other in over a year (nor had I spoken with anyone else in my family). Part of me knew that this was slightly weird, since I was, and still am, a pretty conservative person. But a very large part of me tried to convince myself that it was real, and that the difficulties of the past had nothing to do with the present or, at least, could all be overcome with this true love that had miraculously been rekindled under the pressures of war.

And that was exactly the problem. The relationship had been rekindled precisely because of the war. You fantasize that what you desperately want to be true actually is true. In my case, I did it to the point that I totally convinced myself of its validity. Wiser mortals would have had a few reservations, given our relationship's tumultuous background, but not me. I was convinced that "this was it," mainly because I wanted to be convinced of that feeling. So, we'd made plans to meet in Hawaii, since I had a few weeks before I had to report to 7th Air Force Headquarters in Saigon. All the more reason to be done with my combat tour! Perhaps a trivial event to those who were married or had stable relationships during their tour, but I must admit it had a great deal to do with how I felt about things then. On the one hand, I didn't want to think too far into the future, because some North Vietnamese or Laotian gunner might just cause that not to happen, and yet I was desperately convinced that I had this wonderful romantic future ahead of me and was most anxious to get on with it. As I said, the pressures of combat can drastically warp your perspective.

And so it came to pass that I flew my 124th and last combat mission on August 3, 1968. In many respects, I was glad that it was over, but, simultaneously, there was this vague feeling of unease and frustration that whatever I had done in this war had not accomplished very much at all. I wouldn't have called it a quagmire at the time, but that would have been close to the definition of what I felt. The experience was certainly not what I thought it would be when I first arrived at Ubon, 8 months earlier. I had not swept the skies of the enemy nor had I enabled the successful liberation of North Vietnam or Laos. Essentially, the war was where it was when I had arrived.

I spent the next few days packing my things, going through the usual out-processing events, and saying goodbye to all the squadron folks. It felt a bit strange to realize I was not part of the operation any more. It seemed like a long time ago since I had first arrived at Ubon, but in reality, it had only been 8 months. I had experienced many things that I simply had no concept of at the time I arrived. My simplistic view of how the war would be won had obviously been dealt a rather severe blow, although I found it difficult to admit these feelings, even to myself, and certainly not to other fighter pilots. One does not want to appear to entertain "wimpish" thoughts in the presence of your warrior peers.

It's amazing, as I look back upon events, how easy it was to get around. We had some C-130 transport airplanes at Ubon that were based in Okinawa, so I got a ride on one around 10:00 on the morning of August 5, 1968, after a round of farewells at the squadron. As we took off, I had one last look at the airfield that had been so incredibly significant in my life. It was a strange feeling to say the least. That was my last view of Ubon Royal Thai Air Base. We droned on to Okinawa and finally touched down late in the afternoon. Since I was really hot to get to Hawaii, I immediately went to the Strategic Air Command Operations area where all the KC-135 tankers were located to see whether I could get a ride. The traffic back and forth to the war zone was amazing. I wouldn't think of going on a trip today without having firm reservations in hand, but I didn't even have the slightest doubt that I would be able to get to Hawaii easily. Sure enough, there was a KC-135 tanker scheduled to go to Hickam AFB on Oahu early the next morning. Travel like this is space available, and I was a little concerned that I might have trouble, since there was already a bit of a crowd assembled. As I gave all my information to the Master Sergeant who was filling out the manifest, he asked me if I was on "combat leave." I had never heard of such a thing, but, since I had just finished a combat tour, I said, "yes." I saw my name go near the top of the passenger list. Then it dawned on me. This NCO realized that I might not get on the flight normally, and he also realized where I had just come from. So he took it upon himself to invent a new category of passenger to insure that I made that flight! I never saw the man again, but if he ever reads this I just want him to know how much that was appreciated.

By now, it's about 9:00 in the evening, and the flight was scheduled to leave sometime early in the morning. So, I just plopped down in a chair, with all my earthly belongs, and slept fitfully off and on during the night. Sure enough, we boarded the airplane early the next morning and started the takeoff to Hawaii. Alas, the water injection, which gives the extra thrust on heavy weight takeoffs, failed, so we had to abort the takeoff roll and taxi back to the maintenance ramp. Now, this is August in Okinawa, in an airplane that has no air-conditioning. When the problem was fixed, I, as well as the rest of the passengers, was soaking wet in sweat as we finally took off around noon. Once at altitude, we cooled down and droned across the Pacific and tried to get some sleep in the sparse, uncomfortable seats set up in the cargo area of the tanker. The cabin smelled like old gym socks by now, but I wasn't complaining; I was going to Hawaii!

We finally landed at Hickam AFB, and I caught a cab to Fort DeRussey, where the Army operated an R&R facility on the beach with reasonable prices. I checked in and ran into my old air force ROTC instructor from college, Lt. Col. Robert Milstead, and his wife Jane. He was on his way to Tan Son Nhut Airbase, the same place that I would be going to after my Hawaii interlude. We talked for quite a while, because he had been extremely influential in my decision to get into the air force. My father died just after I started college, and in many respects I looked upon then Captain Milstead as a kind of father figure. I must admit he was one of my heroes, and he and his wife often had cadets to their house for parties. He was always easy to talk to, especially for a young man who needed some adult wisdom every now and then, which I certainly did. After a very pleasant few hours, I went back to my room to freshen up before supper. It would be a few more days before my girlfriend would arrive in Hawaii, so I had plenty of time to explore the place. It was around 6:00 in the evening, so I took a shower before going out. The shower really relaxed me and I felt a bit unsteady, so I lay down to rest a bit before going out to town.

I finally woke up sometime in the early evening. But it was the next evening! I was shocked to find I'd been so exhausted that I had just slept completely through the next day. In retrospect, I guess I shouldn't have been so surprised. I really hadn't had any sleep for the past several days and, combined with jet lag and the stress of finishing a combat tour, I had obviously needed some rest. I felt fine, but when I had to take a flight physical a few months later in Saigon, I was amazed to find that I'd lost 25 pounds. Walking around in a flight suit every day, I hadn't noticed the difference, and my appetite certainly hadn't suffered.

I found a hotel near the beach, closer to Diamond Head, and anxiously awaited the arrival of my romantic interest. She arrived a day later, and we had a week together before I had to find a way back to 7th Air Force Headquarters in Saigon. Reality has a way of intruding on even the most fervently held beliefs, and I must admit that it was a rather bittersweet romantic reunion. We had a pleasant time, but I think both of us felt that the problems and irritations that had driven us apart before had not suddenly been healed and therefore were no longer a problem. But master delusionists that we both were, we still talked as if we would be married when I finally returned from Saigon in 4 months. I bid her a heartfelt adieu at Hawaii International Airport, then headed across the runway to Hickam AFB (a joint-use airfield) to get a flight back to the war zone and Saigon. I wasn't exactly eager, but I was refreshed.

How hard can it be to get to a war? Well, I'm here to tell you it can be damn hard! I checked into the Military Airlift Command Terminal at Hickam hoping to get the next flight to Tan San Nhut Air Base in Saigon. The terminal handled mostly airline contract flights, and they were full of people like myself, who 8 months ago were en route to the war zone, with a quick stop in Hawaii for fuel. Not many empty seats. Undeterred, I walked down to the Military Airlift Command Operations Center. In those bygone days, if you were a pilot or navigator, you could sign on as an additional crewmember; very similar to the way airline crews "deadhead" on flights today. I thought it would be a piece of cake. I was told that I couldn't do this because the next flights out were carrying "dangerous cargo." I was somewhat dumbfounded and asked what type of cargo was involved. I was told that it was paint and bombs. I became somewhat undiplomatic at this point. As red faced as any Irishman can get, I informed them that I had been flying with far more dangerous cargo than that for 124 combat missions and would willingly accept any risk involved. My outburst did nothing to gain a passage on one of the sacred C-141s headed toward Saigon with its load of "dangerous cargo." Defeated, I headed back to the MAC terminal.

Now, one of the rules to get a space-available flight is that you have to be there when your name is called. First come, first served. The immediate impact of this edict was that I couldn't go to the BOQ, get a room, and show up when a flight was available with an empty seat. I actually had to be there in the terminal when it happened. No sweat, I'll just wait around until something shows up, I thought to myself. About 1:00 AM in the morning, I realized that perhaps this was going to be more difficult than I thought, and I was really getting tired. The area where I was waiting was kind of like an open-air bus stop. It was just a covered part of the terminal adjacent to the ramp. Finally, I thought I'd figured out a solution. I went into the little store that was in the terminal and bought a bamboo mat. I figured I could lay that out on the grass just to the side of the terminal in a dark area, and get some sleep. It was only about 40 feet away from all the activity, so I figured I'd hear my name called if any airplane suddenly came in. So that's what I did. In my tan, khaki uniform, and with all my bags, I suddenly became an Air Force homeless person! Nothing happened that night. Nothing happened the next night. Finally, about noon on the third day, my name was miraculously called. We were given a quick briefing and bussed over to Hawaii International Airport, where I had recently left my love interest, to catch a World Airways Flight to Bien Hoa Air Base, which was near Saigon. I could get the rest of the way after that. It was such a horrible experience that I have never tried for a space-available flight to this day, and doubt that I ever will. If I can't afford a ticket, then I won't go. It was really the pits.

We finally took off and headed for Wake Island for a refueling stop. I was seated next to an Air Force Major who was headed back to DaNang Air Base, after R&R. I later found out that he was killed after ejecting from his F-4 right after takeoff in DaNang Bay, about a month later. He was seen in the water OK and motioned for the helicopter to pick up his back-seater. He was never seen again. Apparently, the chute either dragged him down, or the sharks got him.

Immediately next to me was a young Army soldier who was very afraid of flying. As we started our takeoff roll, I informed him that I was World's Greatest Aviator, and that there was nothing to worry about. After about 45 seconds into the takeoff roll, I was starting to get a little worried. With about a 1,000 feet of runway remaining, there was a loud "bang," and we lurched into the air. The F-4 guy from DaNang and I looked at each other: we both knew what had happened. Pretty soon, the captain was on the loudspeaker to announce that we'd blown a tire, and because they lacked good firefighting facilities at Wake, we'd proceed to Clark Air Base in the Philippines for an emergency landing. Lovely, absolutely lovely.

Despite the potential problem, we made it OK, much to the relief of my very frightened Army seatmate. We had to wait a few hours while they fixed and inspected the damage at Clark. I took a long look around. A lot had happened since I'd been here last. It seemed a long time ago. Finally, we were good to go, and took off for Bien Hoa Air Base, about 30 miles from Saigon. We landed in the middle of the night, and I was one of the few that got off, since the flight was going on to DaNang. I was met by one of the F-100 pilots to whom I am forever grateful. I was dead tired, and although there were no quarters for transient personnel, Bien Hoa had a system of "hot bunks"—if a pilot was on alert, you could sleep in his bed, which I appreciatively did. Moderately refreshed, I found some transportation to Tan San Nhut the next morning. Like I said, "How hard can it be to get to a war?" Very damn hard, in this case. But I was back in the war zone. Four months to go.

CHAPTER 21

Saigon

Moderately refreshed after the kindness shown to me by the Bien Hoa F-100 pilot, whose bunk I slept in while he was on alert, I boarded a flight to Saigon. But, in keeping with the rest of the journey, this also was not destined to be a simple trip. As the crow flies, Tan Son Nhut Air Base, where the USAF 7th Air Force Headquarters was located, is only about 30 miles from Bien Hoa. Unfortunately, it wasn't quite the same as driving from Phoenix to Scottsdale on a nice, four-lane highway—the roads were somewhat contested by the Viet Cong, to say the least. Instead, the final leg of my journey to Saigon was by a C-7 Caribou, a twin-engined cargo airplane designed to operate in and out of short airfields, which were common in South Vietnam. Just to make sure I remembered this trip for a very long time, we had to stop at Nha Trang on the way, which was located south of Saigon. This was my introduction to travel in South Vietnam. We landed, and a few passengers and some cargo were off-loaded. More passengers got on, but not what I expected. There were Vietnamese women and children, and goats, chickens, and associated belongings. It certainly was different from what I'd experienced in Thailand, where all the passengers were military, and which wasn't that much different than a trip on a military aircraft in the States. This was different! Lots of garlic smell and other associated odors that I couldn't possibly begin to identify—not offensive, but certainly different. Eventually, we touched down at Tan Son Nhut Air Base, the same place I had been when I went on R&R to Sydney, Australia, in May, a mere 2 months and some weeks ago, but it seemed like a lot longer than that. This visit definitely was not as eagerly anticipated as the first visit had been. But, on the other hand, I only had to spend 4 months here, and then I would be going back to the States. The thought provided some consolation.

By now, it was early afternoon, and I checked in and started to get oriented. Suffice to say, my accommodations were not as sumptuous as at Ubon. My room was pretty sparse: a concrete floor, a small desk, a metal cot, an overhead fan, and a closet that had a gooseneck lamp sitting on the floor. I thought the lamp on the floor was strange until I wiped the sweat from my brow. This was Saigon summer, incredibly humid, and the lamp's purpose was to keep the closet somewhat dry to prevent mildew. No wonder the place had a musty smell. The building itself was rather low slung, with central bathrooms and showers in the middle. Did I mention that there were no windows? Screened upper walls with louvers on the outside provided for a modest amount of privacy and ventilation. The overhead fan was most appreciated. Another surprise. Just on the other side of the sidewalk leading to the latrines and showers was a huge, sandbagged bunker. This was a few months after the Tet Offensive, and there had been more than a few enemy shells land on the air base. It was quite a bit different from the relatively benign living conditions that marked my existence at Ubon. A new experience was about to unfold.

The 7th Air Force Headquarters, or "Pentagon West" as it was sometimes called, was where the Air War in Southeast Asia was run. It wasn't quite that simple, since Pacific Command (PACOM) had overall responsibility for the Air Force and Navy air campaign, but as a practical matter, 7th Air Force made most of the day-to-day decisions that had an effect on Air Force pilots who flew missions. The headquarters was located in a long, two-story building behind a barbed-wire fence that had been strengthened since the Tet Offensive, when insurgents penetrated the base. The headquarters was located right on Tan Son Nhut Air Base, which also served as the civilian airline terminal for Saigon. However, given the wartime situation, especially after Tet, there wasn't that much civilian air traffic. It was a major air transportation hub for the region, and was the home base for an RF-4C Reconnaissance squadron that provided much of the intelligence for South Vietnam and southern Laos.

My role in this endeavor was to be an Air Operations Plans Officer, which, loosely translated, meant that I was to keep track of all the munitions expended and use that information to forecast future needs at all the bases involved in the war. At the time I was in Southeast Asia, we were never short of whatever munition we needed, but that certainly was not the case in the early 1965 to 1966 part of the war. Things apparently were so bad that the Air Force had to buy back 500-pound bombs from NATO. There were documented horror stories of F-4s taking off for strikes in North Vietnam with a meager load of bombs or, sometimes, a totally inappropriate weapon. That was certainly not the situation when I arrived, but I truly gained an appreciation of the logistics and planning effort involved to make sure that never happened again. Not everyone involved in operations at 7th Air Force had actually been in combat, and therefore one of my tasks was to insure that planned mission tasking orders sent out to the wings were appropriate in terms of both ordinance and tactics and made sense from an operational perspective. It was an interesting but rather unstimulating job, and certainly lacked the excitement of my time at Ubon. But, on the other hand, I was reasonably assured that I would make it to the bar every night—something I always didn't feel at Ubon. During my 4 months in Saigon, I saw no enemy activity at all. The Tet Offensive had pretty well emaciated the insurgent aspect of the war in the South, since the Viet Cong and the North Vietnamese Army forces had suffered huge losses. The days passed with little to differentiate them.

One day that did stand out from the rest was when retired General Curtis Lemay visited 7th Air Force Headquarters in the fall of 1968. He had been selected to run as George Wallace's vice president in the Independent Party's bid for the presidency during the 1968 election. As usual, a third-party campaign did not succeed, although it did siphon off many votes from the two major parties. Since the Vietnam War was a major issue in late 1968, it was appropriate that he visit and hear firsthand from General George Brown, the commander of 7th Air Force, how the air war was going. Most of the discussions took place in General Brown's office, but the incident that I remember most was General Lemay's departure after the briefing. It was well known that he was at the headquarters, so there was a fairly large crowd lined up at the doorway as he prepared to leave. It was fairly late in the afternoon, and he had been briefed to death, so when he emerged from the doorway to go to his waiting car and saw the large crowd assembled, an instant scowl appeared on his face. In his previous life as commander of Strategic Air Command and Chief of Staff of the Air Force, he would have barked for everyone to get back to work. This look lasted only a few seconds, as it suddenly seemed to dawn on him that he was now a candidate for vice president. He couldn't "order" people to vote for him, but had to "solicit" their vote just like any other politician. It took him a second to adapt to his new role, and he began to sign autographs and shake hands with everyone there. There weren't any babies, since we were in a war zone, but if there had been, he probably would have kissed them as well. It was truly a sight to see. I always remembered it because ever since I was a young boy growing up with an avid interest in airplanes, he was one of my heroes because of his exploits during World War II and as the head of Strategic Air Command. Truly, one of the "legends of air power," and I was always thankful that I could witness that moment.

One of the highlights of my time at 7th Air Force Headquarters had nothing to do with the place. Since the air war involved quite a bit of coordination with the Navy that operated in the Gulf of Tonkin on "Yankee station," there were Navy officers assigned to 7th Air Force for coordination. I must have looked pretty forlorn one day, or maybe it was my wonderful personality, but for whatever reason, one of the Navy pilots asked me whether I wanted to fly with him to the USS *Coral Sea* for a COD flight the next day. It took me 3 picoseconds to say, "Yes"! Navy ships at sea received much of their day-to-day supplies such as mail and spare parts through a process known as Carrier Onboard Delivery or COD flights. In our case, we would be flying a Grumman S2F, a two-engine, piston-powered antisubmarine plane, which could land on the carrier and had adequate space in the back for cargo. I had never been on an aircraft carrier, and I was ecstatic!

We took off early the next morning from Tan Son Nhut with a stop at DaNang Air Base, just below the demilitarized zone. TheNavy was quite a bit more liberal with its flying rules, so I went on the trip as copilot, although I'd never been in the plane before. Actually, it appeared to be an airplane that could be flown by one pilot but required two because of its design. I was more than happy to fill the square. What a pleasant relief from counting bombs all day! We had an enjoyable flight to DaNang, where we stopped to refuel before heading out to the carrier.

I'm here to certify to my Air Force brethren that an aircraft carrier looks *extremely small* as you fly over it in preparation for landing. I mean really, really small! One of the first things I learned on this trip was that you don't just "show up" and ask for landing instructions, as we would normally do at an Air Force base. The weight and speed of each aircraft are critical since the arresting wire tension must be set to each airplane, and most aircraft coming back from a mission are extremely low on fuel and can't wait while the landing system is reset for each airplane. Each recovering airplane is given a landing time at which time the carrier deck will be set for their recovery. If you don't make the time, it messes everything up, so it's important to arrive at the assigned time. We did, and entered a downwind pattern and then promptly turned final.

The carrier has a very elaborate optical-mirror landing system to guide the pilot down to one of the four arresting wires on the deck. As he turns final, the pilot calls, "Ball in sight," which means he's visually acquired a white "ball" of light on the mirror that represents the glide path. This ball is in the center of a row of green lights and tells the pilot if he's high or low on the desired glide path. There is also a landing signal officer (LSO) right next to this system and he has the final say on whether you can come aboard, since he can see any last-minute change instantly. It's very important that the angle of the tail hook to the deck remains constant. If you see that you are high and try to dive down to the deck, you will raise the hook level and most likely miss the cable. So, you have to adjust your altitude with power to maintain a constant angle of attack. This is somewhat backward to the way most Air Force pilots are trained, although I became somewhat used to it in the F-4, as I got accustomed to the angle-of-attack system. Ideally, the pilot wants to engage the number two cable. The number one cable puts you pretty close to the edge of the carrier if you are low, and could result in a "ramp strike," which means you hit the edge of the carrier first—not a good thing. The number three and number four cables are closer to the far edge of the deck, so those are less desirable as well. Fortunately, the landing deck is canted 15 degrees to the port (left) side, so if you miss the cable, you can still go missed approach and try again. As soon as they touch down, pilots go full military power until they feel the cable pull, then they power back. This gives them enough thrust to make the missed approach, if they missed the cable, and is known in the trade as a "bolter." This stuff is a really big deal, even more so than I had thought. Finally, since the deck is canted, and the carrier is steaming into the wind, you are always correcting back to centerline as you fly down final. You never have to worry about that on a land runway. A quarter of a mile out and this seaborne runway still looks very small!

Finally we touch down. I'm impressed! The actual touchdown was not as violent as some I had made in the F-4 at Ubon during rainy weather. The S2F Tracker has a final approach airspeed of around 110 knots, and the carrier is moving into the wind about 25 knots or more, so this slows your actual ground speed to a reasonable number, but it will still knock your socks off the first time you experience it. As they unloaded our airplane, I got a quick tour around the Coral Sea. I couldn't get over the incredible use of the limited space. We walked around bombs in the passageways. Every inch of space had some purpose. We watched a RA-5C Vigilante come aboard at a final approach speed significantly higher than ours had been. Not much room for error! Two F-4s were scrambled for a search and rescue mission. Now this was something I was familiar with. In the space of about 300 feet, these airplanes were catapulted from 0 to 150 knots. Again, I was impressed. At Ubon, on a hot day, we'd use 5,000 feet of runway to get to that airspeed. My pilot had been excitedly talking about the fact that we would probably get a catapult takeoff ever since we touched down. I must admit, I couldn't understand why that would be such a big deal.

Finally, we were refueled and it was time to go. We would indeed be catapulted off the USS Coral Sea. My pilot was really excited and was fairly quivering with anticipation. I, on the other hand, was a fighter pilot, not easily impressed. I was a bit of a camera buff at the time, and was intent on getting some good pictures. We taxied to the catapult. What a shot! Our wing tip was actually hanging over the right side of the ship, and the edge of the deck looked to be only a few hundred feet in front of us. I was shooting pictures as fast as I could. Meanwhile, the pilot is running up the engines to max power and warning me we're about to launch. When the pilot is ready to go, he salutes the catapult officer on the deck. That signals that he's checked everything and he's ready to go. The catapult officer gives him a second to get his hands on the controls, and then signals to fire the catapult. If something goes wrong at that point, you have no control; you'll get launched anyway. The pilot is grabbing onto the handholds for all he's worth—I'm still taking pictures. Whammo, Bammo! I've never experienced anything like that in my life! We must have pulled six G's, but transversely front to back, not head to toe, as I was used to. I got a black eye from the camera in the process. As soon as we were airborne, we made an immediate hard turn to the right in case we got a cold "cat shot" and didn't get enough of a push to stay airborne. That would at least get us out of the way of the ship, so it doesn't run over us. All was well, and we continued on, back to Saigon. I will never bad-mouth our naval brethren again. I can't imagine launching off on a dark night with no visible horizon. Talk about inducing vertigo, that's got to be a very difficult situation to cope with. Carrier pilots tell me they remember every single one of their night landings, and after this experience, I believe them. It was an incredibly exciting event for me, and I'm very thankful that I had the opportunity to do it. I've long since forgotten the name of my Navy friend that made this possible, but if you ever read this, I never forgot the experience. Thank you!

Gradually, my time in Saigon was drawing to a close. I didn't have much free time, but I did get to downtown Saigon a few times. The French colonial influence was very much in evidence in the architecture and the food. I did manage to have drinks a few times at the Rex Hotel with my old flight instructor, Al Rourke, who first soloed me in the T-37 at Laredo AFB. Al had unfortunately been medically grounded and was in public affairs at the time, but I enjoyed seeing him again. Many of the press briefings took place not far from the Rex Hotel in downtown Saigon, so it was a beehive of activity. I went for Mass once in the beautiful Saigon Cathedral and managed to see the Presidential Palace, which, unfortunately, is where the final surrender to the North Vietnamese took place in 1975. When it happened, it had an air of familiarity about it as I watched it on television. But I'd had enough sightseeing and was eagerly looking forward to going home.

I was scheduled to leave Saigon for the States the second week of December, and was more than ready as the time approached. My enthusiasm was somewhat tempered on Thanksgiving Day 1968, when I received a "Dear Mike" letter from my love interest. In retrospect, it was not totally unexpected, but that provided little consolation at the time. My martini consumption shot up markedly. As I mentioned earlier, a call home to clarify the situation was not really an option, although I did try to do that, alas, unsuccessfully. I remember it as a time of very mixed emotions. Eager to get home, but totally unsure of what I would encounter when I finally did arrive. In retrospect, it would have been a disaster if we had followed through with our plans to be married shortly after I returned, but I certainly didn't see it that way at the time. I mention it here only because it had a large influence on my outlook when I finally did return. The only thing I was sure of was that I would be going back to Homestead AFB as an F-4 instructor, and that provided some solace for my dour mood. Thus, I have rather dark memories of my time in Saigon, even as I write this. It didn't end on the happiest of notes, but it was an interesting experience.

CHAPTER 22

Heading Back Home

The days slipped by as if in slow motion. Finally, the appointed hour arrived, and I was to leave Saigon the next evening, first for a stop in Tokyo at Yokota Air Base, then a transfer to a Continental Airlines flight that would take me to San Francisco. Beyond that, I wasn't too sure. The original plan had called for my love interest to meet me in San Francisco, and we had actively talked about being married there. The letter that I received on Thanksgiving Day had thrown all that into disarray. In those days, I couldn't just pick up my slick, tri-mode cell phone, make a few calls, and straighten everything out. Nonetheless, what had seemed too far into the future to even contemplate a year ago was finally at hand—I had completed my tour, was a combat veteran, and was about to go home. So, despite my melancholy outlook, I was eager to get on that airplane, or as John Wayne would say, "Sister, the time has come for me to ride hard and fast!"

There wasn't much to pack up, since I didn't have a lot with me, so I thought I'd put that off until just before it was time to leave. When I arrived at work, the day before I was to depart, I found out that there was to be a party at MACV (Military Assistance Command Vietnam) Headquarters that night. It wasn't too far away, and many of the people I knew would be going, so why not treat the occasion as a going-away party? Why not indeed? Time has dimmed the purpose of the function, but for whatever reason, it required a uniform, which at that time was simply the short-sleeve tan shirt and trousers. As soon as we finished work at 7th Air Force, we headed over there.

It wasn't a big affair, but there were a few speeches, a nice dinner, and then it was back to the bar. I should have left after the speeches. At a minimum, I should have followed my own rule about martinis—one's not enough, but three's too many. Alas, I ignored my own exceptional advice. Glad to be leaving, unsure about what was in store for me when I did return Stateside, I had way too much to drink. Much later than I should have, I found my way back to my room at the

148

base. Along the way, I had slipped in one of the numerous "benjo" or drainage ditches that line the sidewalks, and was a real mess. I awoke the next morning with a monster headache, a stomach that refused to calm down, and a smelly uniform in a heap on the floor. Afraid that I would miss my flight, the good Lieutenant Colonel Donahue from the office stopped by to see whether I would make it. By that time, further life looked possible, and I started to get ready to catch the flight at the Tan Son Nhut Terminal. I took one look at my rumpled uniform of the night before, decided it was simply unsalvageable, took off the insignia, and threw it in the wastebasket. In retrospect, perhaps it was a suitable metaphor for how the Vietnam War eventually ended. One last swing by the office at 7th Air Force Headquarters to say goodbye to everyone, then it was off to the airplane, or "freedom bird," as it was sometimes called. We lifted off in early evening for the flight to Japan, and just before we entered the clouds, I had my last look at Vietnam. It had been quite a year.

Strangely, I don't remember the flight from Saigon to Tokyo as a particularly boisterous one. As I recall, it was mostly young Army troops who had completed their tours in South Vietnam, and a smattering of the other services, including me. Maybe it was the remnants of my hangover, but I don't recall any large displays of emotion from any of the passengers. Each seemed locked in their own thoughts, and since they had all come over to Vietnam at different times, they most likely did not know very many people on the flight. It would have been a rare event if an entire unit had returned simultaneously. Most of them appeared to be doing the same thing as I—simply sitting there, contemplating what had taken place over the last year. Often, these were the lucky ones, especially the ground combat troops. They were flying back the same way they came over—in one piece. For many ground troops who had been wounded, the return was more difficult, since they had to be medically evacuated to a Casualty Staging Unit in Japan until they were stable enough to be sent to a hospital in the States. Ironically, my future wife, the Fair Linda, was a nurse at the unit in Japan then, although, of course, we hadn't met at this point. We droned on through the night; I dozed intermittently, and, eventually, we landed at Yokota Air Base, just outside Tokyo.

The transfer to the Continental Airlines DC-8 Flight to San Francisco went very smoothly. I think the whole process took only about an hour and a half, and soon we were back on our way. It's a long haul from Tokyo to San Francisco, even by stretch DC-8, and so the atmosphere on this flight was even quieter than the preceding one since we were all pretty tired. With one exception! We picked up some additional passengers on this final leg, and a large group of them were part of a USO show that had been touring throughout the Asian area, including Vietnam. Probably the most prominent of this group was George Jessel. For those of you not of my vintage, he was a very well-known entertainer of the Bob

Hope, Bing Crosby, and Martha Ray era and was often known as "The Toast-master General of the United States." He might have given the title to himself, since he frequently was master of ceremonies at numerous functions. At any rate, he apparently was quite taken by the "General" part of the title, so he appeared on board with this special uniform that he had crafted that had more medals and gongs than I had ever seen—kind of a combination between General Patton, General MacArthur, and Frederick the Great, all rolled into one. He also appeared to have refueled with more martinis than I had taken on the night before, so he was quite a sight. He certainly provided a little bit of levity before the long flight got under way. I don't recall seeing him much after that, and most of us slept, or tried to sleep for the rest of the grueling 12 hours that remained before we set foot back in the United States.

About an hour before the eagerly anticipated landing, the captain came on the PA system to announce that San Francisco was fogged in, and we'd be landing at Oakland instead. Beautiful! I was rather uncertain about what the situation would be when I landed at San Francisco, but now I was really uncertain. I'd passed on my flight information several weeks ago, but that was all before I received the letter calling the possible wedding off. I wasn't sure what I would find, and since the flight had been diverted, and it was evening, I expected I would just find a place to spend the night and figure out everything the next morning when I was rested. I was also uncertain about what sort of reception I, as a military man, would receive. I had read a bit about the turmoil that took place during the Democratic Convention and about the burgeoning antiwar movement, but this was such a change from the mood of the country when I had left that I wasn't sure what to make of it. I had my Class A blue uniform on, with all my new medals, so there wasn't any doubt that I was in the military and had been to the war. I wasn't really worried about it, but I also wasn't sure what to expect either. Another hour or so, and I would have those questions answered.

The pilot successfully groped his way down through the fog to a beautiful landing (must have been a former fighter pilot), and, finally, 1 year to the day that I left, I was back in the United States. Confused perhaps, but very thankful. As I waited for my baggage, much to my surprise, I'm greeted by my love interest; my sister Pat; my old roommate from Big Spring, Dave Kurshan, who now lived in San Francisco; and my good friend from Big Spring, Joe Burley. I was rather stunned. Only later did I find out that since a wedding was planned, they had already made arrangements to meet me on my return; once the whole thing was up in the air, they decided to come anyway. Even now, I'm not sure whether my love interest had totally shared with them her change of heart. For whatever the reason that brought them there, I was overjoyed to see them all, exhausted as I was.

There was the usual excitement of people who haven't seen each other for quite a while. Everyone was talking at once, trying to get caught up in 3 minutes for the past year of life's activities. We picked up my bags, made our way out of the Oakland Terminal, and prepared to drive up to San Francisco, to Dave's apartment. I was quite absorbed with our little group, so I wasn't paying much attention to the larger crowd in the terminal, but I didn't sense any outright hostility toward me as a military person. By now, the flight that I had been on had pretty much emptied out of the building, but nothing caught my attention in the way the other military passengers were treated either. Of course, I wanted to ask my romantic interest just what the hell was going on, but it didn't seem like the time or place to get into that discussion. She was there, so maybe that was a good sign—always the optimist. The conversation of our group picked up as if there had been no long absence after all. Rather strange in a pleasant kind of way. Maybe this was going to work out after all.

The next day was a continuation of the night before, only at least I was rested. It was late morning or early afternoon before we all got together and did some sightseeing in San Francisco. Again, the conversation was a bit stilted between the romantic interest and me, but I determined after moderate interrogation that maybe all was not lost, but nothing would happen in San Francisco for sure. In other words, keep quiet and don't make a scene; we'll talk about this later! Apparently that would have to suffice for now. We all went to a nice restaurant for dinner, and then Dave, who was going with an American Airlines stewardess (that's what we called them back then), suggested that we go to a party that some of her friends were hosting. It was a typical party, and after a few minutes, and the usual introductions, someone asked me the ubiquitous "What do you do?" question. I explained, perhaps a bit flippantly, how I had been defending the world from the Communist hordes in Vietnam and how I had just completed a combat tour as a fighter pilot. I guess I was expecting a bit of interest, since people like me weren't all that numerous at the time. Instead, I got kind of a blank stare. He wanted to know why I had done something like that. He obviously had no interest in the subject and politely excused himself shortly after that. It suddenly dawned on me that 124 missions over North Vietnam and Laos did not meet with the same high regard that my peers and I accorded it. The same scene repeated itself in various ways throughout the night. I confess to feeling a bit of anger. I had seen many very violent things in the last year, and for my squadron mates and me, it had been looked upon as a noble struggle, no matter how distasteful we might have found some aspects of it. Some of these friends did not survive the experience, and their families' lives had been changed drastically. At this party, I had come across several people who could have cared less. As long as the war didn't intrude upon their lives, they had absolutely no interest and were often unaware of events in the war. It was a rather abrupt awakening to how the war was starting to be a very divisive factor for the country. I had not noticed this feeling at the time I departed for Vietnam. There had indeed been a sea change within the country. One that was destined to become more apparent and pronounced as time went on.

I must admit the experience rather caught me by surprise. No one had been out-and-out rude, but I could sense the distaste. Over the years, I have heard some pretty awful stories about the treatment shown to some returning Vietnam veterans. Fortunately, with the exception of the incident I just described, I didn't encounter any outright hostility directed at me personally. Still, at the time, it was disconcerting to encounter the attitude at all.

We spent another day in San Francisco doing pretty much a repeat of the previous day, except, by then, it was pretty well acknowledged that no marriage would take place, and it was time to move on. I decided to go to Dallas with the love interest and my sister to see what, if anything, could be salvaged from this relationship. Joe Burley went back to his base in New Mexico, and Dave, of course, lived in San Francisco. We bid adieu, and the three of us flew on to Dallas. It was a strange time. I spent a few days at their apartment in the hopes that this was all a misunderstanding that could be worked out, now that we were together again. Christmas was approaching, but it was hard to really get in the spirit of things. Finally, the inevitable became obvious, even to an optimist like me, and I made plans to go visit my mother, other sister, and stepfather in Syracuse, New York. My sister, the love interest's roommate, was scheduled to come up there as well in a few days. The Ubon fantasy was definitely not working out as planned.

I can only imagine what my mother must have been going through during all this time. True, she knew the girlfriend fairly well, but it still must have hurt that I didn't come straight home first. The papers of the time frequently had headlines like, "Four F-4s shot down over North Vietnam" on a routine basis. There weren't that many of us (F-4 pilots), and she had no way of knowing if that might be me or not. Years later, when I had a child, I would belatedly come to realize the pain I most likely caused. But, bless her heart, she never once complained about it, and seldom mentioned it. I'm not sure I could have been so stoic if the situation were reversed.

And so, I spent the Christmas of 1968 in Syracuse with my family, which was good. It was certainly a far more joyous occasion than the previous one, where I had been bombing the Ho Chi Minh Trail on Christmas Eve. Many of my relatives lived nearby, and this was the familiar, comfortable environment that I had grown up in. The ill-fated love affair was obviously not going to work out, but disappointed as I was, I think I knew, deep down in my pancreas, that it was not to be. After all, I was the one who had broken the engagement twice before I went off to fight the Great Patriotic War. I spent about 2 weeks in Syracuse, and in retrospect, it was time well spent, as I gradually decompressed, and started adapting to a normal environment. My thoughts were similar to those

I experienced in Sydney during R&R. I gradually began to realize what a strange life I had been living. A little over a year ago, I had left not knowing what the future held, or even if I would survive the war. Now that was all in the past.

The New Year passed, and with it, my leave came to an end. I was due to report to Homestead AFB, just outside Miami, to become an F-4 instructor pilot. It was the same place where I had been checked out in the F-4, a little over a year ago, and now the shoe was on the other foot, and I would be the combat veteran, showing other pilots, new to the F-4, how to fly it, and how to survive in combat. It was also near the University of Miami, where I had graduated 7 years earlier. In a sense, it felt comfortable to be coming back to such a familiar place. A lot had happened in the past few years. As I reported to the base, and got back into the rhythm of flying every day and checking out new pilots, I didn't give much thought to what had happened during my combat tour. I'd survived, had quite a few close calls, but was still standing, and that was all that counted. I truly did not think that the experience had that much of an impact on me. It was to take many years and a considerable amount of reflection before I came to realize what a profound impact the war did have on me. I had come full circle. Checking out in a fighter plane was what I had always dreamed of. I had done that at this very base, and now I was doing the same thing for a new group of pilots who, no doubt, felt the same way as I had. How would they feel when it was all over?

CHAPTER 23

Final Reflections as Time Goes By

Time stops for no one. Life went on, and I soon got into the routine of instructing in the F-4 at Homestead. When I originally checked out in the airplane, we got a few orientation rides in the backseat to familiarize us with the systems, but I was not very knowledgeable about all their intricacies. I came to have a much better appreciation of what the GIBs had to put up with in the back. All in all, not a bad assignment, and I spent 4 years there, including about 3 months deployed to Kunsan Air Base in Korea during the late sixties.

My romantic situation changed dramatically during this period. It soon became apparent that the engagement to my love interest during my time at Ubon was not going anywhere, so it ended as abruptly as it had restarted itself. The year I had spent at Ubon was truly an emotional roller coaster, and this was a perfect example of how the experience can affect one's emotional outlook.

Then I met the Fair Linda in 1971. Captain Linda Leaf was also in the Air Force and was a nurse recruiter stationed in Coral Gables, Florida. I had seen her a few times before, but she was always on the road, traveling to nearby states to interview nurses, so it was hard to meet her. When I finally did, it was a case of "good news, bad news." The good news was that I fell head over heels in love with her after just a few dates. The bad news was that she had orders to go to South Vietnam. What to do? Well, I did a very uncharacteristic thing for old, conservative me—I asked her to marry me right away! I asked her on a Wednesday, we got the license on Friday, and were married on the following Monday after a courtship of about 6 weeks. Part of the reason for the rush was that the Air Force had a policy of compassionate change of assignment. It didn't apply to engaged couples, but if you were married, they would try to assign both together if possible. So, in the end, that's what happened and the Fair Linda was reassigned to the base at Homestead as the nurse in charge of the hospital recovery room. I amaze myself at how sure I was that it was the right thing to do. It's been 35 happy years now, since we made that decision, so I think my judgment has been vindicated.

We were at Homestead for almost a year, when the opportunity to fly the Canadian F-104 Starfighter at Cold Lake, Alberta, presented itself. I always wanted an exchange pilot assignment, and was fortunate to get it. The "Zipper" was one of those classic airplanes that every fighter pilot wanted to fly. So, in quick succession, Linda got out of the Air Force, we packed up all our things, put our house on the market, and embarked on what turned out to be one of the happiest 2-year periods of our lives. Cold Lake was where the Canadians trained their F-104 pilots before they were assigned to NATO forces in Germany. The operation was very similar in many respects to what I was doing at Homestead, and part of my job would be to pass on to the Canadians what I had learned in combat during the Vietnam War. The Canadian exchange assignment was one of the most interesting experiences of my career. Not only did I get to fly a fantastic airplane but I also got a whiff of how other countries view things. Those that knew me at the time probably remember me as somewhat of a hawk about the war in Vietnam. When I arrived in Canada in July of 1972, the war was still raging, and most Canadians were well aware of what was happening. My sense was that their country did not agree with our involvement there, but it did not seem to be an intensely held feeling, unlike the pronounced polarity in the States. The Canadian fighter pilots were interested, but from more of a professional, flying, aspect. More than one of them expressed to me a frustration that having trained as a fighter pilot, there was very little likelihood that they would ever use their skills in anger, and many felt they wanted to experience combat. I tried to explain that air combat isn't quite what they might have thought it was, but the experience was still too fresh in my consciousness for me to be objective and detached about it. As a group, they were some of the best pilots I have ever encountered—very skilled in their craft. I understood the thoughts they expressed about wanting to see combat. After all, hadn't I expressed those very same thoughts just a few years earlier? They wanted to meet the "monster" and see how they would perform. That, I understood. What I couldn't do at that point was coherently explain how I felt about our involvement, and why. That would come many years later.

If my opinion were asked on how the war might turn out, I usually gave the party line that we just had to be patient, it was a righteous cause, we had to draw a line in the sand on Communism somewhere, and soon. At the time, I think I really felt that way. It was almost inconceivable to me that given our immer power and resources, we wouldn't eventually prevail. The December holi
1972 were when the massive Christmas Bombing of North Vietnam tr
that eventually caused the North Vietnamese to return to the barg
Shortly after that, the accords were signed that resulted in

American role in Vietnam. At the time, I think we in the American military tried to convince ourselves that we had somehow prevailed in the end, and that it had all been worth it, despite the incredible cost in lives, money, and material.

Midway through this fascinating assignment, I was back in the United States, at Eglin AFB, to test the new Radar Homing and Warning gear that the Canadians had just purchased for their F-104s. While I was there, the Red River Valley Fighter Pilot's Association (commonly known as the River Rats) was having its "First Real Reunion" at Las Vegas in July of 1973. One became a member of the Rats by virtue of flying one mission north of the Red River in North Vietnam. It was a small group, but we were intensely proud of being members. When the Rats were established in the mid-sixties it was stated that any reunions held prior to the return of the POWs would be "practice reunions." The American involvement in Vietnam came to an end in March of 1973 with the signing of the Paris Peace Accords, and the POWs were finally released that same month. After a several-month period of adjustment it was decided to have the First Real Reunion in Las Vegas that July. It was a long-awaited event, and one that I was most eager to attend. Along with several fellow Rats, we took off in a USAF C-131 transport and headed west.

I had never seen so many fighter pilots and fighter GIBs in one place before. The Las Vegas Convention Center hosted the event, and I saw people who I hadn't seen in years. It was a 3-day affair over the weekend, and, of course, the highlight of the event was the presence of the POWs. At the time they were shot down, many of us thought we'd never see them again. Often, it was several, long years before it was even known they were alive. Whiskey flowed, arms waved, songs were sung, and memories revisited as we all relived our involvement in the long war.

Toward the end, we were finishing dinner, and our attention was riveted to a bank of TV monitors that had been set up in the dining area and were showing slides of the different bases, planes, and gun camera film. We were pretty well lubricated by this point, when, suddenly, all the screens showed the same image—a kind of white/gray shimmering. We looked at each other and wondered what the hell was being shown. After a few seconds, the shape of a C-141 transport could be seen arising from the shimmering on the screens and it became clear what we were looking at. It was a film of the airplane that had picked up the POWs in Hanoi taking off, and the shimmering was merely the heat rising from the runway at Gia Lam Airport in Hanoi. Soon, the screens showed the inside of the airplane as the prisoners finally realized that at long last, they were going home! Their ordeal was over. "God Bless America" and other patriotic songs played on the loudspeakers, and as we looked around, the POWs in the film were there with us. I looked immediately to my right. At the opposite side of the table was Everett Alvarez, the first pilot shot down and captured in

August of 1964. I caught a glimpse of John McCain about the same time. It was one of the most emotional moments I can remember, and one that I'll never forget. I don't think there was a dry eye in the crowd; I know I was teared up.

I think the reason it had such a significant impact was that it was the closest most of us ever got to a successful end to the war. Yes, we'd lost the war, but the full impact of that had not really settled in yet, and the ultimate fall of Saigon was still a few years off. We could still maintain the illusion that we had been successful. A lot of us had not exactly received a warm welcome when we returned home from our part in the war. But at this moment, for one brief span of time, we were all united in the feeling that we had participated in a heroic cause and were proud to have been part of the undertaking, no matter how tragic its eventual result. We felt like heroes — even if only for a moment. It was a moment to savor, and I still do.

Shortly after that memorable event, I had another magic moment. It was about a week after the River Rat Reunion when I arrived home. It was about 2:00 in the morning when the Fair Linda picked me up at Base Ops at Cold Lake and we went home. I thought she was very chipper for so late at night, when she handed me a present, which I thought was a little unusual. As I unwrapped the gift, all became clear. Inside the box were a pair of baby's booties and a card announcing that I would be a father the following April! She was determined not to tell anyone until she could break the news to me in person, and she didn't, despite an awful bout of morning sickness during the first few weeks. Our little Canadian, Saint Erin, the Magnificent, was born the following April in an Edmonton hospital just as our exchange experience was coming to a close.

In retrospect, perhaps it was a fortunate thing that the American end to the war took place while I was on this exchange tour. It afforded me a chance to look at the event through another prism in a detached, somewhat objective, setting. Most Canadians are not bashful about stating how they feel about things, and I think they were fairly candid with me about their thoughts on the war. The period remains one of the happiest of my life.

Stateside Again

The unique Canadian exchange tour ended, and our recently expanded family headed south. I had been assigned to 12th Air Force Headquarters at Bergstrom AFB, Austin, Texas, and would be part of the Standardization and Evaluation Section. All the forces assigned to Tactical Air Command west of the Mississippi River belonged to 12th Air Force, and our particular group gave check rides and inspections to those bases. I was dual current in both the F-4 and F-104, which was a unique experience. It was an enjoyable assignment except for the fact that I was gone every other week, which the Fair Linda did not appreciate very much.

The fighter-pilot world is a relatively small community, and I would frequently run into pilots I had known, many from Ubon days. We would often talk of our experiences as if we had won the conflict. By then the war was in the hands of the Vietnamese. Suddenly, in the spring of 1975, the North Vietnamese surged across the Demilitarized Zone into South Vietnam. The South Vietnamese forces could not stop them, and soon, a full-scale rout was in progress.

As these events unfolded, I was in Springfield, Illinois, giving check rides to F-4 pilots in that Air National Guard unit. When the end finally came, I will never forget watching it unfold on the television in my hotel room. I saw pictures of Tan Son Nhut Air Base being strafed by North Vietnamese aircraft. A tank smashed through the gates of the presidential palace and accepted the surrender of the South—at the very point where I had taken a picture 7 years earlier. The American Embassy was a scene of absolute chaos, as what few helicopters that were available tried frantically to evacuate remaining American personnel and thousands of Vietnamese citizens who were desperate to escape. A similar scene had taken place when DaNang and other bases fell. Vietnamese Air Force helicopters were landing on U.S. aircraft carriers and then were shoved overboard, since there was no more room. It was a heartbreaking scene, and an absolute tragedy for thousands of people. Up to this point, those of us who had fought in the war could talk as if our efforts in Southeast Asia had been somewhat successful. After watching these events unfold, it became impossible to maintain the illusion. For me, it was somewhat of a major turning point in my thinking. It took quite some time, years in fact, for the full magnitude of the event to sink in, but I could not deny that the great adventure of my youth had ended badly. I remember thinking at the time, "All those lives, all that effort and cost—for nothing." It was a bitter moment, and I still remember it vividly.

A few years after that, somewhat disillusioned and moderately less naïve, I moved on to the Pentagon, for an assignment on the air staff, at Headquarters USAF, in the Tactical Fighter Division as the F-4/F-16 program element monitor and, later, chief of Tactics, Forces, and Training. It was quite different, and I must admit, it certainly changed how I looked at the world. As I was beginning to learn, one's view of the world depends on where they are sitting at a particular moment. I found it overwhelming at first. No matter what your title, at some point the DOD budget controls your life. Whatever brilliant tactical fighter ideas you may have, at some juncture it gets exposed to the harsh spotlight of the budget process, and if you can't justify it, it simply doesn't happen. This was somewhat of a shock for an idealistic lad, such as myself.

As I look back upon this period, from 1977 to 1980, one other observation stands out. I did not detect an aura of defeat about the Vietnam War that one might have expected. Quite the contrary. I attribute this to the fact that from a technology, and an individual airmanship standpoint, we had actually done fairly well. All of us had "met the monster" of combat, and we were proud of our accomplishments. We tended not to look at the episode in broad, strategic terms. But the issue simply would not go away and is still a thorn in our sides 3 decades later. Could we have won the war by air power, if allowed to do it the way we saw fit? The controversy still rages.

Toward the end of the air staff tour, another opportunity presented itself. The Office of the Secretary of Defense (OSD) had a position open for a fighter pilot in an office known as Planning & Requirements, whose task was to develop policy guidance for military contingency and deployment planning specifically for Southwest Asia. The OSD supports the secretary, and is mostly civilian, with perhaps a quarter of the staff being military. Except for 1 day a week, the military usually dressed in a business suit, not a uniform. Since all those requisitions passed across my desk, I volunteered myself for the position. A few interviews later, and I was there. One interview bears mention. Walt Slocombe at the time was the deputy under secretary of defense for policy. He was a pleasant fellow, and the interview seemed to be going well. Suddenly, he asked me, "Do you think you can handle this job?" I must admit it caught me off guard. He either sensed my surprise, or was used to asking the question because he then said, "Let me explain." He then described how military officers sometimes have difficulties in assignments such as the one I sought. Walt explained how the military prefer to have most of the questions about a proposed course of action resolved before they commit to executing it. He then made a comment, which I have never forgotten: "Sometimes, you're faced with having to make a decision with only 60 percent of the data that you need, *but* in a time frame that can be very decisive, as opposed to having 100 percent of the information, but when it's too late to have the desired impact—do you think you can deal with that? Sometimes, the military, by its nature, tends toward absolute certainty." Whatever I said was apparently the correct answer because I got the job, but it was a major insight to how decisions are often made at very high levels. I was about to be introduced to the friction between the JCS and the OSD.

I must say that I enjoyed my time on the OSD staff. It was much smaller than the air staff, and I had far more freedom of action. Much of my time was spent on contingency plans, especially in the Mid-East. Again, I learned that where you sit determines your view of the situation. The OSD staff was more concerned about the overall situation and found the internecine attitude of the individual services to be a major hindrance. They also had to deal quite a bit with the State Department, and I often found myself attending meetings across the Potomac River.

The Iran/Iraq War had broken out and was a major focus. Quadafi of Libya was also a consideration, and a significant effort involved a large naval exercise to challenge his contention that the Gulf of Sidra, adjacent to Libya, was not subject to the normally recognized Law of the Sea boundaries. This effort culminated in two Libyan fighters being shot down during the exercise. The planning leading up to this fateful engagement took several months and involved an extreme amount of coordination between the State Department, the National Security Council, and the various military commands. Much of my time was spent coordinating the Rules of Engagement with the JCS, State, and NSC staff. As a young fighter pilot during the Vietnam War, the "Rules" were one of the most frustrating problems we faced. Now, the shoe was on the other foot, and I could see that it was not the simple matter that I had once supposed it to be.

The phrase "Fog of War" took on new meaning in this confrontation. I happened to be in the National Military Command Center when the two Libyan fighters were shot down. We'd expected something to take place, but when it actually happened, it caught everyone by surprise. Things weren't clear-cut, and there was quite a bit of confusion. Russian ships were shadowing the U.S. Navy fleet and suddenly trained missiles on our ships. There were several tense moments until the situation resolved itself, and we suffered no losses during the episode. In many respects, it was a good metaphor for the Gulf of Tonkin Incident that had been so influential in my life. I began to see how a single incident could have great follow-on consequences, and how crucial information was often lacking, even at high levels of government.

Several months later, there would be a major push to duplicate that incident to reinforce the message. It was a touchy situation, and no one was really quite sure how Quadafi or the Soviets would react. I distinctly remember one session in a major policymaker's office with a general from the Joint Staff. This was right after the Falklands War where the British had lost a ship, much to their surprise. I asked, "What would be our response if, for whatever reason, one of our ships was sunk during this exercise?" I received a very annoyed look from the general, who replied to the policymaker, "Don't worry, we have contingency plans." I interpreted that to mean, "assume success, and don't worry about failure." This was exactly the sort of wishful thinking that caused us to expend so much treasure in Vietnam over a lost cause. A "can do" attitude is a wonderful thing, but there are times when decisionmakers have to consider the realistic possibilities. I certainly didn't see it happening at this discussion.

My years spent on the OSD staff were an interesting experience, and it gave me a different perspective on how major policy decisions are developed and implemented. Slowly, over time, I began to grasp how some of the decisions that ~ved so fateful a few decades earlier in Vietnam had come about. I did come to
:isionmakers are often forced to deal with incomplete data, which,
ed with inaccurate assumptions, can lead to faulty policies. All the
to question assumptions.

My joint experiences (working with organizations other than the Air Force) while at the Pentagon proved to be a stepping stone for my next assignment as the Chief of the Office of Defense Cooperation at the American Embassy in Oslo, Norway. The office functioned as the main point of contact for all U.S. military activity and programs between Norway and the United States, especially the Security Assistance Program, and any bilateral programs with the Norwegian government. This is one of those little-known jobs that, while not in the mainstream of Air Force assignments, was, and probably still is, one of the best-kept secrets in the Air Force. It certainly met all my requirements for an interesting assignment.

There was no way I could complain about the office or its location. The American Embassy was located directly across the street from the King's Palace in downtown Oslo. So, it was with great anticipation that we embarked on a very pleasant 4-year stay in Oslo. The job was interesting, the location excellent, and the people I came in contact with were a pleasure to work with. What more could you ask for? Again, it gave me a chance to view policy from a different perspective.

The 4 years passed all too quickly, but one of the major events was a visit to the Soviet Union that my wife, daughter, and I took in the spring of 1985. The opportunity presented itself when a NATO group arranged a tour of Leningrad (still named so at the time) and Moscow. The Iron Curtain was still a very real entity then, although things were starting to thaw imperceptibly. It wasn't the simplest trip to arrange, and there was considerable paperwork to accomplish. We didn't even know whether our visas had been approved until the day before the trip. Intourist, the Soviet agency that handled all tourists within the country, was very suspicious about visitors making contact with Soviet citizens, so normal details like what hotel we might be staying at would not be known until we actually arrived in the country. The preparations were rather bizarre compared to typical trip arrangements. I had to get a special intelligence briefing from my masters at European Command before I went, mainly on things to be aware of as a military person in a country that was still somewhat hostile to the West. But I had a burning desire to go, since it was the dark, mysterious monolith that we in the Air Force and American military had always considered "the enemy" ever since I could remember. Now that it was possible to visit the country as a tourist, I couldn't resist.

Finally, all the obtuse paperwork was in order, and we flew to Helsinki, Finland, and then to Leningrad via Aeroflot, landing late in the afternoon. An Intourist bus promptly met us along with a tour guide, whose job was to keep us within a "bubble," so that they always knew where we were. Our visit gave new meaning to the term "paranoia." We spent a pleasant few days in the city where the Bolshevik Revolution had all started in 1917. This was 1985, and our tour guides gave plenty of lectures about how it was also the 40th anniversary of the victory over Fascist Germany. Since Leningrad was under siege for 900 days by the Germans, it was not hard to see why this was a major event for the Soviets. Our next stop was Moscow, which was equally interesting. However, what is most memorable about the trip to me was my reaction.

To an American fighter pilot, the Soviet Union was always the unseen enemy. When I was a child, we practiced air-raid drills and ducked under our desks in grade school during the forties and early fifties to be prepared in case the Russians bombed us. The Russians had supplied the North Koreans during that war and were a major supplier of aircraft and weapons to the North Vietnamese. Hadn't I almost shot down a MiG-21, nearly been hit by SAMs, and had untold numbers of antiaircraft shells fired at me? With that background for a mindset, a Russian was someone or something I thought of as being a target in front of my pipper one day. This was the enemy—the reason for our existence as fighter pilots. During the seventies and early eighties, we envisioned them as this huge military force that would come storming across the Fulda Gap into West Germany someday, intent on conquest. We attributed their military with great powers and capability. The Soviet Union was definitely to be taken seriously. I was shocked with what I saw!

Although I didn't see much militarily, what I did see was a country tottering on the brink of economic collapse. This was not the huge, powerful, successful country that I had imagined. Whatever money had gone to build up the military had obviously not trickled its way down to the civilian sector. Food was not in plentiful supply at all. The one area that I was not allowed to film with a video camera at all was an open-air food market. There was such a lack of food available that the authorities did not want this publicized. The hotels in Moscow where the tourists stayed were probably better than many other hotels because Intourist wanted to create a good impression. Everything was shabby; cars were not plentiful in the wide streets at all. Even GUM, the large department store opposite the Kremlin, was bereft of consumer goods. People who passed me on the street were not smiling, happy, and whistling "The 1812 Overture" at all. Most looked rather sad. The food in the hotels and restaurants where we dined probably was better than what the average Soviet citizen ate, and even so, it was rather sparse. Any number of people would come up with an offer to trade rubles for dollars, which were very scarce. Almost no price was too high for a pair of jeans. I could not get over how different reality was from my expectations. The entire image I had in my mind about what the potential enemy was like was totally uprooted. Had the situation been like this always? It was an incredible shock to me. The possible enemy we had envisioned as being 10 feet tall was considerably shorter than that!

So what has all this to do with reflections on a war, long ago? Simply that a given mindset predisposes you to presume certain things, which may not be valid, but you have no way of knowing it at the time. This determines your view of the world, and that is one of the difficulties we encountered in the Vietnam War. We assumed certain things to be true, when in reality that was not the case. As I later learned in my MBA studies, the wise person doesn't spend too much time on all the spreadsheets of a business plan, since the numbers can be manipulated to say whatever you want them to say. Instead, the assumptions that are the basis of the analysis are far more important. The Russian trip was truly an eye-opening experience in this regard.

My military career was drawing to a close. The assignment in Norway ended, and I actually felt a twinge of homesickness at the thought of leaving. Norway was a wonderful place, very similar to Upstate New York, where I grew up, and so it was with much regret that we packed up and headed to Phoenix, Arizona, for my new assignment as chief of staff of the Air Division at Luke AFB. About this point in my career, retirement loomed. I began to realize that I was older than most of the young officers and men whom I encountered, and began to feel a little "out of synch" with them in that we didn't have a common core of experience. In the late eighties, most of the younger pilots had not been in Vietnam, and I was aware of the vast gulf that separated us. I did fly in the F-15 Eagle several times, a very impressive experience indeed. I was amazed how the airplane performed compared to the F-4 Phantom that I flew in the Vietnam War. But the time had come for transition to the civilian world, and so I began sending out resumes.

Eventually, I met with success, although I must admit it was not an easy process. I took a position with Martin Marietta, which had a contract with the Federal Aviation Agency (FAA) to do transition planning. In many respects, it was a simple transition. I stayed in the same house, and merely changed where I went to work. Instead of Luke AFB, I would go to an FAA office at Sky Harbor International Airport, which had many new projects to be implemented. Suddenly, after 28 years in the military, I was a civilian. It had been an enjoyable career, but I was eager to get on with my new life.

I stayed in various versions of that role for several years, and eventually Martin Marietta became Lockheed Martin after several corporate mergers and acquisitions. In the mid-nineties, I spent about a year in a very enjoyable assignment with the company in business development. This involved quite a bit on international travel to interest airlines and other aviation customers in an advanced, self-contained Instrument Landing System that the company had developed. I eventually ended going back to the FAA contract, and except for a brief interlude as the manager of a new Pilot Development Program with Mesa Air Group, I was with Lockheed until I retired. At that point, I began to write the book that you are now reading.

Many events have taken place since I first felt the desire to go to a war that I thought would be over before I would have a chance to get there. My atti and thoughts had changed considerably over the years although there was no single event—it was a gradual process. There were many historical changes as well: one of the most significant was the collapse of the Soviet Union. We couldn't have imagined that at the time of the Vietnam War. The Berlin Wall was torn down, and the Warsaw Pact Communist countries were no longer tied to the Soviet Union, and many are now part of NATO. This was inconceivable during the 1960s, when we looked upon the Communist world as one that had both the intent and capability to dominate the world. In many respects, the world turned out to be quite different from what we had imagined during that tumultuous era. All the more reason to reflect back on those events to see what can be gleaned that might be of use in the future, or, at a minimum, to try to make some sense out of the entire experience.

Final Reflections

So, what do I think about as my mind wanders back to that very intense time several decades ago? First, a sense of thankfulness. It was a period during which I wasn't sure I'd see my next birthday. I survived. Sometimes I'm not sure why or how, but I survived. I found the love of my life and enjoy a marriage that has spanned over 3 decades. We've had a daughter who has made us extremely proud. She graduated from a fine Jesuit college at Santa Clara, settled in a good career, and married a fine man. We now have our first grandchild, a wonderful little girl named Olivia. I had a career (actually a couple) that I enjoyed and felt that I made useful contributions in the process. My health is still good, and I've been able to indulge myself in the things that hold interest for me. At the moment, the future holds no immediate terrors. However, this feeling of well-being is sometimes tinged with a vague sense of guilt. Many of those who I flew with during that violent period in 1968 were never able to experience these things—Dean St. Pierre comes to my mind immediately.

Was it worthwhile? I often think quite a bit about this. How could an undertaking that seemed to me so right at the time have turned out so badly? So, no, I don't think it was worth the cost in lives and treasure. Just in terms of F-4s shot down, the war was extremely costly: 193 were lost over North Vietnam, 97 over South Vietnam, while 111 went down over Laos. During the entire war, an incredible total of 3,322 aircraft of all types were lost, 3,265 crew members died, and 497 became POWs. Over 58,000 lives were lost on our side and far more than that on the Vietnamese side. The history and causes of our involvement in the war are generally pretty well understood, I think, but let me just add my perspective. I think it's important that we ponder these issues so that we don't slip into similar situations that we eventually come to regret.

The Vietnam War tore this country apart, and was the longest war in our history. We meant well. Unfortunately, we saw the conflict in terms of the spread of Communism rather than the nationalistic struggle that it really was. We were slow to grasp the limits of military power, and thought that if we only persevered, we would eventually be successful. Alas, that was not to be the case. In retrospect, it was not a conflict that lent itself to attrition warfare as we had come to know it in World War II and Korea. I didn't come to this conclusion readily, and it was difficult to give up thoughts and beliefs that I'd held onto so tenaciously for many years. I amaze myself as I think back of the young hotheaded ideologue that I was, who was absolutely convinced that the war would be over before I could be a player. What did I learn from the experience? Simply that we need to question our assumptions about the necessity of going to war. We should only be willing to commit if some major strategic interests are truly threatened. In Vietnam, that was not the case, although we tried mightily to convince ourselves that it was.

In this respect, I think I differ somewhat from many of my military brethren. I often hear a thought expressed that goes like this: "If they had just let us fight the war the way we should have, we could have won." We'll never know, because we didn't do it, but I don't think it would have changed the eventual outcome, although it might have ended the war sooner. What was a limited war to us was a total war to the other side. Eventually, we would have tired of the struggle. Even if we had occupied North Vietnam, it would have been a guerilla war without end, and, with no vital American interests at stake, it's doubtful if we could have sustained the effort. Are there some things worth fighting for? Absolutely. But I think we have to be more discriminating in determining what they are.

Did I get enough adventure? Without question! In that sense, our situation as fighter pilots and fighter 'gators was somewhat different from many participants in the war. Generally, no one forced us to go. For the most part, we had involved ourselves in the war by virtue of being in the professional military, or by volunteering, or both. While I have many debates with myself about the justness of our cause, I still have strong and pleasant memories of those whom I flew with at Ubon. It was an incredibly exciting time despite, or perhaps because of, the dangers that we faced. Looking back, I find it hard to believe that I did some of the things I did with the Phabulous Phantom. I didn't know airplanes could do things like that and stay in one piece! There was an incredible thrill to having successfully flown a harrowing mission and survived.

Although we never talked about it, I admit that fear was a constant thought that never went away—it was always there, hovering in the back of my thoughts. Maybe others were braver, but I could never totally dismiss the notion. In spite of that, somehow, we did it. No matter what demons might be running through my mind, if the rest of my mates were still there, pressing on to the target, how could I do otherwise? The bravery of your peers was a very powerful force, indeed, and that's the way I remember them. When I took off as part of a thirty-six-ship strike force going to a target in the Hanoi area, I really felt that I was part of a "big deal." I can still hear strains of "The Ride of the Valkyries" in my mind as I think back to those moments.

I think of the MiG I might have shot down. At the time, I was very disappointed that it didn't come to pass—fame and glory denied. I don't feel that way now, and am glad it worked out the way it did. I certainly didn't feel that way at the time. Would I be any happier or more fulfilled today if my hopes had come true and I'd shot down the MiG? The MiG pilot was another pilot, possibly similar to myself. I've come to realize that he probably felt as strongly about his role as I did about mine. To him, we were just another colonial power trying to subjugate them. If I'd read this paragraph 35 years ago, I wouldn't have believed I had written it.

My major question before Ubon had been answered. During that intense year, I had met the monster of combat, and no longer had to wonder how I would react. What I had not anticipated was the difficulty in going on day after day. That proved more difficult than the initial fears of how I would react in combat. I recently saw a picture of me taken just after I had returned. Quite a change! I had lost 20 pounds in that year, and hadn't even realized it.

Not unexpectedly, I also harbor quite a few negative feelings about the war. Despite my idealism at the time, in retrospect I don't think it met the criteria of a "just war" as defined by Saints Augustine and Aquinas. Our premises for the war were flawed, although it took our country decades to accept that, and even now, I'm not sure it's a universally held belief. To a large extent, I don't feel that many of our leaders leveled with us, and many lives were lost needlessly as a result. The number of senior leaders who spoke out once it became obvious the war was not going well was almost nonexistent. Once burned, twice shy, and I'm afraid my outlook on current conflicts is shaped a great deal by my Vietnam experience.

As I was preparing to write this book, I had an epiphany of sorts. Not quite a "Saul on the road to Damascus" experience, but pretty meaningful, nonetheless. In 1972 David Halberstam published a book titled *The Best and the Brightest*. There were others that followed, such as *Vietnam—A History* by Stanley Karnow, and, much later, *A Bright and Shining Lie* by Neil Sheehan. I refused to read them, especially *The Best and the Brightest*, because I assumed the books were written by left-wing, commie, whacko liberals, who would denigrate the military and belittle our efforts. Perhaps the wounds were too raw at that point. It would be another 30 years before I would open up *The Best and the Brightest* and read what was inside.

I was absolutely shocked. By then, my own views on the war had changed considerably, albeit painfully, from what they had been during the conflict. But gradually, over the years, I had come to the belief that the war was essentially a civil war, and we could not have won it, no matter what we did. This was a position that you could not have convinced me of during the war. What shocked me about the book was that Halberstam, a *New York Times* reporter when he was in Vietnam, had seen all this quite clearly at the time. He was a reporter in Vietnam about the same time that I was there, and was about the same age as I. I had a similar reaction to the other books that I mentioned. Thus, my epiphany: Reporters did not have a vested/emotional interest in the outcome. They take a snapshot of what they see, and make some analysis, and that's what they report. Those of us in the military and the government did have a vested interest in the outcome of the war. To a large extent it defined who we were and what we stood for. Any criticism of the war effort was taken as a denigration of our noble sacrifice. We desperately wanted it to work out as we had envisioned it would. We wanted success, validation, and vindication so badly that we would jump through any number of mental hoops to convince ourselves that our strategy was working out the way we thought it should. We tended not to believe reporters, and many in the military felt that they were making the news and slanting it to their viewpoint. In essence, they were able to see things more objectively than we did at the time.

Since they are, after all, mere mortals, I'm sure that some of their biases crept into their commentary on occasion, but on balance, they appear to have seen the situation more clearly than many of us in the military and government did, especially yours truly. It also points out the necessity of reading something before you launch into a criticism of it.

And what of the return from the war? The antiwar protests were somewhat of a shock to the military. Generally, the military had been an admired institution during my formative years, especially during a time of war. When I left in 1967, the dissension was not fully articulated and had only begun to be noticeable. I would read about it while I was in Southeast Asia but was unprepared for how much the country had changed when I returned. It was very strange and unsettling to have our efforts questioned. I did not encounter any outright hostility directed at me, but the presence of it was quite evident. If we had expected a grateful nation to bestow its thanks on us when we returned, we were bitterly disappointed. I didn't realize how deep-seated this feeling was in me until the First Persian Gulf War in 1991. Everywhere you looked, there were yellow ribbons, patriotic songs, and events, especially when the troops started to return home. To be candid, I must admit to feeling a bit of anger and jealousy. As I'd look at some of the cheering crowds I'd think to myself, "Some of these very people were at best indifferent to our return, and often were probably downright hostile." Old resentments die hard.

It wasn't until the Vietnam War Memorial was opened that the issu to resolve itself, or at least as much as was realistically possible. I

Washington, stationed at the Pentagon, when it opened in the fall of 1982, and it was a remarkable experience. I used to go for a run every day during the noon hour over the Arlington Bridge, around the Lincoln Memorial, and then around the Washington Monument and back to the Pentagon, so I passed the "Wall" on every run as it was being built. However, I had only seen if from afar and was unprepared for the first time when I actually saw the memorial when it was opened to the public. It was very emotional, and still is. I had not thought it would have such an impact on me, but it did. I usually advise any Vietnam vet, who has not seen it, to go alone the first time so as not to make a spectacle of themselves—something I certainly did. There was considerable controversy while it was being built, but I think it does exactly what it was designed to do. As you descend the walk and start reading names, and look at the vast expanse of black marble, the sheer enormity of the human cost hits you like a ton of bricks. When you come across the names and dates of death of people you knew personally, it becomes all the more apparent. I can't think of another memorial that has had such an impact on me. The feeling seems to be almost universal as I observed other people with similar reactions during my visits. The site had one very beneficial effect. At last, instead of being forgotten and not discussed, the monument acknowledged the war and the tragic cost of American partici- pation.

I think those of us who fought in the war all hoped, and some assumed, that there would be a successful end to the conflict and that a grateful nation would welcome us home when we returned. I don't think any of us envisioned the war lasting the length that it did. And therein lies part of the problem: a united nation did not send us off to war. After the initial buildup of forces, support became tepid at best and later turned quite against our participation. Unlike World War II, where great wrongs were righted, and the possible imposition of a totalitarian government was thwarted, there was no such result from our efforts in the Vietnam War. Even the Korean War, often called the Forgotten War, while somewhat inconclusive, still had beneficial results. South Korea was free, and developed into an economically viable country, albeit with our continued presence. There was no such ending to the American involvement in Vietnam, which is perhaps why the debate over this conflict has gone on so long. We had a desire for it to be noble, but, over time, came to realize that it wasn't, and that realization has immensely bothered those of us who fought in it. In a sense, it's like a scar that won't heal. The controversy provokes strong reactions even today—decades later.

And, of course, with any reminiscence of the war comes a certain sense of guilt. Guilt over the fact that I survived, while so many others didn't. Did I make good use of the extra time that was available to me, but not to them? Guilt over those I harmed. Did the harm I caused have any good or just result? Somebody had to be on the other end of all the bombs and weapons that I dropped. I often wonder who they were.

At the time, I didn't think about it in those terms. They were trying to kill me, and I got them first, but the thought lingers, nonetheless. Those moments have long passed, but I did want to clarify what it felt like to go through that extremely intense period. In spite of the misgivings about the outcome, it was the defining experience of my life.

I often ask myself, "Would I do it again?"

Appendix A

While my own experiences during the Vietnam War provided the episodes I've related in this book, my absolute favorite war story of that period is not one of mine but that of a very good friend. As you read the story that follows, I think you'll see why.

Lt. Col. R. L. Penn, USAF (Ret.), had a harrowing experience about a year and a half before I arrived at Ubon. I first met him shortly after this incident took place when he was assigned as an instructor at Homestead (Fla.) Air Force Base, where I checked out in the F-4. When I returned from Ubon, he was still at Homestead, and we've continued our friendship to this day. I thank Saint Patrick himself that I never had to experience anything similar! Here's the story in his own words.

MISSION TO THE NORTHEAST HIGHWAY

In most respects it was a typical Route Package Six mission except that we had no electronic warning equipment and it was night. Even those differences were routine to me. My squadron got electronic warning gear after I left, and I had long ago grown accustomed to night missions.

Our relentless daytime presence had caused the Vietnamese trucks to do much more driving at night. Higher headquarters decided to assign two fighter squadrons for operations primarily at night. The 497th and 433rd squadrons at Ubon got the odious task. The 497th Night Owls and the 433rd Satan's Angels both were assigned to the 8th Tactical Fighter Wing commanded by Col. Joe Wilson. I flew with the 497th. One squadron would fly from sundown to midnight, then the other until dawn. Most of our missions were to the North Vietnam panhandle—Route Packs I, II, and III. The big advantage to this was that their defenses were less robust. Surface-to-air missile (SAM) activity was almost none, radar-directed antiaircraft artillery (AAA) was not very effective against a maneuvering target, and visually aimed guns could not see us very well. The downside was there was much more danger of a pilot losing aircraft control or flying into the ground during aggressive maneuvering.

171

The 433rd commander, Colonel Crouch, held a pilots' meeting every Wednesday and he had just instituted a weekly briefing by an outside "expert" on some subject or another. The first briefer, Capt. Chick Waxman, TDY from Fighter Weapons School, finished his briefing, suited up, flew to RP I, got hit, and parachuted into a treetop. Rescue guys had told us, in that case, to stay in a tree until daylight and they'd pick us up directly from the tree. Not Chick; he climbed down, fell off a cliff in the dark, broke his neck and died. The next briefer also had a bad night following his presentation— I think he arrived at the Hanoi Hilton via circuitous routing.

So I was the third lecturer. My pitch was, "You can't get shot down at night." I was very proud of my thesis which involved all sorts of hocus-pocus about the rods and cones in the eye, AAA aiming techniques and tracers, AAA radar gun laying computers, and other stuff which I didn't understand either, but sounded very sophisticated. Anyway, Colonel Crouch thought his guys hadn't been aggressive enough and that this should help. You gotta get in close, and concentrate, to do good work, especially at night.

One way to confirm my theory was to light afterburners at night and get the gunners' attention. The afterburner makes a bright, blue-yellow-white light about fifty feet long that can be seen from miles away. Because they lacked depth perception, visual gunners from maybe four miles away would open up. So, why couldn't the gunners approximate our separation distance, but I could? Because to them, I was just a light in the night sky, but to me, they were shapes against some terrain background.

According to my exalted theory, the gunners' eyes couldn't provide accurate depth perception at night by which they could utilize the adjustments indicated by tracers. For the Soviet 37mm gun, every bullet is a brilliant red tracer. Six guns in a battery, two bullets per second per gun add up to a lot of bright red tracers! However, this tracer-adjusting system doesn't work at night because human sight, in daylight, depends on color-recognizing cones in the eye. But, at low-level night-light, the rods in the eye interpret the available light, and some accuracy is lost—especially in distance recognition. Well, that's what I thought, so I was suggesting that these pilots risk their lives on the validity of my theory. It had been working fine for me!

The sight of those bright red tracers was a thing of great beauty. The closer they came, the more exciting, but they always missed. Tracers are prettier at night because they're so bright. If a pilot is down low, really in the weeds—pretty dicey at night—and 37s are coming really close to the canopy, they seem to go straight initially and well in front. Then, as they pass by the canopy, they appear to curve sharply to the rear. Beautiful! Winston Churchill—perhaps quoting an earlier soldier—is reputed to have said during his experience in Cuba in 1898, "There is nothing more exhilarating than to be shot at without result."

There were also 57mm and 85mm guns. Visually aimed 57mm guns were recognizable by their blue- or green-pastel tracers—loaded about one in six projectiles. These tracers probably provided more useful information to the U.S. pilots with them than to the gunners. The pilot immediately knows he's being shot at, so he can choose whether to deal with the problem at hand or go someplace else. Getting hit by a 37mm projectile may or may not be a major catastrophe, but a 57 packs triple the punch. Obviously, 85mm guns packed a real punch. The 57mm guns could be radar-directed—without tracers—and 85s always were. When the pilot sees a muzzle flash he has one to six seconds to get someplace else other than the position the radar had predicted for him. Really not so difficult to do—unless the sky is crowded with bullets!

There were two railroad and highway routes from Hanoi to China. They formed a V shape from Hanoi—one to the northwest and one to the northeast. During the summer, the Air Force and Navy concentrated extra effort on these important supply routes. It seemed that the North Vietnamese increased their defenses accordingly. On the 7th and 8th of August, the Air Force lost eight fighters in the Kep area—four POWs, two KIAs, and two men picked up in the gulf. Larry Goldberg and Pat Wynne were hit by AAA and killed trying to get out to the gulf. Their airplane had flight control problems and they were trying to get to the water, but apparently the controls failed suddenly and they couldn't eject. The northeast highway/railroad was a tough place!

The enemy truck drivers operated better in the daytime so, presumably, there was more truck traffic during the day. Appropriately, we staged many more sorties in the day against trucks and fixed targets. Still, it would have been a huge mistake to allow them the freedom of night. We ran a few night armed reconnaissance missions and found some targets, but also, importantly, our very presence kept their heads down and slowed their movement.

All Route Package Six missions elicited mixed enthusiasm from the fighter pilots, but Pack VI at night definitely was not relished. For all the losses, we didn't seem to be getting many trucks. The day raids to Route Pack VI usually involved a gaggle of airplanes: EB-66, MiG warning, weather reconnaissance, post-strike reconnaissance, refueling tankers, and rescue forces on alert. Iron Hand was especially important and was included whenever available. Iron Hand was a special mission that involved a fighter—in the earliest applications an Air Force North American F-100F Super Sabre, or Navy Douglas A-4 Skyhawk; and later Air Force Republic F-105 Thunderchief—which had electronic sensing equipment to detect SAM radar activity and its location. This sensing fighter would be accompanied by fighters with bombs. This comprised an Iron Hand package, which would go in first to seek out and suppress SAMs and stay until all fighters were out of the area. Iron Hand motto: "First in. Last out."

Much as the fighter pilots appreciated this escort service, it diverted scarce assets from attacking the primary targets. That's all well and good, except that we didn't have any electronic countermeasure (ECM) equipment and a two-airplane formation doesn't get Iron Hand support. Our only defense was to fly so low that SAMs couldn't get at us. Uhhh? Fly low at night? In mountainous terrain? This was a VERY BAD idea. Not suicide, but very dangerous. Route Packages IV, V, and VI were SAM country—especially around the Hanoi area.

The night tactic was that two airplanes would ingress at a couple thousand feet or so, 420 knots, wingman seven miles—one minute—in trail. Looking at hills on radar from about level creates shadows behind so maps can be interpreted. Even on a fairly dark night, rivers, railroads and breaks in trees can be sorted out visually. We used radar and visual to avoid fatal contact with the terrain and inertial navigation to find turn points. At such a low altitude, with just a few hills around, the SA-2 missile could not track us accurately enough to shoot, and visual gunners could not see well enough to be a threat. When close to suspected SAM sites, fly really low.

In the target area.
The lead fighter carried two pods of eight parachute-retarded flares each. Each flare was one million candlepower. Lead also carried four 500-pound bombs. Wingman carried all bombs. The flares had an ignition delay of about twenty seconds and burned for four minutes. Over a suspected target, lead drops two or more flares. Simultaneously, wingman pulls up, offsets, and rolls in, sort of pointed at the target when the flares ignite. Lead is in a racetrack pattern and drops his bombs about a minute after wingman. Wingman comes around for a second pass after lead. If we have a good target, and four minutes of flare burning time, we could make three or four bombing passes.

The night of 1 June was a bad time for the 8th Tactical Fighter Wing. Dayton Ragland and Ned Herrald were killed attacking a fixed target, the Than Hoa Bridge. On a night armed reconnaissance mission just northeast of Kep, A. J. Meyers and John Borling, two of the finest officers I ever knew, were nailed by ground fire and spent seven years in jail (a.k.a. the Hanoi Hilton).

The Night of 11–12 August 1966

I was selected to lead a two-ship armed reconnaissance to the northeast highway/railroad—the exact objective that Meyers-Borling had had. This would be my 92nd mission north. My backseat pilot—GIB, guy in back—was Bert Finzer, new to the squadron and on his first mission to Route Pack VI. As I briefed the mission, I was impressed by his demeanor—quiet, eager, brave.

We contacted *Red Crown*, a U.S. Navy destroyer very far north in the Gulf of Tonkin that handled radar vectors, refueling rendezvous, and rescue. We refueled over the Gulf of Tonkin and headed to the north of Haiphong, then to the north side of what we called Phantom Ridge. There were two ridges near Hanoi: Phantom Ridge, a low ridge to the northeast, and Thud Ridge to the northwest. By staying north of these ranges we were partly shielded from radars and missiles around Hanoi and Haiphong. Follow the ridge west to the highway—piece of cake. Follow the railroad/highway southwest, climb up to four or five thousand feet and turn gently back and forth—60 to 80 degrees bank—to look down for trucks or trains.

That altitude put us in easy view of all sorts of radars, but with the constant turning there was little defensive reaction. We had no radar warning gear at that time, but surface-to-air missiles could be seen from miles away at night. Defensive measure for SAMs was to turn to place the missile at 60 or 90 degrees off the nose and start a gentle pushover (maybe –2 Gs). The tracking missile also noses down. When the missile, at very high speed, gets close, pull up about 4 or 6 Gs, and the missile can't make the turn. That maneuver worked pretty well, but not quite perfectly. In any event, it obviously can't be initiated from three or four thousand feet above the ground. What to do at night in SAM country? Nothing, I guess. Just try to stay low enough that SAMs can't lock on.

Finzer was excited. Newest kid in the squadron and totally unafraid! I took the opportunity to illustrate my theory that you can't get shot down at night. I would pop up to four or five thousand feet and maintain straight and level for about a minute. It takes awhile for radar operators to see a target, acquire it, and then six seconds for the Puazo Six computer to project the target's future position and bullet impact point, and then fire. As soon as I saw the muzzle flashes I'd make a little turn. Radar-directed guns had time cut fuses, which would explode at the place we would have been, had it not been for the little turn. Bert was enjoying the thrill of being shot at!

I noticed down near the southwest end of the route there were quite a few radar-controlled guns firing. It didn't occur to me why they were there, but I didn't bother 'em. My squadron commander, Jim McGuire, had been in trouble with the wing commander before about my "dueling with AAA." I don't know how he heard about it 'cause I never bragged or nothing like that. (Dizzy Dean says that if it's true, it ain't braggin'.) It was very exciting and I thought a 37mm gun was a worthwhile target—especially if there were no other targets. The CO had different ideas of economics and he thought an F-4 was a substantially more valuable asset. Pilots were in even shorter supply at the time. Anyway, turn on all the lights, or light the afterburner to get those guys shooting, and it's easy to go right down the tracer path straight to the guns. This works especially well with rockets.

I searched the dark highway for targets until my fuel gauge told me it was time to go home. I had risked my life to carry this stuff so far up north and I was not going to haul it back. Besides, it was dangerous to land with flares on board, so if not dropped on a target they would be jettisoned at sea. The taxpayers paid real money for these flares and bombs.

Ah! There's my excuse! I can find only one target—the AAA guns, which had so decidedly announced their presence. I had been keeping their location in the back of my mind, so I turned right for them. I had fuel for only one pass, so I gang-loaded all flares to drop at once. I crossed right over the guns at about 6,000 feet and pickled the flares.

I was in a hard right turn, setting switches to drop my bombs, when the flares lit. The radar guns had been sporadically firing, so everyone knew approximately where I was. The sudden introduction of sixteen million candlepower clarified everything for all of us. I see them. They see me. I was over Kep airfield! That's why there were so many guns in one place. Intelligence had estimated 208 AAA guns of various descriptions around Kep airfield, but I hadn't thought much about it. That's a lot of guns. They really meant to defend their two airfields, even though President Johnson had made them off limits to us—at that time. Wow! Seemed like everybody started shooting at once.

I was hit pretty hard. The airplane porpoised severely. Maybe the artificial feel system had been shot out or damaged. All modern American fighters have full, irreversible, hydraulic flight controls, not hydraulic boost. Without artificial feel, a slight force on the control stick could cause the hydraulic flight controls to deflect fully. Maybe part of the stabilator had been shot away because I had difficulty holding the nose up. I thought the airplane might blow up any second, however . . . two seconds later it hadn't blown up—yet. I yelled to Finzer, "Don't eject." A calm, quiet voice came back, "I'm not." That reminded me to be calm. Pilots are sometimes surprised, but a really superb "stick" never panics and can recover ice-calm composure within a half-second or so. I already had a plan to head to Phantom Ridge—maybe two minutes away—if the airplane wouldn't blow up before then.

I quickly figured that things were more or less OK and I was not anxious to pull the handle that would turn me into a POW. There was no apparent fire because the airplane wasn't lit up. An internal fire? I don't know what that could be. The flight controls were functioning, although definitely not normally. Whoops, fuel seemed lower than a minute ago. Very low.

The attraction of Phantom Ridge was that rescue from there was more likely. Well, not exactly likely, but not completely impossible. I had heard some talk about Navy rescue helicopters going somewhere north of Phantom Ridge. I carried a .38-caliber revolver in a cowboy holster with bullets along the belt, like Gene Autry. I also carried a .380 automatic in my vest. I figured to fight like Davy Crockett at the Alamo—well, at least against a bunch of farmers. A rescue mission deep into Pack VI would have been a long shot, but who knows how long I might be able to hold out in the hills. My friend Rags had convinced me that being a POW is really bad. Worse than really bad.

I got to Phantom Ridge and things were still pretty good. Obviously, there had not yet been an explosion because I'm still alive, so there probably would not be one. Still no fire, and flight controls still functioned. I was heading east for the gulf, staying low enough for the hills to shield me from SAMs. If I had been desperately concerned about sudden, catastrophic loss of control I would have climbed for some bailout altitude, but SAMs seemed the primary threat—psychologically, anyway.

Fuel. Lower than a minute ago.
Finzer said, "We still have our bombs." I hadn't thought about them because I'd been thinking about ejection or explosion. I reached for the jettison button when he said, "Let's look for a truck!" Just then I saw headlights ahead. Some guy driving along with his lights on! I rolled in and pickled the bombs: one, two, three. There was a very bright flash. Direct hit! Must have been hauling ammo.

Who was driving that truck? When he woke up this morning did he think that this would be the last day of his life on earth? I imagine he expected a long, dangerous journey in the night—but this? Did he know what hit him?

Only then, in the pullout, I remembered the damaged flight controls and difficulty getting the nose up. Anyway, I didn't hit the ground. Bert had counted the bombs, "We have one more bomb, let's get that lighthouse."

The lighthouse northeast of Haiphong harbor was a bone stuck in our throats because it was off limits and always operating—taunting us. Facing imminent death or capture, this kid was still fighting the war! By this time I was thinking that rescue was a possibility just as well as death or capture. Focused on rescue, I jettisoned external garbage, went feet wet, headed south, and called *Red Crown* for a refueling rendezvous.

Red Crown had specific orders not to go north of a certain line because the Boeing KC-135 Stratotankers were totally defenseless and were valuable Strategic Air Command assets. This night Captain Martinez violated that standing order.

Fuel was low.

I was leaking fuel—a lot! The tanker headed farther north to meet me. My decision, immediately after being hit, to head northeast for the hills was based on two assumptions, which I held at the time: I might have to eject in a couple of minutes—fifteen miles, that's hill country. Evade capture? Rescue? Alternatively, a southeast heading would have pointed me directly to the tanker and would have saved over a thousand pounds of fuel. But the direct route probably would have proven fatal. The terrain southeast of Hanoi is very flat, much of it covered with rice paddies and standing water. There, the minimum operating altitude for SAMs is quite low, perhaps down to absolute dirt level, because of a technique for optical target tracking and manual missile guidance. It's more convenient to be lucky than smart.

I figured that if I had a severe fuel leak I might as well run it through the engines. I stroked the afterburner to speed the rendezvous. No. That's not a good idea—it certainly wasn't. The shipboard radar controllers apparently were not well-practiced in rendezvous techniques, and it wasn't going well. I spotted the tanker on my radar and took over the rendezvous.

Fuel is almost gone.

My turn point was perfect. I kept my speed up until the final short distance because of the fuel leak. Very high closing speed. I pulled the throttles to idle and slid right in behind the tanker. A rather spectacular join-up! I made it!

Fuel 0000—How accurate is that gauge?

It had been a really fast join-up—dangerously fast. As I advanced the throttles from idle to stabilize under the tanker, I looked at the boom operator. His face and white helmet glowed in the red lights around him. He said, "Forward four." I looked at the digital fuel gage—0000. One engine quit, then the other.

Four feet! In just one or two more minutes the boom operator could have locked the refueling boom into the receptacle and towed me while pumping fuel. Four feet. What might have been. So close! Time's up.

As I eased back on the stick to maintain altitude I slowed rapidly. The tanker quickly disappeared into the distance. It's very quiet without two jets running. It's lonely. And dark.

My wingman, Robinson, was now rendezvousing with the tanker. They continued their jobs—there's nothing they can do to help me. *Rescue is out there. I'm confident.* There were a couple of minutes to reflect. For the only time in my life I thought, "These next may be my last words." Robinson will go back to Ubon and the other pilots will say, "What happened to R. L.? What'd he say?" I didn't have any memorable words. Back to the problem at hand. It wasn't over yet.

Emotions had been alternating pretty fast until now. A half hour ago— some high-stakes combat. Ultimate high stakes. A couple minutes later I was focused on the dreaded POW camp. Then exhilaration on making it to the water. Anxiety and concentration on the race between the fuel gauge and the miles to go to the tanker. The fuel lasted and I'm underneath the tanker.

So, now, finally, I'll have to punch out. Earlier, this was exactly what I had been hoping for—get over the water and eject. Now, instead of being happy with my latest good fortune I was disappointed. My heart sank. Dejected. The adrenalin drained quickly. Up close and real, ejection into the water didn't look like such a hot prospect. Leave this warm womb of a cockpit for the dark, uncontrollable sea? The tanker's lights distanced quickly.

Ejection isn't so difficult a decision if it's a snap decision. But now there's a quiet minute to think. *Think what? Obviously there's no choice. But so many things could go wrong. It's really dark outside. I am far out to sea. This airplane glides better than a brick, but it ain't forever. The clock's running.*

At this time I remembered my Army parachute training at Fort Benning. We always had a reserve parachute. If the main chute malfunctions—does a cigarette roll or Mae West or whatever—the paratrooper simply jettisons it and pulls the reserve. It's very important to jettison the main before pulling the reserve. So what? This time however, I don't have a reserve. Not the best mindset when facing the inevitable. *This is not the time to think about failure.* I could have rationalized that I'd already had my share of failures tonight, but by this time it seemed like everything was going wrong.

OK, Bert, let's go.

Bert's canopy blew. Wind noise was pretty loud. And three hundred miles an hour is a lot of wind. That's what will hit me in the face. I'm in no hurry for that. BANG! Bert's seat fired. I wonder if it hurts.

Sit erect. Feet back. Ready. I pull the face curtain. The canopy blew and the curtain came to a mechanical stop. I pulled down with my arms, head and shoulders, bending forward. Not supposed to do that. Supposed to keep back straight so it doesn't break.

Yes, it does hurt. That's a pretty hard slap. I had other things on my mind. Lot of things on my mind—things to do, and decisions to make. "Things to do" should be easy. It's all automatic—just let it happen. I pulled the handle.

The seat's upward trajectory phase of the ejection should have been a fun ride—a couple hundred feet up like a human cannonball—but that's a blank space. I've lost a couple of seconds there.

As programmed, I was out of the airplane and into the dark night. But I was tumbling in a fast forward roll. Not supposed to happen. I was really spinning! The seat automatic sequence must have failed!

Martin-Baker, a British company, built the ejection seat and some of us were a bit leery of it because it was so complicated. Every step depended on the step before it. Classic Rube Goldberg! If any part failed the sequence stopped. The canopy fires, which pulls a safety pin from the seat. When strapping in, the pilot straps a line to each leg just below the knee to keep the legs from flailing, or being bent backwards around the seat—double ouch!—in a high-speed ejection. During the ejection sequence these lines are jerked back with great force and held tight. After the seat has separated from the airplane and has slowed to lower airspeed—it knows this, measuring my deceleration to be less than four Gs—a small parachute, attached to the top back of the seat, deploys to stabilize the seat. The pilot is still strapped in until it has descended below 3,000 meters, or about 10,000 feet. The main parachute is stowed in the seatback until this time. The shoulder harness normally attaches to the seat until separation when it detaches and becomes parachute risers. Passing 10,000 feet, the pilot's seat belt and shoulder harness are released and a knife of some sort automatically cuts the leg restraint lines. I often wondered what would happen if the leg restraint lines weren't cut before the seat separated—would that 100-pound seat jerk my legs off at the knee?—triple ouch! The small stabilizing parachute is attached to the main parachute which is strapped to the pilot's back. When the straps are released the pilot is attached to the parachute and the seat falls clear. The small parachute pulls the main chute out of its storage space, and Martin-Baker's work is done! If the reader doesn't think that's complicated, he's missing something.

My story almost ended here.

Vertigo is a word used loosely among pilots and others as, perhaps, a more sophisticated word for dizziness. Not so! True vertigo is extremely rare among pilots. Military pilots are taught about spatial disorientation, in theory and in practice. That's different from vertigo. Very different!

Refresher practice for spatial disorientation is provided every year. If a pilot has visual reference to the horizon, spatial disorientation will not be a problem, but if flying by instruments in the clouds, then there is danger of spatial disorientation. The counter action is clear, but not necessarily easy: believe the instruments, fly by instruments, and disregard false physical signs. Eventually the false sensation will go away.

Vertigo is an extreme case of spatial disorientation. The human inner ear has three interconnected semicircular canals containing fluid. Tiny hairs in this fluid sense movement of the fluid, which is caused by different forces on the head and the fluid. If the fluid in two or three of these canals begin spinning, it overrides the central nervous system. The victim may feel that he is spinning in two directions at once. This induced rotation is in no way related to actual head movement. The effect is extreme disorientation. The disorientation can be avoided, at least partially, if the victim is able to recognize true spatial orientation by reference to visual or bodily confirmation of "which way is up." If, however, the victim has no valid reference to constant gravity or sight of the horizon, then the only input is from the inner ear's canals. If the fluid in these canals is spinning wildly, then total confusion results.

A case of vertigo may last only a few seconds, but the recovery can be deadly! Absent clear and reliable visual or physical references, the inner ear fluids will continue running wildly and will continue to give powerful signals to the brain. The brain is totally confused.

My experience with vertigo was severe and terrifying. It was like waking from a very bad dream or being hit hard in the head. *Try to think! What is this? Terror! Total confusion! Something is wrong—very wrong! Concentrate! What's happening? Where am I?*

I was still spinning, but I gradually began to reason. But the reasoning was jumbled and wildly erroneous. I forced my brain to focus and then to reconstruct what had happened:

Where am I? I have ejected.

What's happening? I am tumbling in space.

I'm in the seat. Over water.

The seat has failed! I'm going to spin right into the sea with this aluminum chair strapped to my back!

I'm spinning in a forward roll. How can that be if the stabilizing parachute is out? It can't be! The chute didn't deploy, or it tangled in the seat. Either way, the sequence stops.

Actually, I was not spinning. The fluid in my inner ear was spinning! My brain was tortuously recovering from vertigo.

I was about to make one mistake: I was about to abandon the seat and go it alone. Rube Goldberg had an option in case the seat sequence fails. The pilot can pull a small handle in the seat, which releases the straps, and the pilot kicks the seat away and pulls the parachute ripcord manually. I forgot that. It's understandable. Not only was I not able to think clearly, but also I was in a bit of a rush because it's not far from 10,000 feet to the water (just over a minute). In other words, I was finally in a panic. I had been calm and rational for a couple of hours now, but panic finally took over.

OK, so I had forgotten all about the proper procedure for the manual parachute option, what was I to do? I was not giving up. I was going to fight this all the way to the end! The conclusion to this life was rushing to me!

The unstrap procedure was the same as I did at the end of every mission: leg restraints, seat belt, and shoulder harness. Also, perhaps our frequent practice in emergency ground escape had influenced my imminent mistake. In case of fire, the procedure was to unstrap, scramble out over the windshield, slide down the nose cone, and run. With the practice I'd had, I could unstrap and be on the ground in about three seconds.

Time flies. I had started at about 15,000 feet. *Can't see anything. The spinning had been disorienting. Very. Don't know how close I am to the water.*

I'll not go easy! I'll unstrap, jettison this seat, and dive into the water like Tarzan. From 10,000 feet—or 2,000. Dive into the ocean when I don't know which way is up?

Seems like the only way out.

I started the two-second unstrap: leg restraints. SNAP! The main chute opened! The seat fell away. I'm hanging in the parachute straps. The seat had worked exactly as programmed.

My arms hang limply at my side. That was close! One more second and I would have killed myself! I had almost jettisoned a perfectly good parachute, still in the bag.

It's quiet up here. Exhale. Take a deep breath. Exhale. The vertigo had vanished. My mind clears. All this took about one minute from pulling the handle to parachute opening. *The rest will be easy. I'll bob around in the water awhile, get a little rest, and then the Navy will pick me up.*

This has been an emotional roller coaster. Before the mission I had experienced appropriate apprehension and intense concentration, this increased markedly in the target area. Being vigorously shot at confirms exactly what is going on, getting hit transforms a serious situation to an emergency. This may be it!

Low point:
- Eject immediately?
- Airplane may explode?

Good news:
- The airplane still flies!

Terror:
- Will I be a POW?

Decisive action:
- Head for Phantom Ridge! (1)
- I have two pistols, 100 bullets, a knife, signal flares and a signal mirror.

Grim reality:
- Leaking fuel fast
- Airplane doesn't fly right

Bought time:
- Made it to Phantom Ridge!
- Fuel leak seems slower!
- Feet wet!!

Not over yet:
- Ten minutes of fuel isn't enough

Welcome:
- Red Crown on radio!
- north for refueling rendezvous!

Massive disappointment:
- Four feet short
- "Just in case" last words
- Don't want to do it

Trust Martin-Baker:
- Punch out

Catastrophe:
- Chute failure
- Fight to the end!

All's well:
- Chute opens!

The struggle to live had left me exhausted. I pondered that for a half minute, then decided I'd better get busy. *OK, get started on the things to do next. Total darkness. The sky is no blacker than the sea. Moonrise was supposed to have been at 00:49. But it's only a waning crescent and the sky is solid overcast. No stars. Throw away my helmet; still can't see. Deploy life preserver. Deploy life raft and survival kit. I'm in great shape. I'm ready! Hanging in the chute is a good feeling.*

I'm concerned if Bert is all right. Red Crown *was on the radio, I wonder how far away they are? Are they coming to get me? Do they know where I am? Ah! I'll take out my survival radio and call them. I'll call Bert. Again, irrational. Of course the King is coming to get me. Bert? He's five miles away, in whichever direction. If he's not OK there's nothing I can do.*

Taking out my survival radio was a bad idea. Just then I hit the water. My radio hit me in the face and disappeared into Davey Jones' Locker.

I'm so happy to be in the water I feel like I could swim to shore! *Routine: survival kit and life raft are attached by a long nylon line. Pull 'em in and climb aboard the life raft. Easy. Face the raft, grab with both hands, pull it under my chest, and down. Roll over, and I'm aboard. Pull kit in too. Raft is sort of small—*

I'm in from my knees to my neck. I'm comfortable. Time to rest again. Discard boots. Be comfy.

Sharks? Poisonous sea snakes? No concern. Five-second break is over.

How to contact Red Crown*? My radio is long gone. There is a signal radio in the survival kit, but it's CW only—I can't talk on it or receive. There is a safety plug in the switch attached by a string. Pull string. Oh, but now, is the radio packed with the switch on–and plug in—or off? Not a problem. I'll turn the switch one way for a half minute, then the other way.*

This unorthodox signaling caused some concern on deck of USS *King.* "Here he is!" Then, "He's gone." Did he drown? "He's back! Get a bearing." "Too late."

USS *King* was headed toward the erratic radio signal at flank speed. Wait—we could run over him. Send the helo. Bert must have been doing things right because they picked him up first.

I saw the whirlybird and fired a flare. Bright, bright orange. Beautiful. It burned out, so I dipped it in the water and threw it away—across my body to the other side of the raft. Throw? Why did I throw the flare? Why not just drop it? That got me some burns from hot, wet ashes. Now fire a smoke flare so the chopper can judge the wind. Unhook the raft and survival kit so they don't get tangled in the rotor blades. The downwash blows the raft away quickly. There goes a piece of security that I'd come to love. I've transferred my trust to the chopper.

I'm winched up to the welcome arms of the crewman kneeling in the door. Incredibly strong arms pull me in. *I'm safe! Relax, look around. Bert is back there. What a relief; I'm so glad to see him! His red hair glows in the dark. We made it. Exhale.*

We're quickly back to USS *King.* Deck is lit up. I see the white X and circle on the deck. We approach carefully. A bit of rocking and weaving. Helicopters do that, I guess. Close to the big X. Jockeying back and forth, then wave-off. Hard right turn and we're heading off into the dark.

Another approach. Moving around, sideways, back and forth. Is the ship moving? Is it always like this? Wave-off, hard right turn, into the darkness. We'll run out of gas and ditch. I don't want to go back into that water. Earlier I was so happy to get in it, but that was then. Blood on the deck and all around—am I'm gonna bleed to death? Joke to myself.

Third pass. That surely is a small spot! Touchdown! Several men come out to meet us. Welcome? You bet! These are the most important men in the world.

Next, I was escorted to the medic's operating room. I wasn't exactly expecting the Mayo Clinic, but this place was small. The bright light with reflector dominated the scene. Chief Izquierdo gave me a miniature—1½ oz—bottle of brandy. "Drink this, Captain, and I'll sew you up." *That's it?* "Don't you have a bullet I can bite, or something?" Good laugh. "No. The brandy is traditional. I'll use Novocain for the stitches." Captain Tesh greeted me and put me in the commodore's stateroom for a couple hours' sleep.

Morning. The ship cruised silently, as the crewmen went about their normal duties. I stood at the rail for several minutes—amazed at how calm the sea was. Now that I have time, I reflect on how close I came to the end. Life is so tenuous.

Two or three sailors approached individually, "Congratulations, Captain! I bet ten dollars on you last night." The entire drama had been broadcast on the ship's speakers. Later, it occurs that there must have been an equal number who bet the other way. Clearly, it would have been in bad taste to own up to it.

Chopper transferred us to the carrier USS *Constellation* (CVA-64). Dinner with Admiral Richardson. *I wonder why he chose a carrier for flagship? Aviator. Likes the noise, maybe.* Arthur Godfrey was another guest. In a private conversation, Godfrey invited me to criticize the war, or President Johnson's conduct of it. Although I agreed with what he said about the ridiculous targeting restrictions, I was offended. I'd been doing my job and I wasn't about to criticize the president to a civilian.

Back at Ubon, Colonel Wilson ordered me stateside immediately. I was already thirteen missions past my end of tour. He had been on my squadron commander's back about my aggressiveness, and now, sure enough, I'd gone too far. Wait a minute—whose idea was it for me to go up there in the first place? While this story had a happy ending, there was a tragic and somber aspect to it. Three of the four men who were on this mission did not survive the war. I was the only one who did. Combat is real and unforgiving.

Index

About the Author

During the Vietnam War, Mike McCarthy was an F4D Phantom II pilot assigned to the 8th Tactical Fighter Wing at Ubon Royal Thai Air Base, and flew 124 missions against North Vietnam and Laos from 1967 to 1968. Assignments at the Pentagon in both Headquarters USAF and the Office of Secretary of Defense provided valuable insight on how major policy decisions are developed and implemented. Mike retired as a Colonel in 1990 and currently lives in Litchfield Park, Arizona and teaches at Arizona State University.

Stackpole Military History Series

Real battles. Real soldiers. Real stories.

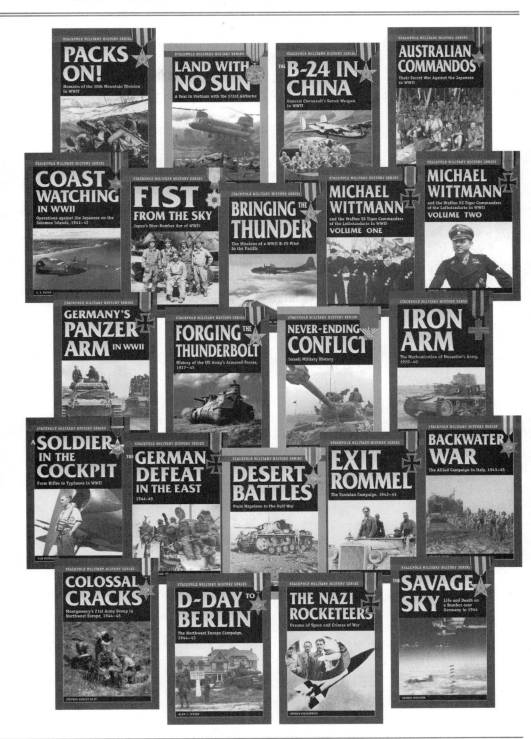

Stackpole Military History Series

Real battles. Real soldiers. Real stories.

Stackpole Military History Series

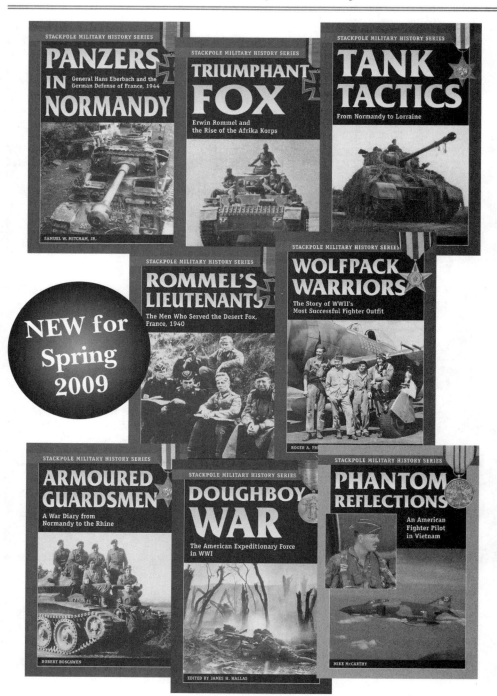

STACKPOLE MILITARY HISTORY SERIES

PANZERS IN NORMANDY

General Hans Eberbach and the German Defense of France, 1944

SAMUEL W. MITCHAM, JR.

STACKPOLE MILITARY HISTORY SERIES

TRIUMPHANT FOX

Erwin Rommel and the Rise of the Afrika Korps

STACKPOLE MILITARY HISTORY SERIES

TANK TACTICS

From Normandy to Lorraine

STACKPOLE MILITARY HISTORY SERIES

ROMMEL'S LIEUTENANTS

The Men Who Served the Desert Fox, France, 1940

STACKPOLE MILITARY HISTORY SERIES

WOLFPACK WARRIORS

The Story of WWII's Most Successful Fighter Outfit

ROGER A. FR

NEW for Spring 2009

STACKPOLE MILITARY HISTORY SERIES

ARMOURED GUARDSMEN

A War Diary from Normandy to the Rhine

ROBERT BOSCAWEN

STACKPOLE MILITARY HISTORY SERIES

DOUGHBOY WAR

The American Expeditionary Force in WWI

EDITED BY JAMES H. HALLAS

STACKPOLE MILITARY HISTORY SERIES

PHANTOM REFLECTIONS

An American Fighter Pilot in Vietnam

MIKE McCARTHY

Real battles. Real soldiers. Real stories.

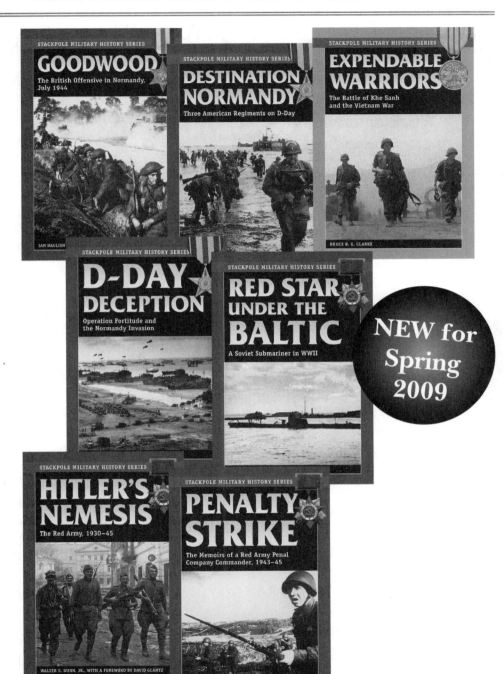

STACKPOLE MILITARY HISTORY SERIES

GOODWOOD
The British Offensive in Normandy, July 1944
IAN DAGLISH

STACKPOLE MILITARY HISTORY SERIES

DESTINATION NORMANDY
Three American Regiments on D-Day

STACKPOLE MILITARY HISTORY SERIES

EXPENDABLE WARRIORS
The Battle of Khe Sanh and the Vietnam War
BRUCE B. G. CLARKE

STACKPOLE MILITARY HISTORY SERIES

D-DAY DECEPTION
Operation Fortitude and the Normandy Invasion

STACKPOLE MILITARY HISTORY SERIES

RED STAR UNDER THE BALTIC
A Soviet Submariner in WWII

NEW for Spring 2009

STACKPOLE MILITARY HISTORY SERIES

HITLER'S NEMESIS
The Red Army, 1930–45
WALTER S. DUNN, JR., WITH A FOREWORD BY DAVID GLANTZ

STACKPOLE MILITARY HISTORY SERIES

PENALTY STRIKE
The Memoirs of a Red Army Penal Company Commander, 1943–45
ALEXANDER V. PYL'CYN

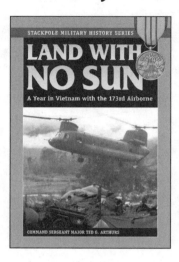

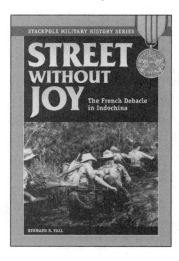

Stackpole Military History Series

THROUGH THE VALLEY

VIETNAM, 1967-68

by Col. James F. Humphries

In the remote northern provinces of South Vietnam—a region of long-forgotten villages and steep hills—the U.S. Americal Division and 196th Light Infantry Brigade fought a series of battles against the North Vietnamese and Vietcong in 1967–68: Hiep Duc, Nhi Ha, Hill 406, and others. These pitched engagements, marked by fierce close combat, have gone virtually unreported in the decades since, but Col. James F. Humphries brings them into sharp focus, chronicling the efforts of these proud American units against a stubborn enemy and reconstructing what it was like to fight in Vietnam.

$19.95 • Paperback • 6 x 9 • 352 pages • 47 b/w photos, 30 maps

WWW.STACKPOLEBOOKS.COM
1-800-732-3669

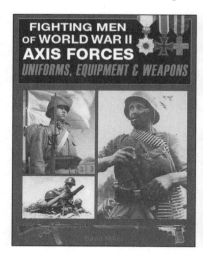